MAUD PUGH
Author of this book.

CAPON VALLEY

Its Pioneers and Their Descendants

1698 to 1940

By MAUD PUGH

★

Volume I

WITH CHAPTER INDEX COMPLETE

Many Illustrations, poems and other
intriguing features of interest
to people of every State
where these descend-
ants are found.

★

CONTAINS INFORMATION AND NAMES
OF THOUSANDS OF PEOPLE IN
CAPON VALLEY

CLEARFIELD

Originally published 1948

Reprinted for
Clearfield Company, Inc. by
Genealogical Publishing Co., Inc.
Baltimore, Maryland
1995

International Standard Book Number: 0-8063-4551-9

Made in the United States of America

DECENDENTS OF LIEUTENANT JONATHAN PUGH

BRIEF AUTOBIOGRAPHY OF MAUD PUGH,
AUTHOR OF THIS BOOK

I was born January 6, 1866, on the Ullery farm in sight of historic old Salem Church near Slanesville, West Virginia. My parents moved twice before I can remember. They were starting life anew, having lost all they had by the Civil War. Father left the farm to manage the Abernathy Mill at Springfield on the South Branch of the Potomac, but after one year there, seeing a better opening he moved to North River Mills, then a thriving village with two burrh flour mills. Here my memory began with Virginia Pugh's pet rabbits in Mrs. Snapp's yard. They were eating clover from the lawn. Virginia was Mrs. Joe Snapp's niece, half sister to Amos L. Pugh, noted elsewhere in this history.

The next thing vividly to be remembered was the high waters and raftsmen coming around the turn above the dam. Now they are stuck on the milldam! Father knows the men, Jerry Hiett is steering the big raft. It is growing dark — men running, lanterns twinkling. Shouting is heard from the raftsmen, answers from the people at the riverside. Will the men have to stay amid the swollen black waters all night? Will the raft be dashed to pieces by the drifting trees that are rushing down this torrent and the men be drowned in the surging water below the dam? Time dragged on. All at once, amid these dreadful fears, a glad shout went up from the river. The raft is *moving* — they are going over now! All is well. The lanterns go twinkling home. Some men are running out over the hill and across Mr. Asa Hiett's field to see them pass the big bend in the river below Croston's ford and glide out past "Deaver's Eddy", under the Ice Mountain. They can follow by the lights on the raft. Now all is quiet and the villagers are at supper talking over the stirring event and hoping the men on the raft will get safely through to Williamsport, the lumber market, before the river is dangerously high for rafting.

3

Other early memories are children playing in the bran on the second floor of the mill, wading in the mill race under the road bridge below the mill wheel, which went cachosh, cachosh, cachosh, while the water, coming out from under the wheel, made a roar like a small Niagara.

People from all over the county came to these mills. Some from a distance would stay all night and wait for their load of grain to be ground. One of these was Capt. Luther Guinnevan, a man of fine form and genial personality, a comrade of father's, now a farmer and fruit grower of Levels, South Branch Mountain, who often brought the Pugh family a bag of good apples. He received a hearty welcome from the children and enjoyed the Miller's hospitality.

Mr. Guinnevan was a good story-teller and everybody sat around the open fire, radiant with a pine light, ate apples and listened and laughed, for these were always clean, good-natured stories and the delight of the children, keener than that felt by the children of today who listen at the radio. Mr. Guinnevan did not come every night and the radio does, and no machine can give the human touch they felt.

Then there was Mr. Asa Hiett, back from the State Legislature, known over the county as "Colonel Ase". He kept a grocery down on the corner opposite the Milldam. No Hollywood comedian could "hold a candle" to him. Small wonder the children all flocked around him. So did the big folks out at Wheeling (Wheeling was then the capital), where he always got the better of his opponent. When not possible with an argument, he did it with a laugh. Even when a small child he was a live wire on a farm. His mother who had a large family, one Sunday stole off to the village church, leaving the smaller children in care of the older ones. She took a seat in a front pew. Amidst the preacher's discourse a redhead popped in at the door and ran barefoot down the aisle, shouting, "Mother! mother! the Miller hen swallered the hook!"

Mr. Hiett's stories abounded in figures of speech which were convulsively funny, but which, like his countenance, radiated good humor.

4

"Colonel Ase" knew that children loved sweetmeats as well as funny tales, so when he stopped at the end of our porch on his way home from the store he never failed to have some raisins, some kisses all done up in paper, or a striped stick of candy for each. We paid him back with kisses and both arms around his neck.

Mr. Hiett had no family of his own. His lovely wife, a Miss Arnold had died soon after their marriage, years before. He was the son of Jeremiah and Lucinda Hiett, one of the "illustrious fifteen". Nor was "Colonel Ase" the only attraction of this village in the early seventies.

There was "Uncle Lige Monendenhall" whose wit and kindly ways endeared him to all, and his sister Eliza, the patient loving invalid; "Uncle Joe Snapp", always humming a tune as he went about his work, and "Aunt Ellen", his sturdy spouse who kept a shining kitchen and baked the best cookies; Mrs. Cordelia Loy Moreland who had the finest flowers and did the most beautiful needle-work — with her dignified husband all spick and span, who owned the general store.

There was Mrs. Sallie Miller with her lovely children, Cora, Annie and Holland, the baby. She kept the fattest cows and the big white rooster; Mr. Billy Miller who owned the Upper Mill with the Great Mill Wheel and the fat ducks on the deep mill race below the school house where the cat-tails grew, and the children skated when the ice was safe; and Miss Harriett Kump who made the pretty dresses for the women and children, and her gray-haired father; the village blacksmith with the big bellows and the shining anvil, who shaped the fine shoes and shod the beautiful horses for the feathered Knights who rode tournament at the Ice Mountain, and crowned the pretty maids and the queens of love and beauty. (One of these was Miss Annie Loy, Now Mrs. Lovett, of Capon Bridge.)

And Mr. Ben Loy in the suburbs of the village, the pillar of the church, whose rugged, kindly personality contrasted sharply with his rustling, smiling wife, and their beautiful daughter, Sallie, who married James Carmichael and went west; and Mr. Wesley Smith with his squirrels for the sick; the sturdy John

Short who made the children's shoes and cut the lacings, too; and Major George Deaver who owned the Ice Mountain and whose wife was "Colonel Ase's" sister.

There was the young Dr. K. Taylor from Slanesville, so starchy and trim on his iron grey steed who brought the babies in his saddle pockets, if the fathers went after him; if not the stork did it, then vanished like Santa Claus.

Two boys from Capon Bridge, alternating, carried the mail on a prancing horse, via the Springfield Grade to Slanesville. The village dogs, dozing on the front steps woke up with a start when they passed, but never a casualty. They held their poses like cavalrymen. Later one of these became a prominent lawyer, the other a sheriff and banker; the latter is still living. (1936.)

Across from the village lived Mrs. Mary Williams whose heart went out to any one far or near, less fortunate than she. The unbridged river at her feet was her opportunity. One day, high up from a third story window she was seen frantically waving at the Miller on the other side of the turbulent stream, "Mr. Pugh, don't let that boy come back across until the water goes down", meaning a young lad from "Pine Hills" who has just swam a pony over in order to get some fishhooks down at the store. She had not seen him enter the stream but by chance saw both boy and pony emerge half drowned.

North River Mills, a rare village of rare people on a branch of the Potomac, of which Ice Mountain, with its Raven Rocks, its caves with ice in July, its spruce, rhododendron and ferns, then the home of the red fox and the wild deer, was its background. At the base of the mountain, on the outskirts of the village, stood the village schoolhouse. Often the baying of hounds among the pines and birches of the overhanging cliffs contrasted sharply with the routine of schoolwork — disturbed classes — the hearts of the children being with the dear, wild things so ruthlessly pursued by the soulless hunter in the name of sport. They were thinking of the beautiful fawn hidden away in the mountain fastness that must starve if the hounds get the mother; they were thinking, too, of the grace-

6

ful, bounding, fleet, sensitive mother, breathless and at bay among the vicious pack. Innocence abhors suffering in anything. The teacher was Chas. N. Hiett, and for one term Bazil Shanholtz, both men being intelligent and well informed. Chas. N. Hiett was County Superintendent of Schools for several terms and later he possessed the largest and best selected library in the county, which was accessible to his students who desired to use it. The teacher not only opened his library to them but selected the reading matter suited to their grade until they were capable of making their own choice. This library was a mine of gold to the Pugh sisters.

Chas. N. Hiett was a born teacher; his students imbibed language, mathematics and literature from him almost without conscious effort. He taught morals, too, in the same way. Mr. Holland Willams and sister Annie, village Sunday-school teachers, aided the school work and laid the foundation for religious thought, but most of all the lives of these villagers, a daily object lesson of clean living and neighborly cooperation molded the character of the village children into wholesome future citizenry. It was the ambition of our parents, above everything else, that we should be educated and receive religious training.

In the spring of 1877 we moved to the farm, four miles south, a part of the old Pugh estate. Here we were still fortunate in our teachers with Chas. N. Hiett again, John W. Hockman and F. M. Frevil. This, the ancestral Pugh farm, had belonged to our Aunt Maria Smith, the house being partly torn away and remodeled. There was much to do everywhere and when not in school we made ourselves useful in all kinds of work indoors and out. We made hay, hoed potatoes and thinned corn. We rode horseback, and drove the cows to pasture. We spun wool, knit, made our own dresses and helped with the garden and cooking, but still found time for reading. I had read and re-read Shakespeare's plays, was familiar with Dickens and Scott and many others of the best old writers. I had read all of the Leather Stocking Tales and decided that Cooper did not know how to make love. I did not like Milton and thought his "Paradise Lost" dull poetry compared with Scott's Lady of the Lake. I thought then, and still think, that Hamlet can be understood by young people and is the greatest play yet written, and the language of it is unexcelled. Our youthful minds, I am glad to say, were not fed on Fairy Tales, nor was our imaginations distorted by such vulgar language and drawings as are found in the so-called funny papers of today, nor our sense of sound dulled by jazz. Our eyes were gladdened by the beauties of nature as God made them — flowers, trees, wild animals, streams, mountains, sunshine and shadows — no city child should be allowed to miss any of these. Without these and good literature the soul is starved and the resultant product may be thieves, gangsters.

October 25, 1884, I passed the teacher's examination and during my first term as teacher of the home school I was 18 in January. For several years then I alternately taught school and took the four-year course at Fairmont, completing with a class of 12 — the Roemer Class, six of whom were young women. We are now scattered to almost as many states. I owe a special tribute to two Fairmont instructors, John H. Roemer and J. Walter Barnes. I had earned a professional certificate and could teach in any county of the State. This certificate was also honored in other States. There were very few High Schools then and they were in the cities only, so I went into the graded work. Young men with influence back of them were the only persons who were able to get more desirable places. Woman had scarcely begun to come into her own. Women teachers in the grades were not much more than mere cogs in a wheel which sometimes, unfortunately for all concerned, was turned by a "Crank".

A real teacher cannot do her best work unless she can be free to use her own personality. So, after I had taught in several of the county seats including Keyser and West Union, I decided to apply for a position as Principal of one of the smaller graded schools in counties where I was already known — these salaries were better too. I began in Springfield in my own county, then, after two terms, went to Frankford

(Fort Ashby) and Ridgeley in Mineral, an adjoining county, five years. From there to the four-room school on Industrial Avenue, Clarksburg. I was now happy in the work but seeking a living salary. It took all I could make to live up to a teacher's standard. I decided to go to the Southern part of the State, on the Norfolk and Western R.R. These counties were rich in mineral wealth with educated board members who sought the best teachers for the sake of their own children, had the money and were willing to pay for them. I now had letters of recommendation from influential people, including County Superintendent, Geo. S. Arnold of Mineral county and Attorney John J. Carnwell of Hampshire county (now ex-governor). I had little trouble in securing what I asked for but teachers in West Virginia are subject to change in position every year and the boards also change often. Every new board had its own favorites to place. I seldom stayed longer than two or three terms in one town but always another place just as good was opened to me.

I had a rich experience among a varied new population in those Southern counties whose good people were from everywhere. Our buildings and equipment were good. We had the best teachers to be found in any of the counties. I was building character for I came in touch with hundreds of children of different ages and grades. I was making many friends. I was helping young teachers who had the ability but lacked the experience. I had the confidence of the county superintendents and served on Examining Boards. I established libraries in new buildings and replenished others with cooperative school programs. I had served as Principal at Nemours, Cinderella, Powhatan and other places. The World War came on and Father fell ill with paralysis. I resigned and went home to care for him. In 1919 I went back as Principal at Yukon. We had an epidemic of flu that closed the school. I was rooming at the Club House with a young primary teacher who took the disease. I nursed her, then took it myself. I barely escaped with my life and my health was so impared that I had eventually to give up teaching and go

9

on a farm where I could do outside work and live mostly in the open air when weather would permit. Since giving up my profession I have been taking data for this history and find it most interesting work. So many of the kin and others everywhere have aided and are aiding me, and their letters have been such an inspiration that I feel very proud that I have undertaken it. It is intended as a memorial to a wonderful people.

(1940) I own the spot where the Lieutenant Jonathan Pugh built the first home of our branch, whose descendants are now found in every state north of Mason and Dixon's line and many south of it. My home consists of 125 acres of the old Pugh estate which we think included all this valley on both sides of North River from Hanging Rock to Hoy, or near it, a distance of three miles and more than two miles wide, much of which was acquired before Hampshire was a county. Several old deeds here yet show where land was bought of the Commonwealth, or Lord Fairfax. The nest has been scattered and the birds have flown away, but the spirit of the Clan goes marching on.

Like many of my name I have remained single and perhaps, like them, not from lack of romance or natural attachments but from circumstances. Life is *not* what we make it. We are creatures of circumstances. My life has been blessed with useful activities and has been and is rich in friends, both men and women.

THAT PHANTOM STEED

A mystical path wends down through the years,
    And memory treds it at will:
Yes, Memory's the steed that carries one back
    To places long silent and still.

An old hitching-post at an old farm gate
    In fancy catches the rein.
The rider is off, a sick mother calls
    For a cup of cold water, again.

Then off through the dark those tiny feet speed;
    And back in a moment — what joy!
As fever-parched lips smile calmly and say,
    "Oh, thank you, my brave little boy!"

A heart flutters fast, the rein is unloosed;
    Away past a lonesome old pine;
Then on, on, on, till a school house appears
    With a myriad of faces in line.

*They are pals, everyone — teachers and all —
    To see them is perfect delight;
What joyous shouts ring loud through the air
    As the steed hurries on in his flight.

He prances along while sleigh-bells ring clear,
    Or he lags 'neath a paling moon.
Beside the road is a half-open gate
    Embowered in roses of June.

Inside the gate is an age-old oak-tree;
    Close by it a spring bubbles fair;
A glimpse of a rose, or lily; perhaps
    A thrush to be freed from a snare.

"Oh, Memory, stop! Pray, linger awhile!"
    But no, no! he heeds not the call —
That phantom-like steed just carries one on,
    Nor does he seem to tire at all.

11

He suddenly stops at a place called Now;
'Tis the place where one lives today;
But he will start again, most any-time
And travel the self-same way.

—LUKE McDOWELL

*(Student in Markwood School, 1893-94.   Maud Pugh, Teacher)

January 8th, 1935

CHAPTER INDEX

Chapter I

13

                              15

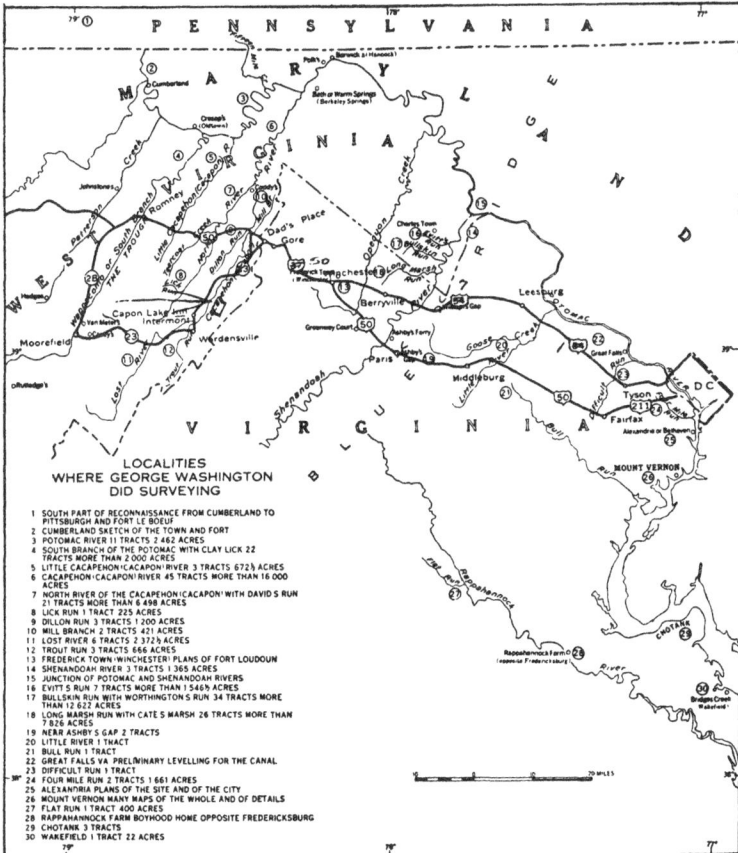

Based upon Plate 18 of the George Washington Atlas, edited by Col. Lawrence Martin
Reproduced by permission of the United States George Washington Bi-Centennial Commission

LOCALITIES
WHERE GEORGE WASHINGTON
DID SURVEYING

1 SOUTH PART OF RECONNAISSANCE FROM CUMBERLAND TO PITTSBURGH AND FORT LE BOEUF
2 CUMBERLAND SKETCH OF THE TOWN AND FORT
3 POTOMAC RIVER 11 TRACTS 2 462 ACRES
4 SOUTH BRANCH OF THE POTOMAC WITH CLAY LICK 22 TRACTS MORE THAN 2 000 ACRES
5 LITTLE CACAPEHON (CACAPON) RIVER 3 TRACTS 672½ ACRES
6 CACAPEHON (CACAPON) RIVER 45 TRACTS MORE THAN 16 000 ACRES
7 NORTH RIVER OF THE CACAPEHON (CACAPON) WITH DAVID S RUN 21 TRACTS MORE THAN 6 498 ACRES
8 LICK RUN 1 TRACT 225 ACRES
9 DILLON RUN 3 TRACTS 1 200 ACRES
10 MILL BRANCH 2 TRACTS 421 ACRES
11 LOST RIVER 6 TRACTS 2 372½ ACRES
12 TROUT RUN 3 TRACTS 666 ACRES
13 FREDERICK TOWN (WINCHESTER) PLANS OF FORT LOUDOUN
14 SHENANDOAH RIVER 3 TRACTS 1 365 ACRES
15 JUNCTION OF POTOMAC AND SHENANDOAH RIVERS
16 EVITT S RUN 7 TRACTS MORE THAN 1 546½ ACRES
17 BULLSKIN RUN WITH WORTHINGTON S RUN 34 TRACTS MORE THAN 12 622 ACRES
18 LONG MARSH RUN WITH CATE S MARSH 26 TRACTS MORE THAN 7 826 ACRES
19 NEAR ASHBY S GAP 2 TRACTS
20 LITTLE RIVER 1 TRACT
21 BULL RUN 1 TRACT
22 GREAT FALLS VA PRELIMINARY LEVELLING FOR THE CANAL
23 DIFFICULT RUN 1 TRACT
24 FOUR MILE RUN 2 TRACTS 1 661 ACRES
25 ALEXANDRIA PLANS OF THE SITE AND OF THE CITY
26 MOUNT VERNON MANY MAPS OF THE WHOLE AND OF DETAILS
27 FLAT RUN 1 TRACT 400 ACRES
28 RAPPAHANNOCK FARM BOYHOOD HOME OPPOSITE FREDERICKSBURG
29 CHOTANK 3 TRACTS
30 WAKEFIELD 1 TRACT 22 ACRES

Compliments of J F Baylis, Capon Lake Inn, Intermont, West Virginia

"The Pioneers," sculptured by A. Phimister Proctor

—Photo by couresy of W. C. Brown.

The old Linsley Institute Building at Wheeling, the first Capitol of West Virginia.

Arthur I. Boreman, of Parkersburg,
first Governor of West Virginia

CHAPTER I

A TRIBUTE TO WEST VIRGINIA

Bruce Barton, author of "The Man Nobody Knows," has written this tribute to West Virginia for the "Parade of the States" Monday night programs of the General Motors Corporation, part of an educational plan to make the country as a whole better acquainted with the individual states—their history, secenic beauty, industries and people.

From the east you see a mountain wall. From the west you look up toward the headwaters of hurrying streams. There among the tops is West Virginia, the Mountain State.

Rivers go roaring down with the power of a million horses, to flow at peace among fields and pastures and hillside orchards. Industry hums in the valleys, paved highways course beneath the Warriors' Road where moccasined feet once trod. Deep in the earth the wells go reaching for West Virginia's oil and natural gas, and deep lies her coal that can be mined for twenty centuries more.

West Virginia raised the barrier of her mountains against early comers from the east, but there were breaks in the barrier and men passed through to empire. At the falls of the Great Kanawha a royal governor staked the claim that won the West from France. George Washington came this way a-measuring land while he was yet a young surveyor. The oak tree from which whole states were mapped, the earliest corner tree in all the Mississippi Valley, is standing yet at Marlinton.

Trees, trees, always trees—West Virginia dwells in their shade. Here is the botanist's paradise, the native home of more than sixteen hundred flowering plants. Here one may pay tribute to the mother-trees of Grimes' Golden Apple and the Golden Delicious. National forests lure you, and two that the state preserves.

Your wanderings will bring you to strange rivers that dive under mountains and flow mysteriously for miles before they return to the light. You will find a spot where ice is forever forming, no matter how hot the sun. You will stand

19

where your gaze can sweep across a score of mountains. You will look on Harper's Ferry, with its memories of John Brown, and on other fields of battle. You will taste the waters and the welcome of White Sulphur and other Springs, famous since colonial days as spots of lovliness and rest.

This is the state where the mother of Lincoln was born. Stonewall Jackson was a native son. James Bridger, scout of the Oregon Trail, learned his craft in these woods. True mountaineers they were, these sons of West Virginia and truly did they live her motto that "Mountaineers are always free." In our own time the Mountain State has given Dwight Morrow, John W. Davis and Newton D. Baker to the nation.

West Virginia, we honor you as the Old Dominion's daughter; we distinguish you as the youngest state east of the Mississippi. You have the culture of the Old South, the enterprise of the industrial North, the rugged spirit of that West whose gates you opened. Through the blue air that tops your mountains, we salute you. West Virginia, hail!

HELLO! WEST VIRGINIA

Bentztown Bard in the Baltimore Sun

The National road o'er the mountain Frederick and Braddock and then,
Boonsboro, Shepherdstown—yonder that ribbon of river agains
That ribbon of Upper Potomac, and Martinsburg next in line—
Hello! Miss West Virginia, as sweet as a flower on a vine.

Home by the old way, ascending through Harpers Ferry and by
The Jefferson pike to old Frederick, under its Maryland sky!
The Shenandoah's sweet music, and o'er the Potomac again —
Hello! Miss West Virginia, Sweet land of the memories of men!

A circuit of magic, the morning all crystal with kiss of the dew,
Around the great loop of the mountains, with every sweet minute a view.
A B. & O. train in the distance, a peak of great rocks 'gainst the sky—
Hello! Miss West Virginia, with a twinkle of love in your eye!

This picture was taken in Morgan County, near Great Cacapon, and shows the B. & O. Railroad, the Potomac River, the old C. & O. Canal, and the Western Maryland Railroad.

W. VA. STATE CAPITOL

HAMPSHIRE COUNTY, NOW, WEST VIRGINIA

This division of the Old Dominion was first Spottsylvania County, 1720 to 1734, then Orange County, 1734 to 1738. In the year 1738 the portion of Orange County, Virginia, west of the Blue Ridge, was made into two new counties, Augusta and Frederick, since there were already many settlements there. Frederick county embraced the lower, or northern part of Shenandoah Valley with Winchester as the county seat, and Augusta, the southern or upper, with Staunton as the county seat. This division embraced the whole Northwest Territory which extended to the Mississippi River and from this Hampshire, the oldest county in West Virginia, was chiefly formed in 1754, in pursuance of an Article passed by the General Assembly on December 13, 1753, and then included Hardy, Mineral, Grant counties, parts of Morgan and Pendleton, Hardy being cut off from it in 1785, and Mineral soon after the Civil War, and Grant from that fourteen days later, 1866.

Hampshire is now a part of the Eastern Pan Handle of West Virginia. It contains 640 square miles and approximately 409,600 acres, drained in a north easterly direction by the Potomac and its tributaries, Capon and North rivers, Little Capon, and South Branch, named from east to west.

Climatic conditions are fairly uniform through the county, summers warm with few hot spells, and winters cold. It is adapted to agriculture, and may be divided into three classes: first, smooth upland, suited to general farm crops, orchards and pasture. Second, river bottom lands that are very productive, suited to corn, wheat, oats hay, potatoes and gardening. Third, mountain acres, more or less stony and too steep for cultivation, that are forested but some of this land is cleared and used for orchards or summer sheep pasture.

The width of the valleys of the streams vary with the size of the stream.

The Allegheny Mountain Spurs, included in and bounding the county are Patterson's Creek Mountains on the west, South Branch Mountains, Short Mountain, Side Long Hill and Spring Gap, North River Mountains, Timber Ridge, Ice Mountain,

21

Castle Mountain, Capon and Bear Garden, Little North Mountain and Great North Mountain. The average elevation of these are: west is about 2,200 feet, and on the east, 2,000. The highest point in the county is 3,060 feet above sea level, four miles east of Sector.

Romney, the county seat, named for a Cinque Port in England, at first was intended to be a central location but after the other counties were cut off and changed, and new developments came about, has been a very inconvenient location for the Eastern Districts. They do much business at Winchester and Martinsburg, and more recently the Eastern section is outvoted by the more thickly settled upper end — Western part of the county — where the population has increased by proximity to railroads and these districts have thereby lost representation; consequently the farmers' roads and other improvements have been neglected, which has caused dissatisfaction, and much of the best blood of the county has been lost to other states by continuous exodus from the beloved Capon Valley, which includes North River and its drains. Capon Valley, being nearest Jamestown and accessible to the Old Indian Trail from New York and Pennsylvania to the Carolinas was naturally the home of early settlers. They filtered in by way of what is now Harper's Ferry with their pack horses. There is good reason to believe that there were pioneers here as early as 1698 or soon after. (See Philadelphia records).

These settlers were largely British people, Welsh, Scotch, Irish and English, and brought with them samples of the home comforts, as well as the brain and refinements of the homeland. They, being cut off from it by lack of roads and transportation, very soon set about making provision for their future needs by building mills, roads, tanneries, factories, ferries, forts, etc. The flax hackler, the distaff, the spinning wheel, the hand looms, the swift flying needle, the press board, and goose irons were necessary adjuncts. They grew their own flax and wool and manufactured it in the home, used wild fruits and pounded the corn in a mortar at first, dipped their own candles and burned pine knots, which were plentiful, in the wide, open fire places which they constructed from native stones; made their own moccasins from buckskin — not brought down for sport, but which provided meat for the household. Without matches they struck a spark with flint into flax lint, or borrowed fire, if a neighbar lived close enough. They used honey from a bee tree to preserve the wild fruits and made sugar from sugar maple sap, grew tobacco which they cured and used as money, made their own brooms and utensils; had their own forge for blacksmithing where they made most of their farming tools and even nails for the erection of log houses. These logs were chiefly hearts of virgin pine, hand hewn with a broadaxe, rafters of poles covered with oak shingles, hand riven and planed, or clapboards formed the roof. Few doors and windows adorned these pioneer homes. They were expensive and hard to make. Some of these log houses built perhaps 200 years ago are still occupied by the descendants of the builders, and the logs, preserved many years by weatherboarding, are still sound.

Old church records prove that there was a settlement of Quakers in Quaker Hollow, and perhaps Sandy Ridge, before 1730. Old records of the Welsh founders of Pennsylvania and Glenn's Book of Welsh Genealogy give data to show that one Evan Pugh ("who married Mary"), son of Robert Pugh, who married Sarah Evan, daughter of Rev. Evan Lloyd Evan, that traced back to Capt. Madog, of the Era of Lancaster, emigrated to Virginia soon after 1698. These pioneer founders were both Quakers and Church of England people but this particular Evan Pugh and his father, Robert, were Church of England people. Church history again shows that there was a settlement of Church of England, or Episcopalians, on North River, a branch of Capon, large enough to form a parish at a very early time before the county was organized and that old Zion was the second church in that valley to be erected.

There is a tradition in the Pugh family of the Lieut. Jonathan, son of Evan, line that he helped build the first Episcopal church in this section, consequently the first church of that denomination in West Virginia. It was then called the Church of England. There are records here to show that he had lived on North River, north of Hanging Rock before 1757, since his third child, the Capt. Jonathan Pugh, was born there August 21, of that year and that he held a commission under the Royal Governor Botelourt, 1768. He later fought with the Virginians for Independence in the Revolution. He was burried here, October, 1794.

It is also an established fact that among the Sandy Ridge-Quaker Hollow pioneers was a John Hiett and his son, Ebon, Quaker minister, the founders of the Hiett family of this county here very early in the century. They, too, were British people as were the Monroes and others of the earliest settlers and may have known each other before coming to Virginia from Pennsylvania, as these families have intermarried and been neighbors and friends ever since pioneer days.

History speaks of a Robert Pugh, whose sons Joseph Edwards the builder of Fort Edwards, 1747 and 1748, the first Indian Fort in West Virginia, willed 400 acres on both sides of Capon. This Robert married Joseph Edwards' daughter, Mary, and reared twelve children, several of whom were born in the 1750's and one of whom is the reputed founder of the Capon Bridge settlement. This complete family record is preserved and given elsewhere in this book.

Trustees for Capon Springs, 1787, Elias Poston, Henry Frye, Isaac Hawk, Jacob Hoover, John Winterton, Valentine Swisher, Rudolph Baumgardner, Paul McIvor, John Sherman Woodcock and Isaac Zane.

LORD FAIRFAX

By a grant from Charles II, all the lands bounded by the Rappahannock and the Potomac to their head waters became the property of various English proprietors of whom Lord Culpepper was one. He eventually bought out the others and, by inheritance, this vast estate, about six million acres, descended to Lord Fairfax. He came to Virginia in 1747

24

and was so pleased with the country that he decided to live here. At that time he was middle aged, tall, dark hair and complexion. A scholar, a man of letters. He never married.

In 1748 Fairfax employed Washington, then a boy of 16, to survey his lands. He had met the youthful surveyor at Mt. Vernon, the home of Washington's brother Lawrence, whose wife was a relative of Fairfax. The day of this meeting was a regal date in the life of Washington and a fateful day to the distinguished nobleman, for in the three years spent in surveying the lands of the wilderness, Washington in every way fitted himself for leadership in the Indian Wars to follow, which paved the way for his appointment as Commander in Chief of the American Army; and the eight years' struggle that put an end to Great Britain's rule brought ruin to Lord Fairfax and his ambitions.

From the first, Fairfax had paid a small yearly rental to the King and had exacted a few cents per acre from persons living on his lands. "The Pepper Corn paid on Lady Day". If they had taken up and improved the lands without title he charged more. Immediately after his coming to this country he began selling his lands but the rental continued and thus he laid the foundation for an income that would enable him to live royally —but when the Revolutionary War broke out, Virginia began passing laws to break up such estates.

Thomas Jefferson was the leader. He wanted a law to prevent a man from selling his land and still keeping it — prevent him from collecting rent forever. "Estates should be held in fee simple." This stopped the rent on the land already sold by Fairfax.

Lord Fairfax early planned a princely home at Greenway Court in Clark County, the heart of the Valley, twelve miles from Winchester but completed only one building and in it his steward lived. He lived simply in a log cabin and had 150 slaves in cabins around about, and seemed happy.

He, as a friend of Washington, was not molested during the war though known to be a British sympathizer. General Washington visited him occasionally. He took to his bed at the defeat of Cornwallis at Yorktown and died soon after at the advanced age of 92. After the war his estates were confiscated as belonging to a Tory and all his unsold lands thrown open to the public, but a lawsuit of long duration followed in which the Fairfax legatees won out. This of course included Hampshire county.

Lord Fairfax lies buried in a crypt under the Chancel of the Episcopal Church in Winchester, Virginia, of which city he was one of the founders — See tablet erected in front of its court house.

Famous Old Bible

Among the relics of the old Fairfax family of Yorkshire are the famous Bible, prayer book, and psalter of Archbishop Neile. They date from 1618, and were given to the first Baron Fairfax by this celebrated primate of York, who was the son of a tallow chandler, became dean of Westminster, and passed through five bishoprics on his way to the primacy. As bishop of Rochester he had as his chaplain Laud, afterwards the celebrated archbishop of Canterbury. The Bible contains an entry of the baptism of Thomas Fairfax, the general who was commander in chief of the army of the parliament (1645-50). He was one of Charles I's judges, but afterward became a supporter of the restoration.

CHAPTER II
PUGHS, AS FIRST SETTLERS

The first Pughs to come to this country of whom we have any record were among the early founders of Pennsylvania, who arrived only a few years after Penn's original colony and settled in Chester and Philadelphia counties, as follows:

Ellis Pugh, born at Grath Gowen, Quaker minister; wife, Sinah, from Dongelly, Merioneth, Wales. Arrived, 1687. Settled in Rodnor Township, Chester county, Pennsylvania. Later, in Plymouth, Philadelphia county; died, 1718. Had a son John and other sons. (See letter of A. H. Pugh) Mrs. Ellis McClure, Miss Georgia B, Pugh and others.

William Pugh, "Friend", of near Dongelly, Merioneth, Wales. Yeoman, removed to Pa., 1688; wife, Katherine. Child, Ann, born in Wales.

Robert Pugh, of near Bala, County Merioneth. Yeoman, removed to Gwynedd, Pa., 1698. Church of England. Freeholder of 200 acres in Gwynedd. Wife, **Sarah,** daughter of Evan Lloyd Evan of Ucheldre. Children: **Sarah,** who married Samuel Bell; **Mary,** who married Roland Roberts, Evan, "who married Mary" and removed to Virginia, soon after 1698. **Ellen,** married John Rogers. (They were the ancestors of the Capon Valley Pughs).

William Pugh, Church of England, from Bala, Merioneth, Wales. Yeoman. Removed to Radnor, Pa., before 1700. Freeholder there. Wife unknown. Children: William and others. Died 1708.

David Pugh of Radnor, Pa., before 1701, and Freeholder of 174 acres, constable and supervisor before 1703. Wife, Catherine. Children: Jonathan and others, and Hannah, who married James Miles.

Evan Pugh, Church of England, of near Bala, Merioneth, Wales. Removed to Gwynedd, Pa., 1698, which seems to indicate that Robert Pugh and his son, Evan, removed from the same place in Wales and settled at the same time and place in Pennsylvania, where Evan was a Freeholder before going to Virginia. His wife's name was Mary, according to some genealogists, which may have been a second marriage.

This information of emigrant ancestors is largely obtained from a book of genealogy by Thos. Allen Glenn of Wales, and seems to be borne out by Pennsylvania records. According to Librarian Spofford's examination of Glenn's book in the Library of the Historical Society of Pennsylvania in Philadelphia, September 30, 1933, Sarah Pugh, daughter of Rev. Evan Lloyd Evan by his second wife, traces back through "a Deirwa Ddu ap Madog" or Madoc. In other words, Sarah Pugh traces kinship back to Madog. See Glenn's Welsh Founders of Pennsylvania, Vol. I, page 204, and pedigree in Vol. II, page 100; also, Vol. II, page 78.

All historians and readers are familiar with the story of the Welsh Prince Madoc who "sailed westward with a fleet, A. D., 1170, discovered a vast and fertile continent", returned to Wales, sailed again with ten vessels and was never more heard of. (See R. P. Anderson's "America Not Discovered by Columbus".

Humphrey Lloyd, 1559, Nova Hespania, part of Florida traditions there of a strange race who had honored the Cross, and an Indian tribe in Mexico which spoke the Welsh language —all in line of proof that the Welsh Prince reached America on his first voyage of the 12th century, left a colony, but having been lost on his second voyage they were absorbed as natives. Other traditions show their influence on the Mayas, some of their notions being similar to that of orthodox Christians.

In the Glenn Book the matter of whether Sarah was the wife of Robert or Evan Pugh is somewhat confused, but is clarified by the fact that Robert had three children; namely, Sarah; Evan, who removed to Virginia; Ellen, and elsewhere Evan is said to have "married Mary".

The Welsh Founders of Pennsylvania honored the discoverer by naming one of their first settlements there Gwynedd — the Prince's father was Owen Gwynedd.

There is a tradition in the family of the Lientenant Jonathan Pugh that the first Pughs to come to this country were four brothers to Pennsylvania, and it seems probable that four of these men were of the same family, since they are practically from the same place in Wales and settled at first in, or near, the same locality. It is noticeable, too, that the children of the different families, all down the line bear the same family names.

It was then, and is now, a common thing for brothers and sisters to differ on religious matters. And it is not strange that some of these Church of England faith should later remove to Virginia, as the Old Dominion largely held to that church.

The people immediately showed their frugality and their determination to adopt this country as their future home by becoming Freeholders, and by taking a wholesome interest in local affairs as shown by records.

COPY
(Verbatim to the History)

"Glenn's Welsh Founders of Pennsylvania, Volume I, page 204.

Evan Pugh of near Bala, County of Merioneth; Yeoman, removed to Gwynedd, Pa., 1698. Church of England. Freeholder of land in Gwynedd. Wife, Sarah, daughter of Evan Lloyd Evan (otherwise Evan ap Evan), of Ucheldre; parents of Llanfor, according to earliest MS.. but later MSS differ (see Pedigree in Volum II).

(This chart is on page 100 of Volume II).

In a footnote Glenn says there is doubt as to whether Evan or Robert Pugh is the correct name of Sarah's husband.

The above Evan Lloyd Evan traces back through a Deiews Ddu ap Madog about 1400, Glenn, Volume II, page 78."

THE FIRST SETTLER IN WEST VIRGINIA FROM KNOWN RECORDS, A WELSHMAN, MORGAN MORGAN

Since this volume is devoted to two families of Welsh pioneers — Pughs and Offuts of Capon Valley — our readers will be interested in a Welsh pioneer who settled on another tributary of the Potomac nearby, very early.

Morgan Morgan cut the trees and hewed the logs, as did the Pughs and Offuts, for his dwelling at Bunker Hill, 1727. He is said to have been the first military officer, peace officer and first hotel proprietor in the community that grew up around him.

His son, Zackwell Morgan, founded Morgantown, our university city. A mound of stones marks his grave as an Old Indian fighter, near Morgantown. Among the State's prominent men who are his descendants, Francis H. Pierpont, the war governor of Virginia and E. F. Morgan, Governor of West Virginia are outstanding examples.

CENSUS OF 1790 IN HAMPSHIRE COUNTY GAVE THE FOLLOWING AMONG THE RESIDENTS
Fron the list of Levi Ashbrook, 1785

Samuel Pugh, Capon; Thomas Pugh, Capon, near what is now Gore; Jacob Pugh, Capon and North River; Bethuel Pugh, North River, Jonathan Pugh, North River, adjoining each other; Robert Pugh, Capon; Jonathan Pugh, Jr., North River.

William Murphy; James Murphy; Hugh Murphy.

Daniel Westfall; John Westfall, Sr.; John Westfall, Jr.; Jacob Westfall; Henry Westfall; Eleanor Westfall (widow); Cornelius Westfall.

Ebenezer Wood; Richard Wood.

CHAPTER III

PUGH FAMILY

Historical and Genealogical Research of Atty. A. D. Pugh, Des Moines, Iowa, dated 1927.

To go back to the migration of the family to this country, I found from the source mentioned at Philadelphia that there were at least five of the Pughs among the Welch founders of Pennsylvania, viz.:

David Pugh, of Rodnor, Pennsylvania, before 1701. Constable, Freeholder of 174 acres before 1703, in Rodnor. Wife, Catherine, Children: Jonathan, Hannah, who married James Miles, and others.

Ellis Pugh, "Friend", of Drithdu, near Dongelly, County Merioneth. Wife, Sina, Yeoman, removed to Pennsylvania in 1687.

William Pugh, Church of England, of Bala, County Merioneth. Yeoman, removed to Rodnor, Pennsylvania, before 1700. Freeholder there. Died, 1708. Wife unknown. One child, William.

William Pugh, "Friend", of near Dongelly, County Merioneth. Yeoman. Removed to Pennsylvania, 1688. Wife, Katherine. child, Ann born in Wales.

Robert Pugh, of near Bala, County Merioneth. Yeoman. Removed to Gwynedd, Pennsylvania, 1698. Church of England. Freeholder of 200 acres in Gwynedd. Wife, Sarah, daughter of Evan Lloyd Evan, of Uchldre. Their children were: Sarah, who married Samuel Bell; Evan, who removed to Virginia; Ellen, who married Roberts of Merioneth, and it seems that Sarah also married Rawland Roberts of Gwynedd, which I take to be a second marriage.

There is also further reference to Evan Pugh, Church of England, of near Bala, County Merioneth. Removed to Gwynedd, Pennsylvania, 1698, Freeholder in Gwynedd (Which I

31

take to indicate that Evan and his father, Robert Pugh, came at the same time and from the same place in Wales.)

The book from which I obtained this information of emigrant ancestors is now out of print and I could not obtain a copy. I have asked my son Jonathan H. Pugh, instructor at the University of Pennsylvania to try to find one at a second-hand store. Its author is Thos. Allen Glenn of Wales. It gives a large amount of pedigree of the family in Wales, showing in general, descent from an Old Lord named Madog or Madoc, as I remember it. The book is not easy to understand unless one has more experience than I have in reading Welch ancient pedigree.

I did not find that Evan was one of Penn's party but I did find the above reference to his coming soon after Penn's coming, which I think fairly verifies this family tradition. Evan, who migrated to Virginia might easily have been the father, or grandfather of my great grandfather Jonathan of Hampshire county, Virginia, who held the Lieutenant's commission in the Colonial Army, 1768. I feel that I can verify the accuracy of this commission. My father remembered the signature of the Colonial Royal Governor appended to it as Bofetourt. He was governor about the years 1768 to 1769 and died 1770 in Williamsburg, Virginia.

I know nothing of the descendants of my grandfather's older brother Jonathan who remained in Virginia, except that he had a son Jonathon, I think, about as old as my grandfather John. It seems quite likely to me that some of his children migrated to Ohio. Some of the descendants of Aaron near Lima, Ohio, look very much like members of my family, and I believe Ohio Aaron came from Virginia. They do not seem to have descended from any of my grandfather's other brothers.

I frankly admit that I think it is a benefit to me to know my breeding, for the more I know of it the better I know myself.

With all those fine emotions which one member of a good family should feel for the other members of it, we are,

Yours respectfully,

(Signed). A. D. Pugh

32

From "Historical Collections of Gwynedd" (Jenkins) 1884, p. 149, with additions from "Hopewell Friends History" 1936. Pugh — Evans Families who came to Pennsylvania, 1698

ROBERT PUGH married Sarah Evans, sister of the four brothers, dau, of Evan ap Evan, the marriage doubtless in Wales.

Children of Robert and Sarah Pugh:

Evan, who went to Virginia to live. One of his sons became a Baptist minister, and one a justice of the peace in good circumstances. Document of 1797.

Sarah, married Samuel Bell. "They left one daughter, Hannah wh married Evan Rees of Providence township.

Ellin, married John Rogers, 4-21-1717. In 1744 they removed to Frederick County Virginia.

Mary, married Rowland Roberts. They had a son Elden who was father of John Roberts, Esq., in Montgomery township.

No further history of Evan Pugh.

Children of Evan and Hannah Rees were: Samuel, removed to near Stroudsburg, Pa.; Evan; Daniel; Sarah, all of Providence township, Montgomery county, Pa., and of the Baptist Church.

Children of John and Ellin Rogers in Frederick county, Va., were: Evan, married Sarah Ballinger in 1749; Owen, married Lydia ———; Edward, married Hannah Borden; Thomas, marmarried ———; William married Elizabeth Branson; Eleanor, married Benjamin Barrett; Sydney, married Isaac Wright. The Barretts removed to Highland County, Ohio.

Rowland Roberts' descendents are given in "Historical Collections of Gwynedd", p. 195, 199.

Kindness of Mrs. Matida W. Evans, West Chester, Pa., 1939.

From the Genealogical Research of A. D. Pugh, Attorney at Law, Des Moines, Iowa, kindly turned over to the writer for use in this book.

My great grandfather, Jonathan Pugh, settled in Hampshire county, Virginia, near Romney. He held a Lieutenant's Commission in the Colonial Army in 1768, which he gave to his son Jesse who gave it to my father, Jonathan Gilbert Pugh, but it was lost during his absence in California in '49. He married Margaret Wood, who died about 1812, having out-lived her husband some years. Their children were: Daniel, Jonathan, David, Hananiah, Jesse, John; daughters, Sydney, Margaret and Lucy.

Jonathan, it is thought, inherited a part of the old homestead and remained in Virginia (now West Virginia).

David settled in northeast Ohio and had two sons, Jonathan and Nidy. Both sons went to California and Nidy afterwards returned and settled on the Des Moines River in Iowa.

Jesse settled at New Lancaster, now Lancaster, Ohio, and had two sons, James and John, and a daughter, Susan, who married a Mr. Smith. James married a sister of a lawyer and moved to Nebraska about 1876. John settled in Morrow county, Ohio.

Hananiah settled in Newark, Ohio, and was killed by a falling tree. ("He is one of the first fifteen settlers with their families, 1804, in Newark, as noted in the Historical Collections of Ohio by Henry Howe. He is thought to have married a Miss Dar-lington. He was born in Virginia about 1779 (As per Gilbert Cope's Darlington Research)". He had two sons, Merryweather and John.

Sydney married for her first husband, Harvey Westfall, Hamp-shire county, Virginia. Their children were a son, Harvey, and two daughters, Sydney and Mary. Sydney married a Carmichael and their children were a son, James, and other sons and daugh-ter, Mary, who married a Crall. Their children were, John Abraham, James and Susan. After the death of Mr. Westfall, Sydney married Christopher Lamberton, of Mansfield, Ohio. They had three sons: Jonathan, Robert and Christopher who settled in Arkansas. One was killed.

My grandfather, **John Pugh,** was born September 12, 1782. Removed to Mansfield, Ohio, about 1812 and established the first tavern in that city on Main Street, on the site now occu-pied by the Masonic Temple. He also ran a tanyard several blocks north of the tavern, on the ground now occupied by the Baltimore and Ohio Terminals.

About 1812-13 he married **Florinda Murphy** from near Hagers-town, Maryland. Her father was Asa Murphy and her mother, a Shipley, who was related to the Cockey family of Maryland. Florinda had a sister Mary and another sister, both of whom married Teals of Indiana. Florinda also had two brothers, Asa and Benjamin; Asa of Huntington, Indiana; Benjamin, near Columbus, Ohio. Asa had a son Pugh Murphy. Florinda, born January 12, 1797, died August 23, 1847.

The children of John and Florinda Pugh: Hanibal H., John Wood, Jonathan Gilbert, Euphemia (Effie), Margaret Ann, Elizabeth Amanda and Alverda Tomanis.

Hanibal H. went south with one Hedrick, last heard from on Red River, Louisiana. Reported killed.

John Wood, a physician, married Harriett Rutger, daughter of Dr. Rutger, Mansfield, Ohio. He lived in Nevada during the Civil War and was Speaker of the House there. He removed to California about '49 where he lectured on anatomy and had the first anatomical chart in the state. He had one child, Josephine, who married a man named Crocker, near Sacramento, California.

Euphemia (Effie) married Alfred Foulks of Rome, Ohio. Children: John Pugh Foulks, who was 16 when the family crossed the plains to California. George W., Louisa Satira, and Josephine. After the death of her husband the family moved to California. There Josephine married Abraham Clark Freeman, well-wnown law author of San Francisco. George W.'s son, George Guy Foulks, lives at Elk Grove, California, on a ranch located by my father, Jonathan Gilbert Pugh, in '49.

Maragaret Ann married James McNulty of Pennsylvania, settled at Ashland, Ohio, conducted the McNulty House there for years. Their children were Horace Pugh, Agnes, Flora and Isabella.

James McNulty went to California about 1850, died of cholera. Margaret Ann then married William McNulty of Pennsylvania, their children being William, James, and Edward Bird.

Horace Pugh McNulty was a dentist of Ashland, Ohio. unmarried. Agnes married first an Atkinson, then Asa Holt of New York. Flora married George Moulton, Minneapolis, Minnesota. Isabella, unmarried, lived with her brother at Ashland; now deceased.

William James McNulty was a civil engineer of reputation and ability for the government. He located much of Missouri, Kansas and Texas Railway. Inspected Cottonbelt Railroad when sold. Was engineer for the City of St. Louis for years. He married May Sprengle of Ashland, Ohio. They had two sons: Hugh Pugh and Naulta Neil. They removed to California where he died in 1911.

Edward Bird McNulty married and settled in Duluth, Minnesota, where he was a prominent and successful dentist for many years. He has two sons, and is now deceased.

Elizabeth Amanda married Hugh M. Colwell of Lexington, Ohio. Later settled in Muscatine county, Iowa, and afterwards moved to near Holden, Missouri. Their children were: Samuel Pugh, Thomas Cummins, Hugh M., Florinda and Anna Agnes.

Alverda Tomanis Pugh went with my father to California about 1850 and there married Solon Moore, formerly of Missouri, and settled at Oakland. Their children are: Horace, Henry, Ida, Florinda and one other. Her branch still reside at Oakland, where she died in recent years.

Jonathan Gilbert Pugh, my father, was born January 12, 1825, died April 13, 1894. He served through the Mexican War in Taylor's Division, and as lieutenant of Home Guards in the Civil War. He went to California by water in 1849, returned around the Horn and took an expedition across the plains in 1852 in association with one Jacob Beem of Pennsylvania. Again returned to Ashland, Ohio, and engaged in business there for a short time. Located land in Iowa in company with George Carpenter, lawyer of Mansfield, Ohio. Pioneered in Iowa and Kansas. Settled in Muscatine county, Iowa, in 1857; removed to Poweshiek county, Iowa, in 1875, about 1880 prospected and located a mine in Colorado. Moved to Des Moines in 1893.

In 1857 my father married Harriett Victoria Baker. Their children are: Bobt. Wood, lawyer, Williamsburg, Iowa, now

JOHN PUGH FAULKS

"Jack Faulks" as given in A. D. Pugh's
poem, "The Overland Trail". Great
grandson of Lieutenant Jonathan Pugh,
of the Indian Wars. This picture was
made some years after the Civil War.
He died in California.

DR. JOHN WOOD PUGH
Son of John Pugh of Mansfield. Noted
Anatomist and Physician in California
where he died and is buried.

deceased; George H., Garfield, Colorado; Frank Edward, Tacoma, Washington; Albert D., Attorney, Des Moines, Iowa, Clara Pugh, teacher, Des Moines; Mrs. S. B. Doty, Oakes, North Dakota, Effie Pugh, teacher, Chicago, 500 Diversity Parkway; Zada Pugh, teacher, Des Moines; Harriett, died in childhood; and Mrs. Clementine Arands, wife of Dr. A. L. Arands, St. Paul, Minnesota, and White Bear Lake.

THE BAKERS

My mother's great grandfather was Mushack Baker who came from Pennsylvania to Ohio in very early times, settled on Paint Creek, near Bainbridge, Ohio. He married Ann Watson and both are buried at the Falls of Paint Creek near the Rapid Forge. Their chidren were: Ephraim, Charles, James, Maurice, Benoni and Ruth.

Benoni Baker, my mother's grandfather married Elizabeth Stewart, related to Fraziers and of Scotch descent. Their children were: Isaac, my mother's father, Benjamin, Nancy, Elizabeth, Sarah and Mary.

Isaac Baker married Clarinda Clayton Anderson, of near Scottsville, Fluvianna county, Virginia. Their only child was Harriett V. Baker, my mother, who died here in Des Moines, Iowa, 1904.

Benjamin Baker married Mahala Blackburn and died at Bainbridge in recent years.

37

CHAPTER IV

PUGH FAMILY

Evan Line

John Pugh, 1st, was son of Evan, who came to Virginia from Pennsylvania soon after 1698.

Evan was son of Robert Pugh who married Sarah, daughter Evan Lloyd Evan, an Episcopal Bishop of Wales who traced his lineage to Madoc, or Madog. This Robert Pugh family removed from Wales to Pennsylvania about 1698. Robert and Sarah remained in Pennsylvania—Philadelphia records—see else-wher, this Volume.

Evan and wife, whose name, according to Gilbert Cope the historian, was Mary, were found here when the first records were made, with the following sons, all at the age to do business; namely:

Jonathan, who was lientenant in the Indian Wars; the above John who, between 1765 and 1770, removed to Orange county, North Carolina to escape from the Indian Wars. Jacob who appears on Wills and Deeds here before 1777 when his name is found on the roll of men of Captain Foreman's Company. Killed in the Indian massacre at Grove Creek, near Wheeling. Captain Foreman and his Company from Hampshire county were enroute to assist the besieged garrison at Fort Henry, now Wheeling, when they fell into an ambush where he and thirty men lost their lives. He may have left a son Jacob, per old records.

It seems that Jacob was married and had children as some are later given in court records as daughters of Jacob Pugh.

An Evan Pugh also appears in records for a time late in the century, who was doubtless, Evan, Jr.

Robert Pugh, who may have been the youngest of these brothers, married Mary Edwards, daughter of Joseph Edwards, the earliest Fort builder in what is now West Virginia. They joined lands with James Caudy, the noted Indian fighter, on either side, near where Capon Bridge now stands.

John Pugh never returned to Virginia but sold his lands here on both sides of North River from North Carolina.

The farm adjoining Lieutenant Jonathan to the North-East, which was a Fairfax land grant of 1765, he sold to Betheul Pugh and wife (who was a Tansy), 1770. This land is now known as the Jerry Hiett place. Betheul Pugh was born about 1740, married about 1765, died without children, about 1822. Aaron Malick, born 1801, said to Asa Hiett, that he dug Betheul Pugh's grave at what now is the Jerry Hiett burial ground, when he was a young man. A large tree, wild cherry, stands between the graves of Betheul and wife, close up to her grave. It is a beautiful tree, tall and symetrical. Since the graves of the husband and wife are unusually far apart it would seem that the tree may have been of a decade's growth or more before the second grave was dug. It is almost certain that Betheul was John's son and there is no record of more than one Tansy family here, so Betheul's wife must have been a sister of Mary Ellen Tansy Pugh, wife of Captain Jonathan, and of Mrs. Elizabeth Tansy Hiett, wife of John Hiett, the 2nd, in Virginia They had one brother, Arthur Tansy, an architect who doubtless came here to rebuild the old Pugh Mill. He is buried in the Henry Pepper grave yard, which was a John Pugh farm.

The Tansy family were Quakers before the War for Inde pendence but on taking sides with the patriots were expelled from the church and left Maryland for Virginia, according to records of Society of Friends. It is possible that they were in Maryland for a time before coming to Virginia. Others of the Tansy family went south. See Tansy Family, this Volume.

Jonathan Pugh, known as Lieutenant Jonathan, whose commission was dated 1768 and signed by Governor Batetourt of Virginia, was born about 1720 in Capon Valley, Now Hampshire county, West Virginia, but then a part of Spottsylvania county, Virginia. There is no **positive** record of his life before marriage. What we have is fragmentary, received from various sources.

We think the old Bible with his family record may have been lost when the early home of his grandson, John Pugh, was consumed by fire — though much was saved.

Some of these old deeds, letters and documents have been handed down from generation to generation of those of the descendants who remained on parts of the old estate to the fourth generation, and are now in possession of John, and Finley Pugh and the writer. His Commission was given to the son Jesse who emigrated to Ohio late in the seventeen hundreds and was afterwards the property of his grandson, Jonathan Gilbert Pugh, of California and Iowa. The Lieutenant's Cavalry Saber is now owned by John Pugh of Hoy, West Virginia.

The Lieutenant espoused the cause of the Colonies and fought in the Revolution. The old sword sabre gives evidence of hard fighting. Morgan's men were familiar with his estate and one of his scouts, returning to Winchester from a reconnoiter up the creek that joins North River in sight of the Lieutenant's original residence, named the stream Tearcoat.

Early in the 1740's or before, Jonathan Pugh married Margaret Wood, English ancestry. The census of 1790 made from what was then Hampshire county gave several men named Wood, among them "Richard Wood", who was doubtless the father or brother of Margaret, since the following deed has been handed down in the family and is yet preserved. We believe they were near relatives of James Wood, founder of Winchester — as they were both here at this early date.

Deed

"From Beverly Randolph, Governor of Virginia, to Richard Wood, a tract of 429 A." dated October 12, 1768. This deed mentions a corner in Hanging Rock Run south of "U.S. 50," the southernmost limit of the Lieutenant's estate.

Deeds for several tracts of the estate have not been found and they may have had the so-called "Tomahawk Title" for them, since they seem to have been the oldest tracts. It is well established that the Pugh estates extended from one-half mile

41

below the mouth of Tearcoat to Hanging Rock Run, a distance up the valley of three miles or more with the line running to the top of North River Mountain.

The following children were born to Jonathan Pugh: **Margaret,** who married a Parsons, a slave holder, resided on South Branch, died without heirs.

Daniel, identified by a legal document in the hands of the writer dated the 15th day of March, 1793, in which he is shown to be a joint owner with his father of a slave named Dick, with witnesses present as follows: "James Daily, Isaac Parson, Wm. Fox"; also, by record in the Clerk's office at Romney in sale of Fairfax Confiscated lands: "1791, Dan'l Pugh, 9600 acres, on both sides of Patterson's Creek, including the greater part of the Philip Martin Manor." and by the wills of Daniel and his father Jonathan — W. B 2 — Romney, W. Va.

Lucy, wife of Francis Taggart, mentioned in the will of Jonathan, I.

Jonathan, Jr., in after years known as Captain Jonathan, born August 26, 1757, died August 21, 1834, is the oldest of the Jonathan Pugh line who remained in Hampshire county.

David, who settled in northeast Ohio.

Jesse, who carried his father's commission with him and was one of the first settlers in New Lancaster, Now Lancaster, southern, Ohio.

Hananiah, born 1779, one of the first fifteen married settlers of the city of Newark, Ohio, 1804. — From Howe's Historical Collections.

Sydney, who married Harvey Westfall (Westfalls, given in census of 1785) in Hampshire County, Virginia, then went to Ohio and became one of the founders of Mansfield. After the death of Mr. Westfall she married Christopher Lamberton of Mansfield. (Noted in A. D. Pugh research.)

John, born September 12, 1782, emigrated to Ohio in 1810 or 12, one of the founders of Mansfield. There is also some evidence that there was another daughter, the wife of one Hezekiah Davisson, who had a son, Thos. P. Davisson, and she was later married a second time. This is from an old letter but the matter is not clear. He is an executor on Daniel's will, 1794.

There is a legend among some of the Western branches that the Lieutenant was married twice, the first time to a French woman. If this is true, the Mrs. Davisson may have been their daughter. The Davissons lived in Marietta, Ohio, near Parkersburg, Virginia, 1812. Romney was the nearest post office to the ancestral home at that time and this letter was addressed to Captain Jonathan Pugh who lived in Hampshire county near Romney, Virginia. Thos. P. Davisson was asking his "Uncle Jonathan" for legal advice — he spoke of the Ohio Pughs as "uncles and aunts" but this present generation is not able to place him. The name Davisson looms large in **old Virginia** literature — they were not lost in their day. He wrote a beautiful hand. Here is hoping that this description will bring a response from some one who knows. There is also a legend that the first Jonathan was a member of the Virginia Assembly which has not been verified, though the writer has the antique silver watch, one of the very first made, that he is said to have carried while there. It is from Aunt Effie Monroe who held the watch and who had a wonderful memory. This watch has a double case, a chain spring and winds with a key. It did duty until after 1860. It once fell by accident into a well, was recovered by Mr. Alexander Monroe who dropped it, and to his great relief was found to be still running.

The old people still living in my childhood told me that my great, great grandfather was hospitable and had a humorous turn of mind, that he possessed a fund of good stories that attracted his fellow officers and friends, and won the love of servants. But back of it all was the proverbial backbone for which the name is notable. His wine bottle and glasses, and the turkey plate that graced his table are still preserved, as was also the platter made in London upon which reposed the roast pig with the red apple in its mouth, until the 1880's.

The silver and pewter were lost in the Civil War days, though some of the former was cunningly secreted in unusual places, and the latter stowed away in the basement of the "Old Mill".

The old mahogany desk of the ancestry is in John Pugh's home. John loves the old relics; he also owns a part of the old plantation and posseses some of the happy traits of his grandfather's grandfather, and is the only one of his immediate branch who is the father of sons to carry the name down, but the western Pughs of the line have sons.

The home of the first Jonathan was a log structure, hewn by hand from the hearts of virgin pine, impervious to water. The nails, too, were products of the brawny arm. The house, commodious in its day, had immense double stone chimneys with deep and wide fireplaces, having great wooden arches, the one in the kitchen equipped with hooks and appliances made at the forge to support the pots and kettles for cooking. There was ample room, too, for the ovens for bread and cakes.

The dining room, which was also the living room, contained the mahogany corner cupboard which went out of the family in 1926 with the sale of the effects of T. D. Pugh, the last of the fourth generation here to pass away. On the tall mantel stood the candles and in a corner the flax wheel, around the room the Windsor chairs.

This living room was radiant with a shining brass fireplace set, dog irons, shovel and tongs, the most beautiful perhaps to be found in the Old Dominion, not even Mt. Vernon has their equal. The father of the writer once owned them. Here in early days was enacted many a Yuletide scene, for the Pughs, being Welch, loved the old-time British customs.

Legend has it that feasting and merrymaking at Christmas time among them continued for a week or more, and that the colored servants engaged in it with as much joy and zest as did the whites. Together the boys brought in the Yule log, "Uncle Dick" played the fiddle, Uncle Ned met the quests at the door. The horses pranced, the sleigh bells jingled. "Grandmother", with "Aunt Dinah" and Aunt Cloe" prepared the feast at the end of which grandfather served the wine or apple jack.

The colored people had their full share of all the good things either in their cottages or at the great table in the kitchen as

Home of Lieutenant Jonathan Pugh

The Ancestral Jonathan Pugh fire place.

they chose, there being an air of freedom and good cheer everywhere and no labor during the whole season.

Most of the good food had been in course of preparation for days ahead. The fragrant bread baked in the Dutch oven, over coals from hickory wood burned in the fireplace, "tended" by Aunt Dinah.

The pound cake, the tangle breeches, the mince pie, the cookies, the honey from the bee tree, the deer and the "possum" were all here and ready. No Chef from a Ritz or a Waldorf Astoria ever prepared anything half so toothsome as that of the colored cook of the old South.

The world lost much with the passing of the fireplace, the symbol of good cheer.

> "The quaint, old customs are no more,
>   The Yule log and the coach and four,
>   The powdered wigs and buckled knees,
>   Gone are the old time ways like these."

Traces of the colored servants' cottages remained until 1870. My father cared for Aunt Clara, the last to remain after the Civil War. She, like all Pugh servants I heard about, was very black, with thick lips and a happy, loving disposition, and all the old-time negro dialect. She, you will note by reading the Lieutenant Jonathan's will, came down to us from our great, great Aunt, Lucy Tygart, and died, age about 87.

The Pughs and their colored people, like the Offutts and theirs lived happily together, no stories of sales or runaway slaves ever came down to us — they were busy and happy and well fed.

Slavery, however, was a misfortune for the South and wrong in principle but She was only partly to blame for it. The East and Northeast trafficked in slaves and passed them on to the South where the climate and soil were suited to them, and there the government allowed them to take root, which should never have occured.

They were sometimes driven through in herds like cattle from the Eastern Seaports and sold to planters on the way.

45

Many was the scene enacted on this North Western Turnpike, after its construction, as told by the older people now passed on. Since this institution had been allowed to exist it should have been dealt with by pacific means, not by war. We had great men in those days, men with fine minds capable of dealing with such gigantic sectional matters, but man's old enemy, hot-headed anger, prevailed, and force and bloodshed were the consequence, from which this nation has never fully recovered. The best brains on both sides were sacrificed and the negroes left among us — the South's problem still.

We think that it was Lieutenant Jonathan who built the old burrh flour mill with the great water wheel on his plantation, perhaps the very first wheat flour mill in Hampshire county. It was a three story structure with stone basement and logs above. It had a hipped roof of hand riven shingles, in the memory of the older people. It may have been covered with clapboards at first, for the second Jonathan repaired and reconstructed it in his day and it served the people until the Civil War.

Two large pairs of round stones, called burrhs, one stone supported above the other were made to revolve rapidly by the water power generated by the wheel, crushing the grain between them let down from the hopper above.

One pair was for small grain that, with bolting cloth produced wholesome flour for bread, cake, etc; the other stones of a coarser kind were for feed, meal, etc.

This big wheel was a beautiful sight in action and was the motive power for the whole plant which, with a pressure on a wooden arm inside the mill, a child could turn on or off.

Many large trees grew up about this old mill which enhanced its beauty, situated at the foot of the mountain on the riverside.

The writer and sisters, with some young friends, explored this mill not long before its fall. We secured some souvenirs, things not considered valuable by marauding forces of the Civil War, hidden there by the owners. The miller's house hard by, long deserted, had fallen into decay. Parts of the stone chimney still stand. The mill fell and was washed away by the floods of the eighties, only parts of the wall and some iron work remain,

1933; also, the mill race, wide and deep, dug through the farm from a bend in the river where the dam once stood. What a piece of engineering for spade and mattock and shovel. Partly filled in, it still serves as drainage for the land.

After the new type of mills made commercial grain products available and the people heard of the bleached flour, the burrh flour, though more healthful, gradually fell into disfavor and the mill that so long served the whole country side with the staff of life suffered the fate of the inevitable law of change. The descendants of the pioneer, now found in every state, are not aware that it ever existed.

Flax as well as grains was cultivated on this estate. Sheep roamed over the hills and from these were produced food and clothing for all the people on the plantation, it being manufactured right at home.

We are told that Jonathan Pugh took an active interest in community welfare, helping to build the first church on North River, an Episcopal, then Church of England, as already mentioned.

Strange as it may seem there is no certainty of knowledge of his burial place, but tradition says that he and Margaret lie on a part of what was then his estate, a mile or more south of the old home, in a pioneer graveyard on land now owned by James Frye. It seems that the Bakers and other pioneers also lie there. All traces of this graveyard have been obliterated by the present owner.

It is evident, too, that a residence had been erected there, the most desirable lands of the Pugh estate and the old people had moved into it before his death. Their son, Jonathan, Jr., is known to have occupied the first built home at that time. The descendents of the son John say that he lived with his mother for ten years or so after the death of his father, until her demise, then went to Ohio. This house built of logs was still standing until the lands were sold to the present owner by the Henry Hiett family, who reside on still another tract of the old estate. The Hiett and Pepper families were also early pioneers and they and the Pughs have been friends and neighbors since the division of the Pugh estate. Some of the descendents have intermarried. The Hietts are English and among the very earliest to settle in Capon Valley. They are a people of very high character. The Pepper family are of German lineage, intelligent and thrifty.

Back near the foot of the mountain on the Pugh estate, now a part of what is known as the Henry Pepper farm, was a bloody Indian battle between the Five Nations and their enemies of other tribes. This occurred before the French and Indian wars and the whites were not molested. Indian arrow-heads are still plowed up on this field of battle, the date of which is not known.

Old deeds found among the Pugh papers, handed down to 1934.

No. 1: From Beverly Randolph, governor of Virginia, to Richard Wood, a tract of 429 A., dated October 12, 1768. This deed mentions a corner in the Hanging Rock Run.

No. 2: A tract of 24 A. from Lord Fairfax to John Fox-Croft and Charles Thompson, dated 1771.

No. 3: A tract of 111 A. from the Commonwealth of Virginia to Jonathan Pugh, dated 1779.

N. 4: From the Commonwealth of Virginia to Jonathan Pugh, a tract of 349 A., dated 1789.

No. 5: (To the second Jonathan) A tract of 33½ A. from Thos. Randolph to Jonathan Pugh, bearing the date of 1818. This is evidently that tract commonly called the "Flat".

No. 6: (2nd Jonathan's son John N.) A tract of 50 A. from the Commonwealth of Virginia, John Floydfi Governor, to John Pugh and adjoining the lines of Jonathan, Sr., and Jonathan Pugh, III, dated 1828.

See other deeds and records at Romney in Volume II of this history.

Will of Jonathan Pugh, W. B. 2, Pages 374, 5, 6.

"IN THE NAME OF GOD AMEN: I, Jonathan Pugh of Hampshire Co. and State of Virginia, being of sound mind and understanding, do make this my Last Will and Testament, as follows:

In the first place I commit my soul to the Author of All Being, my body to be buried where my Son, Daniel lies in case it be convenient.

I give and bequeath to my loving wife Margaret Pugh one-third of the land I now live on, during her life, also two negroes, Dick and Trusty for her life.

I will that after her death that the aforesaid Dick and Trusty be apparised and that in case the said negroes should be desirous of going to either of my children in particular and such child to pay the value of the appraisment as aforesaid (to be disposed of as hereafter mentioned) then such child be permitted to take said Dick and Trusty at such appraisment, otherwise that the said two negroes be sold at public sale and the amount be equally divided among my children, male and female, also, in case they should be taken at the appraisment then the money to be equally divided amongst all my children as above.

I further give to my beloved wife a third part of my movable estate.

To my son Jonathan, I give and bequeath the plantation whereon he now lives, to him and his heirs and assigns forever.

To my sons David, Jesse, and Annanias and John I give the plantation on which I now live containing Four hundred and forty-Seven acres, to them and their heirs forever — to be equally divided amongst my aforesaid sons, David, Jesse, Annanias and John, quantity and quality without surveyorship, but should one of my aforesaid sons, David, Jesse, Anninias or John die before they arrive at the age of twenty-one years without issue of their body capable of inheriting such childs proposition of the aforesaid plantation on which I live, as aforesaid, then, and in that case, my will is that the part of the aforesaid plantation so divided as aforesaid go to be equally divided amongst the surviving of the said David, Jesse, Annanias and John and their heirs forever.

To my son David Pugh I give and bequeath a tract of land containing about Two hundred acres, to him and his heirs forever, which said tract of land is bounded by lands of Francis Keyes on one side, lands of Jas. Currethers, Wm. Bab and Lord

49

Dumore on the other sides, lying in the Co. of Hampshire, aforesaid.

To my sons, Jesse and Annanias, I give and bequeath a tract of land containing about 429 A. which land I purchased of John C. McCook, lying in the County and State aforesaid, to them and their heirs forever — equally to be divided between said Jesse and Annanias in quantity and quality without surveyorship.

I give and bequeath to my son John a tract of land about 148 A., joining the land heretofore devised to my son Jonathan and the land I sold to Wm. Myers, to him and his heirs and assigns forever.

To my daughter Lucy Taggart I give a negro girl named Clary.

I will that my Executors hereafter named, sell my personal estate, not disposed of, and from the amount thereof pay and satisfy my debts and that the balance with the debts due me be equally divided amongst all my children, male and female.

I hereby constitute and appoint my son Jonathan Pugh and my son-in-law, Francis Taggart, Executors of this my Last Will and Testament, revoking and disannulling all former and other wills made by me.

In testimony whereof I have put my hand and seal this 20th day of September, 1794.

Jonathan Pugh   (Seal.)

Signed, sealed and published as the last will of Jonathan Pugh and acknowledged to be the same and   in presence of the witnesses, F. G. Keyes, Jacob Emmert, and John Pepper.

At a court for Hampshire Co. held the 15th day of October, 1794, This, the last will and Testament of Jonathan Pugh, deceased, was presented in court by Francis Taggart and Jonathan Pugh the Executors herein named, proved by the oath of the witnesses thereto and ordered to be recorded. Executors gave bond in penalty of Ten Thousand Dollars.

Test: Andrew Woodrow, Cl Court."

AFFIDAVIT

STATE OF IOWA, POLK COUNTY, S. S.

I, A. D. Pugh, depose and say that I am of legal age, a lawyer by profession, having my office at 1016 Paramount Building, in the City of Des Moines, Iowa, and reside at 2707 Grand Avenue in said city:

That I am the youngest son of Jonathan Gilbert Pugh, who was born in Mansfield, Richland County, Ohio, January 11, 1826; and the grandson of John Pugh, who was born on North River in Hampshire County, Virginia, — now West Virginia, — September 12, 1782, who was the yougest son of my Great-Grand-Father, Jonathan Pugh, of Capon Drains, Hampshire County, Virginia, whose will was proved in a Court for Hampshire County, Va., October 15, 1794, and Recorded in W. B. 2, Pages 374, 5, 6, and who was Commissioned a Lieutenant in the Colonial Forces of Virginia in 1768, by the Royal Governor of the Colony, Baron Norborne Berkeley Botetourt, 1768-1770, and who later served in the Virginia Cavalry in the War for Independence:

That this Commission was given to my Father when he arrived at manhood by his Uncle, Jesse Pugh, because he had been named for his Grand-Father, Jonathan; that thereafter, this Document was lost during several year's absence of my Father in California, before he married and established a home of his own, but he remembered the signature of the Paper and the rank thereby conferred, and the rather short tenure of office of Governor Botetourt corroborates the date of its issue; that my Father and Mother have often told me the story of this Commission substantially as above set forth, which they said had been told them by my Grand-Father, John Pugh; that my Father has often related to me the Gift of the Commission to him by his Uncle, Jesse, and that he remembered it was a Lieutenant's Commission issued to his Grand-Father, Jonathan Pugh, by Colonial Governor Botetourt of Virginia, and was thereafter lost during his absence from Ohio in California; that I have made some examination of contemporaneous colonial, biographical and historical authorities and records with a view to verifying this memento of Colonial times, and consider that they fully support the authenticity of this pre- revolutionary ancestral commission. Any further deponent sayeth not.

A. D. PUGH

Subscribed and sworn to by said A. D. Pugh before me this 15th day of January, 1942.

R. W. NEUMANN

Notary Public in and for Polk County, Iowa. My Commission expires July 4, 1942.

There was no Post Office between Romney and Winchester before 1812 — after that came Pleasant Dale, Capon Bridge, Cold Stream and Slanesville.

Pughs, Albins, Bakers, Malicks, and Martins had settled in the Pleasant Dale-Hanging Rock region before the Indian Wars.

Among my many new Book Friends from New York to San Francisco I wish to note Mrs. E. B. Cooper and family of Winchester and White Rock Lodge.

CHAPTER V

Will of Dan'l Pugh, W. B. 2, Page 349. Romney, Hampshire County, W. Va.

"IN THE NAME OF GOD AMEN: I, Dan'l Pugh of the Co. of Hamps. Va., being weak in body but of sound mind and memory, Blessed be Almighty God for the same, do make and publish this my last will and testament in manner and form following:

First: I give and bequeath to my beloved wife, Sarah Pugh, the sum of three hundred pounds current money, money to be paid her by my Executors, hereafter named, within five years after my decease, or sooner if the situation of my estate will admit, but it is my will that she receive no part of said legacy until she has released her right of dower in and to my lands of which she may be dowable as my wife.

Item— I give and devise to my son Hannibal Pugh two tracts of land in Harrison Co. Viz: One of Seven Hundred and Ninety A. being on Maxwell's Run, the other of twenty-five A., adjoining the town of Clarksburg, to him and his heirs forever. I devise that all my other lands of whatever description and whether claimed or held by deed survey, entry, or in any other manner, may be sold by my Executors (if they find it necessary) for the pay't of my just debts and the legacy aforesaid to my wife, or such credits as they may judge proper, and after my debts and the legacy to my wife are discharged and disposed of — the residue of my lands (if any remain unsold) One-half I devise to my son Hannibal Pugh and the other half to my daughters, Amy and Juliana Pugh to be equally divided between them in quantity and quality to them, my said son and daughters, and their heirs and assigns forever — but if no lands should remain unsold, then the residue of the money arising from the sale of my said lands and all my outstanding debts when recovered, I give and bequeath to my son and daughters as aforesaid and in like proportions and whereas I have brought suit in the District Court held at Winchester against a certain James Parsons for five negroes, Viz: Sambo, Rachel (Daughter of Hannah) Tes, Sarah, and Rachel (Daughter of Barl) and it is my desire that the negroes if recovered should remain to my children, I therefore give and dispose of them in the following manner Viz: Sambo and Rachel (Daughter of Hannah) I bequeath to my son Hannibal, Rachel (Daughter of Barl) to my daughter Amy, and Tes to my daughter, Juliana — To them and their heirs forever — and whereas I am informed that I cannot recover Sarah (the said Parsons having sold her) but only a compensation in damages — It is, therefore, my desire that that compensation be equally divided between my daughters Amy and Juliana.

All the rest residue and remainder of my estate of whatever kind I give and bequeath one-half to my son Hannibal, and the other half to my daughters Amy and Juliana, to be equally divided between them.

To my executors I devise the custody and tuition of my children, requesting them to have my daughters brought up and educated in a manner suitable to their sex and fortune, and to have my son educated liberally, if he discovers talents worthy of much cultivation, otherwise to have him educated in a manner adapted to the common business of life.

Lastly, I do hereby constitute and appoint my trusty friends, Isaac Parsons, Jonathan Parsons, Hezakiah Davisson and John Prunty, Executors of this, my last Will and Testament, and revoke all former wills made by me in writings, whereof I have hereunto set my hand and seal this 26th day of May, in the year of our Lord, 1794.

Dan'l Pugh   (Seal)

Signed, sealed, Published and Discharged by the above named Dan'l Pugh to be his last will and Testament in the presence of us who have hereunto subscribed our names as witnesses in the presence of the Testator.
Edward Dyer, John Brown and Francis Taggart.

At a court held for Hampshire Co. the 10th day of Sep. 1794. This last will and Testament of Dan'l Pugh, deceased, was proved by the oathes of John Brown and Francis Taggart, two of the witnesses thereto and is ordered to be recorded.

Test: Andrew Woodrow, Co. Clerk."

DESCENDANTS OF THE LIEUTENANT JONATHAN AND MARGARET WOOD PUGH

Amy Pugh McNeill

Strother McNeill, born June 22, 1773, died January 1819, was the son of Daniel McNeill, the first. Strother was married twice. First, Mary Ann Renick; second, Amy Pugh, on February 11, 1810. She was the daughter of Daniel and Sarah Pugh.

Strother and Mary Ann Renick MeNeill children:

1. Eliza McNeill, born 1799, died 1854, married, 1822, James Williams.

2. Sallie McNeill, born 1805, died 1854, married, February 25, 1825, George Casey Harness.

3. Daniel McNeill, never married.

4. Billy McNeill, never married.

5. Thomas McNeill, married first, Ann Nevill, June 18, 1831; second, to Kate Mask.

Children of Strother and Amy Pugh McNeill:

J. Hanson McNeill, married Jemimah Cunningham, January 19, 1837; wounded at the Bridge of Mt. Jackson in the fall of 1864 and died a month later. See later revised foreword— This Volume. Hannibal McNeill, died, aged 4 years. Kitty McNeill, died, aged 11 years. Mary Ann McNeill, died, aged 15 years. Adaline McNeill, died, aged six years. **George W. McNeill,** married Margarette R. McMechen. She was the daughter of Samuel McMechen, Sr., born October 5, 1820.

Children of George W. and Margarette R. McMechen McNeill.

1. James William McNeill, born September 28, 1845.

2. Susan Catherine McNeill, born February 2, 1848; never married, died, aged 86, October, 1933, at Moorefield, West

Virginia. George W. McNeill, died, June 8, 1862. Margarette R. McMechen McNeill died October 10, 1898.

James W. McNeill and Emma Jane Crabill were married May 12, 1870. Their children were:

1. George W. McNeil, born February 28, 1871, died November, 1934; married to Sarah C. Van Mater (Sadie), September 25, 1895. She was born October 11, 1872, died February 1, 1934; daughter of Isaac and Martha Peer Van Meter.

2. Irvine Seymour McNeill, born September 5, 1875, married Florence M. Lemley, March, 1895.

3. Ambrose McNeill, born October 25, 1876, died November 5, 1916; was married to Ella M. Welton, July 4, 1899.

4. Roy Newell McNeill, born May 8, 1877, died unmarried, November 26, 1900.

5. Margarette R. McNeill (Pearl), born May 5, 1879, married to Benjamin Seymour McNeill, September, 1903. He is son of John W. McNeill and Mary McNeill Pancake, daughter of John McNeill Pancake. They have four children.

6. Bessie T. McNeill, born August 31, 1881, died unmarried.

7. Nina Renick McNeill, born May 5, 1885, married Frank V. Carpenter March, 1910. One son, Frank V. Jr., died aged six years.

8. Anna C. McNeill was married to James Price, March, 1918; no children.

9. Emma C. McNeill was married to Floyd Fisher, September 26, 1916; no children.

Their mother, Emma Crabill NcNeill died June 16, 1918. The father, James W. McNeill, died after his wife but I do not have the date.

George and Sadie Van Meter McNeill has seven children: James, Elizabeth, Roy, Vanse, William, George and Jake.

Irvine Seymour and Florence M. Lemley McNeill had seven children: Katherine, Donald, Taylor, Jesse, Irvine, Barbara and one other. Residence, Harrisonburg, Virginia.

Benjamin Seymour McNeill and Margarette R. (Pearl) Mc-
Neill; residence, Columbia Avenue, Cumberland, Maryland,
have four children:
1. Adrian S., born June 1, 1902.
2. Campbell P., born July 8, 1904.
3. Crabill, born July 18, 1906.
4. Susie, born December 6, 1908.
All are married at this writing.

McNeill Family Record

Marriages

John Hanson McNeill and Jemima Harness Cunningham were
married, in Hardy County, Virginia; by Rev. Davis Kennison
of the Methodist Episcopal Church, on the 19th day of January,
1837.

Robert Bell Sherrard, and Elizabeth Inskeep Van Meter were
married in Hardy County, Virginia; by Rev. William N. Scott
of the Presbyterian Church; on the 1st day of August, A. D.
1843.

Jessie Cunningham McNeill and Sarah Elizabeth Sherrard
were married, in Alleghany County, Maryland; by Rev. Lewis F.
Wilson of the Presbyterian Church, on the 14th day of August,
A. D. 1865.

Wm. D. Ewin and Sarah Emily McNeill, were married in
Cumberland, Md., on the 13th day of June, 1865.

William Strother McNeill and Mary I. Pryor, were married,
in Davies County, Missouri by the Rev. John D. Vincil of the
Methodist Church, on the 10th day of Nevember, 1859.

John Hanson McNeill, II, and Mary Jane Reed were married
in Daviess Co., Mo.

Robert Sherrard McNeill and Ida Inez Wright were married
in Champaign Co., Ill., Feb. 6, 1896.

William A. Roberts and Katherine P. McNeill were married
in Piatt Co., Ill.

Margaret S. McNeill and Ralph W. Smith were married in
Champaign Co., Ill., June 15, 1907.

Richard Dulaney McNeill and Nina Johnston were married

in Seymour, Ill., Jan. 28, 1903. (no children)

Jesse Cunning McNeill, Jr., and Olive Bergner were married in Champaign, Ill., March 9, 1904.

Sallie Sherrard McNeill married J. A. Bell, Douglas Co., Ill.

McNeill Family Record
Births

John Hanson McNeill, son of Strother and Amy Pugh McNeill was born in Hardy County, Virginia, on the 12th day of June, 1815.

Jemima Harness Cunnigham McNeill was born, in Hardy County, Virginia, on the 8th day of March, A. D. 1819.

, Children of J. H. and Jemima H. C. McNeill follow:

William Strother McNeill, the first child of the above named, was born in Hardy County, Virginia, on the 11th day of November, A.D. 1837.

George W. McNeill, son of John Hanson McNeill, was born in Bourbon County, Kentucky, on the 26th day of October, A. D. 1839.

Jesse Cunningham McNeill, was born in Bourbon County, Kentucky on the 22nd day of September, A. D. 1841.

William (or Wellum, not clear) was born in Bourbon County, Kentucky, on the 18th day of March, A. D. 1843.

Sarah Emily McNeill was born in Hardy County, Virginia, on the 18th day of July, A. D. 1844.

John Hanson McNeill, II) was born in Daviess County, Missouri, on the 7th day of October, A.D. 1859.

Sherrard Connection

Robert Bell Sherrard was born in Berkeley County, Virginia, at the house of his grandfather, Wm. Wilson on the 30th day of January, A. D. 1818.

Elizabeth Inskeep Sherrard was born, in Hardy County, Virginia, on the 27th day of November, 1824. Children:

Sarah E. Sherrard was born at Bloomery, Hampshire Co., Virginia, on the 13th day of August, 1844.

Robert Van Meter Sherrard was born, in Hampshire Co., Va. on the 1st day of May, 1846.

Ellen Bell Sherrard was born at Bloomery, Hampshire Co., Va., on the 8th day of July, A. D. 1848.

Samuel Alexander Sherrard was born at Bloomery, Hampshire County, Va., on the 11th day of November, 1849.

William Wilson Sherrard was born at Bloomery, Va., on the 29th day of September, A.D. 1852.

Mary Stewart Sherrard was born at Bloomery, Va., on the 23rd day of January, A. D. 1854.

Edward Hogue Sherrard was born at Bloomery, Va., Feb. 9, 1858.

Annie Kate Sherrard was born at Bloomery, Va., on the 20th day of May, A. D. 1856.

David Hogue Sherrard was born at Bloomery, Va., on the 9th day of February, A. D. 1858.

Margaret Sanford Sherrard was born, at Bloomery, Va., on the 5th day of March, A. D. 1860.

Emma Graham Sherrard was born in Hardy County, Va., on the 9th day of October in the year A.D. 1865.

McNeill Record

Births

Children of Jesse C. and Sarah E. Sherrard McNeill

Robert Sherrard McNeill was born at Oakland, Hardy Co., W. Va., on the 27th day of September, 1866.

John Hanson McNeill was born on the 6th day of March, 1868.

Elizabeth Van Meter McNeill was born April 3, 1869.

Jemima H. McNeill was born June 13, 1870.

Thomas W. McNeill was born May 29, 1871.

Jesse Cunningham McNeill was born in Davies Co., Mo., Jan 18. 1873.

Catharine Pollock McNeill was born in Davies Co., Mo., June 14, 1874.

Samuel Sherrard McNeill, was born in Piatt Co., Illinois, August 14, 1875.

Richard Dulaney McNeill was born in Champaign County. Ill Aug. 14, 1877.

Margaret Sanford McNeill was born in Piatt Co., Ill., July 10, 1880.

William Wilson McNeill was born in Piatt Co., Ill., Feb. 9, 1882.

Sallie Sherrard McNeill was born in Piatt Co., Ill., Aug. 22, 1884.

Reece McNeill was born in Piatt Co., Ill., Dec. 6, 1886.

McNeill Record

3rd Generation

Births

3rd Generation in the West

Gladys Champion McNeill, daughter of R. S. and Ida McNeill was born in Piatt Co,, Ill., Feb. 10, 1897.

Doris Wright McNeill, daughter of R. S. and Ida McNeill, was born in Champaign Co., Ill., Nov. 22, 1900.

Mary Sherrard McNeill, daughter of R. S. and Ida McNeill was born in Calhoun County, Iowa, September 1, 1908.

Ruth Burgner McNeill, daughter of J. C. and Olive McNeill, was born in Logan Co., Ill., Sept. 18, 1907.

Jesse McNeill Smith, son of R. W. and Margaret Smith, was born in Champaign Co., Ill., May 1, 1908.

Elizabeth Bell, daughter of T. A. and Sallie Bell, was born in Champaign Co., Ill., Dec. 15, 1907.

Catherine Bell, daughter of T. A. and Salle Bell, was born in Douglas Co., Ill., Oct. 1, 1909.

Allen McNeill Bell, son of T. A. and Sallie Bell, was born in Douglas Co., Ill., Aug. 5, 1911.

Virginia Bell was born in Douglas Co., Ill., October 10, 1915.

Mildred and Dorothy Bell were born in Douglas Co., Ill.

Deaths

William Strother McNeill, son of Capt. John H. and Jemima H. C. McNeill died May 18, 1904 in Daviess Co., Mo., age 66 yr. 6 mo. 7 days.

Mary J. McNeill, wife of Wm. S. McNeill, died in St. Joseph Mo.

Robert V. Sherrard, son of R. B. and E. I. died in Piatt Co., Feb. 1908.

Ellen Bell Sherrard, daughter of R. B. and E. I. Sherrard, died in Moorefield, W. Va., Aug. 1908.

Margaret Sanford Sherrard died at Moorefield, W. Va., May 27, 1879.

David Hogue Sherrard died at Moorefield, W. Va., date unknown.

Emma Graham Sherrard died at Moorefield, W. Va., Jan 27, 1892.

William (or Wellum) McNeill died August 9th, 1843, age 4 mo. 3 weeks.

George Washington McNeill, son of John Hanson was shot whilst on Picket, near Lexington, Mo., Sept. 17, 1861 and died in one hour, aged 21 years, 10 mo. and 22 days.

John Hanson McNeill, Captain of Partisan Rangers, in the Confederate Service, was wounded near Mount Jackson, Shenandoah County, Va., Oct. 3, 1864; and died on the 10th of the the following November, aged 49 years, 5 months, lacking two days. He was buried at Harrisonburg, Va., with Masonic honors, on the 11th day of November, and on the 5th of Jan., 1865 his remains were removed by his company and re-interred in the cemetery near Moorefield, Hardy County, Va.

Robrt Bell Sherrard died in Mansfield, Piatt Co., Ill., January 27, 1884.

Jemima H. Cunningham McNeill died in Champaign Co., Ill., April 10, 1900.

Edward Hogue Sherrard died at 7 o'clock P. M., on the 10th day of September, 1855, aged 5 months and 7 days.

Mary Stewart Sherrard died at 1 o'clock A. M. on the 15th day of October, 1862, aged 8 years, 8 months, and 22 days. Her disease was congestion of the brain, and her illness of but seven hours duration.

Elizabeth Inskeep Sherrard, the cherished wife of R. B. Sherrard, died at Oakland, Hardy County, W. Va., at 3:45 in the

61

morning of January 27, 1867, aged 42 years and 2 months. Her disease was typhoid pneumonia with which she was taken just one week before she died. Her funeral sermon was preached on the 29th of January by Rev. Geo. W. White, from Job. 23 Chapter, 10 verse. She lived a righteous life and her last end was peace. "Don't put off preparation for Eternity," were her words.

Samuel Alexander Sherrard, son of R. B. and E. I. Sherrard, died in Moorefield, Hardy County, W. Va., on the 24th day of Feb., 1876. He lived the life and died the death of the righteous, aged 26 years, 3 months, and 13 days.

John M. McNeill, son of J. C. and S. E. McNeill, died, Sept. 11th, 1868.

Elizabeth V. McNeill, thier daughter, died Jan. 5, 1873.

Jemima H. McNeill, another daughter, died July 9, 1870.

Thomas W. McNeill, their son, died July 5, 1872.

Samuel A. McNeill died in Piatt County, Ill., May 7, 1879.

William W. McNeill, died in Piatt Co., Ill., June 4, 1883.

Reece McNeill died in Piat Co., Ill., Dec. 31, 1886.

Captain Jesse Cunningham McNeill, son of Captain John Hanson McNeill and Jemima H. McNeill, died in Mahonet, Ill., March 4, 1912, aged 70 years, 5 months and 12 days.

Robert Sherrard McNeill, son of Jesse C. and Sarah Sherrard McNeill, born September 27, 1866, died September 16, 1926, married, February 6, 1896, Ida Inez Wright, born June 26, 1866, died, January 17, 1936. Children:

1. Glady Champion McNeill, born February 10, 1897, married Robert G. Clapper, November 11, 1916, who was born August 12, 1892.

Children:

Edith Roberta Clapper, born September 22, 1919.

Rosemary Sherrard Clapper, born July 3, 1922.

Robert G. Clapper, Jr., born October 23, 1925.

2. Dora Wright McNeill, born November 22, 1900; married Lou M. Jones, March 15, 1920, who was born, May, 1899.

Children:

John McNeill Jones, born December 29, 1920.

Joyce G. Jones, born April 14, 1922.
James Paul Jones, born May 1, 1923.
Joseph Jones, born January 18, 1925.
Donald Jones, born January 29, 1926.
Jack Jones, born 1930.
Richard Grant Jones, born January, 1937.
3. Mary Sherrard McNeill, born September 1, 1908, married
Clyde M. Taylor, June 7, 1931. Child: Baby Taylor, born
March, 1933, died, March, 1933.

McNEILL FAMILY
Pugh-McNeill Connection

Descendants of Strother and Amy Pugh McNeill
John Hanson McNeill, Captain of McNeill's Rangers, and
wife, Jemima Harness Cunningham, began life near Moorefield,
Hardy County, Virginia, on a farm. After the birth of their
first child, William Strother McNeill, they removed to Bourbon
county, Kentucky, where they lived until about 1844, when
they returned to Hardy; later, and before 1859, when their
youngest son, John Hanson, Jr., was born, they removed to
Davis county, Missouri. About the period of the beginning
of the Civil War they seem to have returned to Hardy county
when he organized his company of Partisan Rangers. Two
sons, William Strother and George W., remained in Missouri,
where the former married and spent his life and the latter
was shot while on picket duty near Lexington, September 17,
1861; died the same day, while the third son, Jesse Cunningham
McNeill, succeeded his father in command of the Rangers, John
Hanson having met death in an attack on Federals on guard
at the Bridge at Mt. Jackson, Shenandoah Valley, November 10,
1864.

It would take a volume to recount the many dashing move-
ments and successes of the first Captain McNeill and his
Rangers. As a military leader he possessed the courage and
shrewdness of a Jackson, the cunning of a "Swamp Fox".
Little is known of his private life. It took a Civil War to

bring out and establish his genius. For some of the major exploits of Captain J. H. McNeill and his Rangers, see Maxwell and Swisher's History of Hampshire County.

Jemima, following the Civil War, went again to the middle west with her sons and died at the home of Jesse C. and Sarah Sherrard McNeill in Illinois, 1900, sad at heart since the baby son, John Hanson, Jr., and family had just moved to Washington State. She lies buried among her descendants, Captain Jesse C., his wife, and others at Mansfield, Illinois, while her distinguished husband rests beside his McNeill ancestry in the cemetery near Moorefield in his native state.

Of the children born to John Hanson and Jemima H. C. McNeill, all but one reached adult age, and four married. They were William Strother, Jesse Cunningham, Sarah Emily, and John Hanson, Jr.

Captain Jesse C. and Sarah E. Sherrard were married at the home of an aunt in Allegheny county, Maryland, in order to keep from taking the despised "Amnesty Oath", 1865. He had been wounded in the ankle during the war and was always slightly lame. His Cumberland Raid, in which the Generals, Crook and Kelly were taken as given in this volume is the high point of his career in the war between the States.

Their son, Robert Sherrard McNeill, was born at the home of his grandparents on South Branch, with the family and friends present; also, the old colored "mammy". They removed to Davies county, Missouri. Crossed the "Father of Waters" in a ferry boat, by the overturning of which they lost practically all their possessions, excepting an old chest that came from Holland with Srome, remote Van Meter ancestor. It is now the property of Mrs. Gladys Clapper of Mohamet, a granddaughter of Captain McNeill.

The next living child was Jesse Cunningham, Jr., born in Missouri. Mrs. Sarah E. McNeill said that while living there she felt sometimes that she must die for a sight of the mountains of Virginia.

Hard years were theirs for need of medical care and other necessaries of life and they lost three children in succession,

64

but had fine lands and fat cattle. About 1875 they removed to Mansfield, Illinois and bought land near the Van Meter holdings. During this time Mrs. McNeill was a Sunday-school teacher in the Presbyterian Church. In 1894, they removed to Seymour, Illinois, with their sons Robert and Richard on good farms near by. Captain Jesse C. and wife were congenial people, who kept a youthful viewpoint and were tolerant. They loved to entertain and the family reunions were a joy to all.

The McNeill men were Masons and Democrats. They took an active part in community life. Every place where they lived was bettered by their presence in it.

Robert Sherrard McNeill organized the first telephone company in his county and was a school director. The young people all joined the Methodist church, since there was no Presbyterian church in Seymour. Catherine Polluck and William A. Roberts lived in Piatt county. Margaret was organist in Seymour. After her marriage to Ralph W. Smith, they removed to Champaign county where their son, Jesse C. Smith was born.

Jesse C. McNeill, Jr., and Olive McNeill removed to Logan county and their daughter Ruth was born there.

T. A. and Sallie Sherrard McNeill Belle lived in Douglas county where their children were born. Richard Dulany, named for Colonel Richard Dulany of C.S.A., and wife, Nina Johnson, residence, Seymour, Illinois, are still living (1937). He is the only survivor of the Captain J. C. McNeill family and has cutody of the McNeill family records in the middle west which he has graciously allowed the writer to use in this work.

One who has for years known the family says that they were never too successful financially but generous and warm-hearted (a Pugh trait). In other words none ever got rich but are comfortably situated and helpful to others.

After the removal to Illinois, Captain McNeill came upon an old colored man in Danville who had been one of his father's servants and whom he had known all his life in Virginia. They were rejoiced to see each other but the old man was in want. Captain McNeill helped him and kept in touch with his needs while the old man lived.

The McNeills educated their children and the third generation are taking advantage of college work now available for young people. Mrs Clapper's daughter drives ten miles from home to the State University; another is in High and the son, in Junior High. She herself is a teacher as is, also, a sister, Mrs. Taylor, whose only child is deceased, the other sister has a large family of children.

John Hanson McNeill, Junior's descendants are in the Northwest. A branch of the family, Mrs. Fred Bruns, lives at Bonner's Ferry, Idaho.

CAPTURE OF GENERALS CROOK AND KELLEY FEBRUARY 21, 1865, by McNEILL'S RANGERS

As related to the writer by Jack Markwood and according to J. B. Fay, another one of the participants
Given by MAXWELL & SWISHER

"The debatable ground between the two opposing armies in Northern Virginia ran parallel with the Potomac and embraced sometimes the length of two or more counties southward. During the latter part of the war this region was dominated by three famous Confederate partisan leaders, Mosby, Gilmer, and McNeill. Their forces sometimes intermingled, but ordinarily the operations of Mosby were confined to the country east of the Shenandoah; those of Gilmer to the Valley of Virginia; While McNeill's field of action lay to the westward along the upper Potomac and South Branch.

Captain J. Hanson McNeill's command was composed principally of Volunteers from Virginia and Maryland, thought nearly every Southern State and not a few of the Northern had representatives in the ranks.

Moorefield, on the South Branch, was the principal headquarters of this command (McNeill's native home community). In a daybreak attack on a company of Pennsylvania Cavalry who were guarding the bridge over the Shenandoah, near Mt. Jackson in the fall of 1864, Captain McNeill met his death.

His son, Lieutenant Jesse C. McNeill was next in command.

"In February, 1865, Lieutenant (now Captain) McNeill consulted me (J. B. Fay) about the feasibility of going into Cumberland and capturing Generals Kelly and Crook. After giving McNeill every assurance that his design could be successfully carried out, he determined to make the attempt.

"I was commissioned to proceed at once to Cumberland and prepare the way for our entry, by learning the number and position of the picket posts, the exact location of the sleeping apartments of both generals and any other information deemed necessary. Selecting C. R. Haller as a comrade, I started.

The desired information was procured and it was found that six or eight thousand Federal troops occupied the city and on this particular night Generals Hays, later President of the United States, Lightburn, and Duval were also temporarily there, but this was unknown to the party who otherwise might have made a greater harvest.

At the same time Sheridan's Army was in Winchester and another Federal force at New Creek, a few miles west — both these points nearer to Moorefield than Cumberland.

Captain McNeill, with twenty-five picked men of his own and about a dozen seasoned veterans from Companies F of the Seventh and D of the Eleventh divisions of Rosser's brigade, Virginia Cavalry, all well mounted, joined these messengers at the desired rendevous. The men and horses were fed and rested, and at nightfall they were on their way, proceeding over obscure and difficult mountain routes where snowdrifts of uncertain depths made it necessary for the troops to dismount. They descended into the valley and crossed the Potomac into Maryland. A council was then held to decide what route would be best as the night was far spent.

To gain time the most hazardous road was decided upon because it was the shortest.

The attempt to pass quietly through two lines of pickets promised but doubtful results. The attempt was made.

McNeill and Vandever followed by Keykendall and Fay rode ahead as an advance guard; the rest of the troops under Lieu-

67

tenant I. S. Welton, close behind. It was not an hour and a half till dawn. The New Creek road runs close to the base of Wills Mountain parallel with the Railroad and river, all very close together at the mouth of a deep ravine. About two miles from Cumberland the road turns to the left up a ravine and over a hill to the city. A Calvary picket was encountered here, captured and forced to give the countersign which was "Bull's Gap." These men, mounted on their own horses, were taken in and out of Cumberland, when they were turned loose, minus one horse, but glad to escape with their lives.

Keykendall and Fay led in the approach to the next inner Post which was fully a mile away, located at the junction of this road with the Frostburg Pike. This Post consisted of five men of the First West Virginia Infantry who were busily engaged at cards in a shed made cozy by a log fire. As the Rangers drew near, one of the number got up, reached for his musket and advanced to halt them. To his formal challenge Keykendall answered, "Friends with the countersign." When requested to dismount and give the countersign, there was an instant forward dash and the pickets were captured, disarmed and left at their post with the request that they remain there until the return which the Rangers had no intentions of making by that way, McNeill's men knowing that their work would be done before these men could raise the alarm. They were now inside the picket lines and before them lay the "slumbering City".

Here the troop was halted and two squads of ten men each, charged with the capture of the generals. Sergeant Joseph W. Keykendall, Seventh Virginia Cavalry, a soldier of great courage and coolness, Scout for Early, who had once been a prisoner in General Kelley's hands, was placed in care of the men detailed to secure that general. Serg. Joseph L. Vandever, a man of imposing figure, was given charge of capturing General Crook.

The duty of destroying the telegraph lines was intrusted to Fay and Haller, with assistants. The troop then rode down the pike and into Green Street, over the Bridge, across Will's Creek and up Baltimore Street, the chief thoroughfare, the men whistling Yankee tunes and joking with guards and patrols as they passed. Some wore Federal uniforms but the light was too dim to distinguish grey from blue anyway.

A part of the men halted in front of the Barnum House, later Winsor Hotel, where General Kelley slept, and the others rode on to the Revere House where General Crook had his headquarters. J. G. Lynn captured the sentry and ordered him to lead them to General Kelley's sleeping apartment. They went first to Adj. Gen. Melvin and asked him where the General was. He directed them to the next room, the door of which was open. When General Kelley was awakened he was told that he was a prisoner and directed to make his toilet as hastily as possible. He complied, inquiring to whom he was surrendering. Keykendall replied, "To Captain McNeill by order of General Rosser." He and Adj. Gen. Melvin were hastily mounted.

At the Revere House a similar scene took place. The sentinal was taken and a little colored boy opened the door. When asked if General Crook was in the house he said, in a frightened tone, "Yas, sah, but don't tell him I told you." Gassman rapped on the General's door and he called out "Who's there?" He was told, 'A friend', and the General said, 'Come in.' Several of the troop entered. Vandever advanced to the bed and said "General Crook, you are my prisoner." 'What authority have you for this?' asked the General. "The authority of General Rosser of Fitzhugh Lee's Division", said Vandever. General Crook, rising up, asked, "Is General Rosser here?" 'Yes,' replied Vandever, 'I am General Rosser. We have surprised and captured the town.'

When they reached the sidewalk a clerk came out with a lantern and inquired, "How many Johnnies have you got, boys?" John Taylor snatched his hat off, John Cunningham ran through his pockets and W. H. Malony grabbed him by the back and jerked his overcoat over his head. By this time he was disillusioned. The Rangers rode down street in an orderly manner to the Bridge, having secured headquarters' flags.

Here they stopped at the stable to take some fine horses, among them Philippi, General Kelley's charger. They then secured the guards at Canal Street and left the city on double quick, until halted at the canal bridge, about a mile below on their new return route, by a picket. Moving on, one of the pickets was heard to say, "Sergeant, shall I fire?" Vandever, in front shouted, "If you do I will arrest you. This is General Kelley's bodyguard and we have no time to waste. The Rebels are coming and we are going out to meet them." When the column was about five miles away the boom of a cannon was heard giving the alarm.

Sixty miles was between them and safety but they were elated and happy with no thought of fear — their expedition had been entirely successful, their pursuers from New Creek and Cumberland were twice in sight, but knowing all the by-paths and short cuts the Rangers evaded them, but had to abandon their intention of exhibiting to their friends and sweethearts the fruits of their daring expedition by passing through Moorefield, since Ringgold's cavalry was hot on their trail with fresh horses. Convinced that they would be overtaken, McNeill led his men into the woods skirting the road and, taking a well-known trail, passed through the ridges east of the town to a place of security seven miles above, where they camped for the night. In 24 hours they had ridden ninety miles over stream, valley, hill, mountain, and ravine. The prisoners received the very best attention possible and next day they pursued their march to Richmond successfully eluding pursuit from four directions.

A dispatch went out from Cumberland to General Sheridan at Winchester next morning, reporting the whole transaction and stating that only ten minutes had elapsed until the alarm was given by the darkey watchman at the Hotel, expressing belief that is was McNeill, not Rosser.

(Captain Jesse C. McNeill of this extraordinary performance was a son of the first Captain McNeill of the Rangers who was the son of Strother and Amy Pugh McNeill, Strother McNeill being the son of Daniel McNeill the first, and Amy Pugh being the daughter of Daniel and Sarah Pugh. Daniel Pugh was the oldest son of Lieutenant Jonathan Pugh of the Indian Wars who married Margaret Wood. Daniel was older brother of Jonathan Pugh, Jr., who was Captain of 1st Battalion, 114 Reg., Virginia Militia in the war of 1812. All records of this Pugh-McNeill Genealogy are given in this book. Sarah Hiett Pugh, daughter of Pioneer John Hiett, was sister of Martha Hiett Caudy, ancestor of the Caudy Family of Capon — See Vol. II, Will of Jas. Caudy I).

On February 24, 1865, General Robert E. Lee sent the following dispatch to the War Department of the Southern Confederacy: "General Early reports that Lieutenant McNeill, with thirty men on the morning of the 21st, entered Cumberland, captured and brought out Generals Crook and Kelley, the Adjutant General of the Department, two privates and the headquarters' flags, without firing a gun, although a considerable force is in the vicinity."

Records at Richmond, near the close of the war, showed that McNeill's Company had captured more than 2,600 prisoners, or about thirty persons for each man. Usually there were sixty to seventy men in active service with McNeill.

The men who took part in the capture of Generals Crook and Kelley were the following:

Captain ("Lieutenant") Jesse C. McNeill, Serg. Joseph W. Keykendall, J. B. Fay, Jacob Gassman, John G. Lynn, Serg. Joseph L. Vandever, G. S. Harness, John W. Markwood, D. E. Hopkins, J. W. Mason, R. G. Lobb, H. P. Tabb, I. S. Welton, Joseph A. Parker, George H. Johnson, C. R. Haller, Sergs. C. J. Daily and John Cunningham, Wm. H. Maloney, Geo. F. Cunnigham, Chas. Nickols, Isaac Parsons, Benjamin E. Wotring, I. E. Oats, John Mace, F. W. Bean, Mr. Tucker, John Acker, Wm. Poole, Wm. H. Haye, J. W. Duffy, I. S. Judy, I. L. Harvey, J. W. Crawford, J. G. Showalter, John Taylor and I. H. Welton.

The writer was a boarder during one school term at the hospitable home of J. W. Markwood ("Jack"), near Burlington, West Virginia and heard the story first hand from him as one of the party. She also knew Mr. Vandever, Mr. Johnson and Mr. Maloney, participants.

Juliana Pugh, daughter of Daniel and Sarah Hiett Pugh, was married to James Westfall (on record in Moorefield, Hardy county) December 30, 1809.

DESCENDANTS OF LIEUT. JONATHAN AND MARGARET WOOD PUGH
THEIR OLDEST SON, DANIEL, AND SARAH HIETT PUGH
(Daniel died before September 10, 1794, that being the date of probation of his Will given elsewhere in this book.)

Hannibal Pugh, only son of Daniel and Sarah Hiett Pugh, was born February 27, 1791, married Sydney McNeill, daughter of John and Amy McNeill (born February, 1797, died May 16, 1868) on ———, 1828. Hannibal died February 13, 1856, aged 64 years, 11 months and 16 days. Children:

John William Pugh, born April 18, 1829, killed in Civil War; member of Co. F., Imboden's Cavalry, George F. Sheets, Captain at first, then after he was killed at Brickston Station, Isaac Keykendall was Captain. The name of John W. Pugh is engraved on the monument which is the Hampshire Women's Memorial to the Confederate dead.

First Confederate monument erected
after the Civil War   1867.
Indian Mound Cemetery
Romney, W. Va.   0556

CHAPTER VI

Captain Jonathan Pugh and wife Mary Ellen Tansy.

Mrs. Bethuel Pugh, Mrs. John Hiett, Arthur Tansy.

Children of Jonathan II, and Mary Ellen Pugh.

CAPTAIN JONATHAN PUGH

Captain Jonathan has always been closely associated in the minds of the descendants of the Lieutenant Jonathan with the Pugh lands since he was the only member of the Lieutenant's family to remain here and bring up a family of his own; but we have cause to know that he inherited only his share of the old estate, as handed down to his children, (see his father's Will). The rest had all been sold off and settled upon before 1812. Among papers found was a bond given by his brother John dated 1803 to John Wolford for a deed for a part of his share, witnessed by Jonathan.

There is also a deed, dated 1818, showing that Capt. Jonathan, bought land and added it to his share. Capt. Jonathan was born August 26, 1757, died August 21, 1834. About 1777 to 1780 he married Mary Ellen Tansy of British extraction from eastern Maryland. She was a sister of Arthur Tansy, a noted architect of that day, who was also a fine cabinet maker. A piece of his handiwork in the form of a deed chest, which was last the property of Mrs. Effie Monroe, who left it with the request that it should be passed down in the Pugh name. It is now at Finly Pughs.

This chest is mahogany and bird's-eye maple, finished with lock. His signature and the date are on the bottom of the chest, yet perfectly legible, 1933. There is also a corner cupboard of his work in the family.

Capt. Jonathan and Mary Ellen had the following children (spoken of elsewhere in this book): Arthur T., Daniel, Jonathan III, John II, Maria and Lucy, all of whom married but Daniel. Arthur T., who married a Miss Carter of North River and went west is lost to us (1940.)

Johnathan and Mary Ellen Pugh lived on what is still the Pugh land that includes the old home site and that of the mill property. They were slaveholders and some of the slaves remained in the family as house servants until their death after the Civil War. These servants were too polite to sit at the table with the whites when solicited to do so, but fared well at their own table, where they joked and enjoyed the meal much more.

They spoke of the whites as "Mars John" or "Mars James" and "Miss Pluty" or "Miss Maria" and the whites called them "Uncle Ned or Aunt Clara". Aunt Clara remained single and lived to be quite old. She had had a lover who died when young. She was very black and so proud of her chaste character and that of her parents. She lived with my great Aunt Maria Smith who died in the early seventies, afterwards with my father. She evidently same down to us from the Lieut. Jonathan and his daughter, Lucy Taggart. She spent much time with other colored people in other places, but came to father when she liked and father supplied her needs and at death buried her according to her request among her colored friends. We were all fond of her.

Jonathan Pugh, Jr., was captain of a Company of Virginia Cavalry, 1st Battalion, 114 Regiment which was called out during the war of 1812, but too late to reach the scene of action before the war closed. He remained Captain of Reserves as late as 1822. His company roll is here among his papers and will be given elsewhere in this book. In this company were the ancestors of many of Hampshire's prominent and best citizens of past and present, and also some of those who have gone to build up other states.

Among the officers and men are: Williams, Loy, Carmichael, Fahs, Cooper, Pepper, Baker, Smith, Edwards, Monroe, Powell,

Ambler, McCauly, Emmitt, Stewart, Gallaway, Carter, Wilson, Delaplain, etc.

Capt. Jonathan Pugh was also Deputy Assessor for the 6th District of Virginia, with one Jacob Hull, Principal Assessor, receiving his appointment the 8th day of May, 1815. The letter of appointment is given elsewhere. Jonathan, Jr., and Mary Ellen Tansy Pugh lie buried in the Pugh burial ground in sight of the "Old Home".

He and Francis Taggart were executors on the Will of Jonathan, I. The name Tygart is also spelled Taggart in the old records, but we believe it is the same family name.

CHAPTER VII

Johnathan Pugh, III, and wife Nancy Offutt and other children: Arthur Tansy Pugh, killed at New Hope, Solomon J. Pugh of Cumberland, Md., and descendants, John Paterson and Nancy Offutt Pugh.

Descendants of Lieutenant Jonathan and Margaret Wood Pugh continued through their son, Jonathan, Jr., (Capt. Jonathan) and Mary Tansy Pugh.

Jonathan Pugh, III, of Virginia, son of Captain Jonathan and Mary Tansy Pugh, was born on the old plantation, April 14, 1795, where he remained until his marriage to Nancy Offutt, June 14, 1827. He seems to have purchased a part of the Offutt estate near Slanesville on the Old Martinsburg Pike, where they lived until his death, February 29, 1832.

Nancy Offutt, daughter of Solomon and Elizabeth Offutt, Welsh lineage, whose genealogy is given elsewhere in this book, born on the Offutt estate, January 15, 1805, was married again, March 3, 1836, to John Patterson of the same community. She died January 2, 1872. Jonathan and Nancy lie buried in the front row of the Offutt Cemetery, which has a beautiful outlook, on the old estate, between No. 45 and the Old Martinsburg Pike. Their descendants are now found in nearly every state from Pennsylvania to the Golden Gate.

Children of Johnathan and Nancy were Arthur Tansy and Solomon Jonathan Pugh.

John Patterson deserves mention in the Pugh history because of the interest he took in the orphaned children of Arthur Tansy Pugh. Even after the death of Nancy Pugh Patterson, the paternal feeling remained and he practically adopted Lucy May Pugh, daughter of Arthur Tansy Pugh, and Lucy's only living daughter became, by his will, sole heir to to his estate, on the demise of his second wife, Margaret Smith Patterson.

He was a warm-hearted Irishman, humorous and thrifty, a typical Celt. "Grandfather" and "Uncle John" to the whole kinship, both Offutts and Pughs, and the home of John and Nancy Patterson was well known over the county for its hospitality and good cheer, which continued under the Patterson-Pepper regime, after the marriage of Lucy to Joseph Pepper. John Patterson died July 3, 1899, aged 87 years, 6 months and 21 days, and Margaret Smith Patterson, in the winter of 1928. The home is now in the care of two step-grandchildren whom he loved.

Arthur Tansy Pugh, born July 12, 1828, near Slanesville, Virginia, married Margaret Wolverton about the year 1850 or 51, was killed in battle of New Hope, Virginia, in a charge, June 5, 1864. He, like his brother, was compelled to sunder the home ties to answer the call of his State in the Civil War. Arthur enlisted late, leaving a wife and seven small children, never to return.

His was one of those heart-breaking cases of a soldier, lost in battle and buried among the unknown dead. Where the wife hopes and fears and at last gives up in despair, realizing that the husband and father would have returned if life had been spared. A comrade saw his horse come out from the battle riderless with bloodstains on the saddle. Nothing was ever heard of him afterwards.

Another comrade and neighbor, John O. Saville, father of William Saville, the present owner of the nucleus of the Offutt farm, saw Arthur fall from his horse on that fatal day when so many Hampshire boys lost their lives at New Hope, and said he saw him "crawl under a house, but the Yankees were charging and we could do nothing". His body perhaps lies among the unknown dead of Shenandoah Valley, most likely at Harrisonburg, Va.

Arthur was a member of Company C., 18th Virginia Cavalry, of which he was then an uncommissioned officer. His name is enrolled on the Confederate monument at Romney, erected by "The Daughters of Old Hampshire, as a Tribute of Affection to Her Heroic Sons Who Fell in Defense of Southern Rights".

This monument was dedicated September 26, 1867, and has been decorated with appropriate ceremonies every year since. The Commissioned officers of this Regiment and Division were General John Imboden, Colonel Imboden, 1st Lieutenant S. B. Patterson, D. H. Higby, 2nd Lieutenant, and M. Guinevan, Captain. After the death of the latter, his brother, Luther Guinevan, was made captain. Other Hampshire boys, at various times, in Guinevan's Company, relatives of Arthur Pugh, were: C. M. Milleson, Joseph Hiett, Sol. E. Pugh, Sol. J. Pugh, J. J. Pugh and Peter Yost, the latter was the husband of Elizabeth Pugh, daughter of John N.

The children of Arthur Tansy and Margaret Wolverton Pugh were:

Nancy Jane, born December 18, 1852, still lives (Wisconsin, 1934).

Lucy May, born August 1, 1854, deceased.

John Thomas, born June 15, 1856, still lives, 1934 (Idaho), died January 8, 1936, and was buried at Solman, January 10, 1936.

Solomon J., II, born December 12, 1857, still lives (Missouri, 1936).

Miranda H., born November 16, 1859, deceased.

Mary Elizabeth, born July 17, 1862, deceased.

Martha E., child, died January 18, 1864.

Margaret Wolverton Pugh, born July 4, 1827, died July 20, 1879, must have been a woman of much energy and strength of mind to be able to bring up a family in such strenuous times as the Civil War and the years that followed, not to mention the grief and suspense that was hers following her husband's disappearance. All of her children lived to adult age, excepting the one lost during the war, but she must have had help and sympathy of the whole kinship, among them the strong arm of John Patterson.

Children of Arthur T. and Margaret Wolverton Pugh.

Nancy Jane Pugh, eldest daughter of Arthur and Margaret Wolverton Pugh, married **William McKinley,** of Cumberland. Mr. McKinley was of Scotch lineage, rather tall, with black eyes, and a ready wit which made him popular among his

79

guests, he being proprietor of a hostelry. Mrs. McKinley was of medium height and an interesting conversationalist; they were a congenial couple.

The McKinleys moved to New Rochelle, N. Y. Mr. McKinley died in 1883. His wife, at this writing, resides with their only daughter, Mrs. Pearl Thursinger, 24 South Allen Street, Madison, Wisconsin.

The McKinleys had three sons, **Arthur T.**, the oldest, has often visited in Hampshire where he is favorably known, is married and living at 718 Fourth Street, Modesta, California. **Gabriel E.**, the wanderer of the family, was for a time a Railroad man, later found the army and went to the Philippines. At present his whereabouts is not known to his relatives here, June, 1933.

Virgil P. McKinley was born December 3, 1885. He is tall, broad shouldered but his health has not been of the best, so, he has vacillated from city to country, crossing the continent several times, finally choosing the country life near Augusta, West Virginia. He received his first liking for the farm as a child on frequent and extended visits to his Grandfather Patterson, with whom he was a favorite. His is an amiable disposition, does not seem to care for the society of the fair sex and is likely to remain a bachelor, and inherited Pugh family trait. Later — Virgil McKinley died at the old Patterson Home, April 23, 1940. Burial at the Jake Pepper place, April 25.

Lottie McKinley died in Lonaconing during childhood.

Lucy May Pugh, whose smiling face and genial disposition made a lasting impression on all who knew her, chose as her life companion Joseph Fahs Pepper (born Nov. 18, 1848), again uniting the Pugh family with the Pepper family, among one of the oldest and best of Hampshire's fine people. They were married August 26, 1873, and took up their abode at the Patterson place where they continued during their lifetime. Their family consisted of two daughters, Ida May and Margaret Frances, and a son, Chas. Arthur, born May 11, 1881, but died in infancy.

Ida May, born October 31, 1877, died September 17, 1882. **Margaret Frances** was born July 14, 1874. Fannie, as she is familiarly known, is the sole survivor of her branch of the Pepper family to bear the name, her mother having passed away after a sudden illness September 10, 1881 and her father died December, 1926. Margaret Patterson died January, 1928. Fannie tenderly and faithfully cared for the old people, and she and a cousin are now dispensing hospitality in a quiet way while she rests from her labors and keeps up the traditions of the old home. Fannie died June 13, 1942. Buried at the Pepper place, 3:30 P. M., June 15th.

John Thomas Pugh was born June 15, 1856, on a part of what is now known as the John Paterson Farm located on "No. 29", now "45". His father having been lost on the field of battle, June 5, 1864, he began very early to earn his own living. About 1879 he left his mother's home in Hampshire county, West Virginia, for Peculiar, Cass county, Missouri, the home of a relative, John Urton, Mr. Urton paying his way. He traveled with John Urton's father, Alfred Urton, who was on his way to Missouri to buy a farm and locate there.

In 1872, Mrs. Pugh removed to Cumberland, Md., and in 1873 John T. went back there to see her. In 1874 he went to Chicago and from there to Iowa and worked on the C. B. & Q. Railroad. Then to Kansas City, Missouri, and later returned to Peculiar where he worked for John Urton again.

John T. was in the West several years before his brother Solomon J. joined him there. He made but one trip back home. Leaving Urtons the second time he went to Denver, Colorado. From there to Boulder, San Louis Valley and Cripple Creek. While at Cripple Creek he made money.

In the Thunder Mountain Gold Rush of 1902, John T. went to Idaho where he settled and bought a claim. Here he is known as the "Prospector". His business has been that of locating veins of ore by radium, with his home at Salmon, Lemhi county, where he still resides, June, 1934. About four years ago he was poisoned while working underground and has since been unable to work. He has no family. During his wanderings, among other things he learned to cook, and at Cripple Creek for a time was Second Stewart at the National

Hotel. At other places he ran restaurants on his own. Besides the places named, he has visited Butte, Montana, Portland, Oregon, etc. Despite his rovings, Mr. Pugh has lead a clean life and is loved and respected in his home town, for his pride of character. The Postmaster at Salmon says he considers Mr. Pugh a very fine old gentleman.

Solomon J., second son of Arthur Tansy and Margaret Wolverton Pugh, was born December 12, 1857, near Slanesville, Virginia (now West Virginia). He went West at fourteen to Kansas City, Missouri, and married Eliza Jane Ash about the year 1891, residing at Lee's Summit, Missouri, where he, at this writing (1934), still lives, 1943. Died 1945.

Solomon J. and Eliza Jane Ash Pugh, have the following interesting family:

Ralph Waldo Pugh, born May 24, 1892, married Muriel Bullips. He is engaged in the garage business and resides at Salinas, California.

Walter Arthur Pugh and wife, Bertha R., have one daughter, Gertrude Claire, now, 1941, is a graduate of University of California, Art Department. Walter was born March 19, 1894. He is in the clothing business as salesman and lives at Berkley, California, later Oakland.

Hattie Margaret Pugh, married F. H. Maher. They have three promising children who are making their mark at school and who are proud they can trace their ancestry to the F.F.V's. They have not yet visited the birthplace of their grandfather and the battle ground where his father lost his life, but are looking forward to it when their education is completed. They are Edward, 19; James, 16; and Jeannette, 13, (1932). Jeannette is the champion speller of her school, having proved herself such repeatedly, as per a clipping from Omaha Daily. Mr. Maher, their father, is a traveling salesman and their residence is at 2107 Spencer Street, Omaha, Nebraska. Mr. Maher died January, 1948.

Nancy A. Pugh, married to Luther R. Thornton, lives in Chicago. They have two children, Theadore, aged 15 and Mary, 13. Nancy Pugh was born October 31, 1903 and named for her great grandmother, Nancy Jane Offutt, wife of Jonathan Pugh, III, and for her Aunt Nancy Jane McKinley, of Madison, Wisconsin. The writer would like to know her if only for the name's sake.

Wm. E. Pugh, born May 15, 1906, single, lives in Idaho.

John Thomas Pugh, named for his uncle, the Prospector, was born May 10, 1909 and was married September, 1932 to Rose Brucia. He is in business at Monterey, California.

Miranda H. Pugh, fifth child of Arthnr T. and Margaret W. Pugh, was born near Slanesville, Virginia, November 16, 1859, moved to Cumberland, Md., with her mother about 1873, and later married Joseph Porter of Lonacoming, Md. Both are deceased. Their children are:

Lelia Porter, who married E. M. Sales and resides at 1217 Morrow Street, Williamsburg, Pa.

William Porter, who married Miss Brown of Lonaconing, where they reside, 57 E. Main St., is the only one of the family ever personally known to the writer. He is of medium height, weight about 160, fair, with blue eyes, dark hair, a young face that radiates good humor. William at present, is a motor bus operator to and from this city. This is a most excellent opportunity to know people and to fix regular habits in a young man.

Margaret and **Joseph Porter,** deceased.

Mary Elizabeth Pugh, youngest daughter of Arthur and Margaret, well known to the writer whose home she often visited, was much like her sister Lucy whom she resembled in looks. She was a dressmaker, industrious and independent. She spent most of her life in Cumberland and Lonaconing. We often saw her on vacation for she loved the open country. She and her cousin, T. D. Pugh, were fast friends, and saw much of each other when she was here for an outing, but for some reason both died single.

Generation of Johnathan Pugh, III, and Nancy Offutt Pugh.

Solomon J. Pugh, son of Jonathan III, was born near Slanesville Virginia (now West Virginia), April 30, 1830, died in Cumberland, Maryland, April 16, 1901. He was married to

Margaret E. McDonald, daughter of James and Elizabeth Stump McDonald, March 20, 1860. He was much liked and of fine physical appearance, being tall and well proportioned. His wife was small, "a lovely little woman". She was born near Pleasant Dale, Virginia, July 14, 1835, and died in Cumberland, March 14, 1889.

Mr. Pugh espoused the cause of the Confederacy as a member of Co. C., the 18th Virginia Cavalry, Imboden's command, being Orderly Sergeant when he was captured and sent to Camp Chase, Ohio, where he spent several months as a prisoner, was later exchanged. When the war was concluded the family moved to Cumberland, Mr. Pugh having secured a position with the B. & O. R.R., with which company he remained until death. He lies in Rose Hill cemetery, beside his wife.

The following children were born to Solomon J. and Margaret E. Pugh: **Annie Imboden** and **James Fundenburg**, who died in infancy, buried in the Offutt graveyard.

Furman Gilbert, popularly known to business as F. G. Pugh, began his life in L. M. Shepherd's store, where as a boy he won the hearts of the Cumberland people and laid the foundation of a succssful business and social career. In 1896 he entered as a partner with his brother-in-law, Oliver S. Wilson, in Wilson and Pugh Wholesale Hardware business of which he is now, 1934, the senior member, being also president of the Commercial Bank, president for many years of the Cumberland Board of Education, a 32nd degree Mason, an Elk, a Rotarian, Director of Fort Cumberland Hotel, a member of Chamber of Commerce, and a regular attendant at Center Street Methodist Episcopal Church. Mr. Pugh, a favorite with the gentler sex and of a magnetic personality, has chosen to remain single. Died aged 78. See Vol. II for his death date, also page 85 of this book.

Maud Lee Pugh, sister of F. G., with whom he now resides, 1934, and who has always been very close to him, married Oliver S. Wilson, May 28, 1896. Mr. Wilson was the founder of the Wilson and Pugh Hardware Firm and charter member of Commercial Savings Bank and its president for some years, besides being connected with other Allegheny county enterprises. Mr. Wilson died in 1923. The Wilsons have two sons, one in the retail hardware business and the other an attorney at law.

Mrs. Maud Lee Wilson lives at 15 South Liberty Street., Cumberland, Maryland, where she, like her mother, is a charming hostess. The brother and sisters spent some time in Florida this winter, (1932.) Maud Lee Pugh Wilson died at her home, October 13, 1940.

Florence Elizabeth, the younger sister, who, after Maud Lee's marriage, kept the home fires burning until 1903, went to the altar with Wm. Riely Deitz, October 28, of that year, W. W. Bernes, officiating. Mr. Deitz was then with the Wilson and Pugh firm. Mrs. Deitz is a typical Pugh, of her father's type that combines dignity with graciousness, she is yet living, March 22nd, 1947.

William E. Pugh, the cherished younger brother, followed his mother to the Great Beyond, passing away February 4, 1890.

This branch of the Pugh family is of the blond type, blue eyes and fair complexion, and strong Pugh characteristics.

From CUMBERLAND NEWS, *Wednesday, November 30, 1938, Abbreviated.*

DEATH CLAIMS FERMAN G. PUGH

Cumberland mourned today the death of one of its outstanding citizens, Ferman G. Pugh.

Mr. Pugh, who for more than half a century had been prominent in the commercial, banking, civic and educational activities of the Queen City, died early yesterday morning (5 a. m) at the home of his sister, Mrs. Oliver S. Wilson, 15 South Liberty Street.

He was 78 years of age and had been ill only since Sunday. Besides Mrs. Wilson, another sister, Mrs. Wm. R. Deitz of this city survives.

$100,000 Bequests Are Made To Two W. Md. Hospitals

Cumberland, Dec. 6—The will of Furman Gilbert Pugh, probated today, provided bequests of $100,000 each for "relief of sickness, and suffering" in two hospitals.

Both bequests become effective upon the death of Maud Pugh Wilson and Florence Elizabeth Deitz, sisters of Pugh, for whom the money will be used as a trust fund.

His will directs that, with termination of the trust fund, the money shall be divided equally between the board of governors of Memorial Hospital in Cumberland and the Sisters of Charity of the Allegany Hospital, Inc.,

Other bequests included $10,000 to the Cumberland Public Library, $5,000 to Centre Street Methodist Episcopal Church, $10,000 to Mary B. Wickard, Lavale, and $5,000 to Lena McDonald, Winchester, Va.

CHAPTER VIII

John N. Pugh and wife, Sarah Offutt
Residence, burial place of eleven children and their descendants

SON OF JONATHAN, JR. AND MARY ELLEN TANSY PUGH

John N. Pugh, born December 28, 1800 on North River Virginia, died May 19, 1887. He grew to manhood on the old plantation, married Sarah Offutt, (born Dec. 25, 1808, died May 25, 1880), February 21, 1828. He built the first frame residence on the old homestead just a short distance from his father's home and lived there during his whole life. He was Capt. of Malitica, a farmer and a stock raiser, and he and his wife had both, in youth, been accostumed to servants in the home. Consequently they took life rather easy. A large family of boys and girls that were born to them learned, at an early age to do their share in the homemaking. The girls learned to spin and weave, do fine needle work and tailoring. The beautiful counterpanes and quilts are still in the family. They did their own cleaning and pressing, and made their own clothes without a sewing machine since Howe's invention had not come into general use yet. And what astonishingly beautiful stitches they put into things with the "Bright little needle, the swift flying needle, the needle directed by beauty and art."

They raised geese and picked the white feathers to cool their fowl in the warm days and made beds and pillows, the downiest and sweetest ever slept upon. The boys clipped the wool from the sheep's back and washed it in the creek, took it to the carders and brought the rolls back in the spring wagon. The girls spun it and colored it, wove it into flannel for the household, and blankets and counter-panes for the beds. Their warm, beautiful woolens for winter spelled their handiwork from the sheep's back to their own. They never thought of it as drudgery. They sang and the house resounded with voices and laughter while they worked.

These boys learned to be farmers, gardners, fruit growers, millers, stock raisers, carpenters, bookkeepers, teachers, as well as soldiers and athletes. They could shoot like the Green Mountain boys, ride like troopers, swim like swans. So, in later life, they did not need much training when called to arms to defend their State they shouldered the gun and mounted their own horses and were off, ready for action. Their names follow:

Euphemia (Effa), born Dec. 18, 1828, died July 31, 1913, at 3:15 a. m., buried August 2, at 11:30 a. m., at the Pugh burial ground.

John James, born February 20, 1831, died October 31, 1920, Sunday, 7:40 a. m. buried Nov. 3rd, 2:30 p. m. at Salem Church.

Azbernia, born March 16, 1833, died May 4, 1911, buried at Offutt Cemetery.

Jonathan, born March 18, 1835, died February 19, 1914, lies in Pugh graveyard.

Elizabeth Hester, born April 16, 1837, died October 7, 1925, buried in Pugh graveyard.

Owen Van Buren, born March 11, 1839, died at Harrisonburg, 1863 and is buried there.

Joseph Arthur, born Nov. 11, 1841, died April 19, 1926, buried at J. Pepper Cemetery.

Solomon Edgar, born June 12, 1844, died October 29, 1923, buried at the Offutt graveyard, Oct. 30th.

Algeron Wood, born June 28, 1847, died August 13, 1870, 8:15 a. m., buried at Cambria, Missouri.

Thomas Dye, born May 19, 1849, died August 25, 1928, buried at Augusta.

Robert O., born Dec. 1851, died March 30, 1908, buried by Sol. E.

John N. Pugh had the Pugh physique with high forehead and straight nose, and regular features but his black eyes and hair were characteristic of his mother's people, the Tansys. He was at one time a militia captain and was always called Captain John Pugh but was too old for active service in the

JOSEPH ARTHUR PUGH

Alexander Monroe, son of Elexander, The Baptist Minister (who went to Kentucky) and Effie Pugh Monroe. She is eldest daughter of John N. and Sarah Offutt Pugh. This picture was made soon after the Civil War.

Civil War. All five of his sons who were old enough espoused the cause of their State as Confederates.

Sarah Offutt, wife of John N. Pugh

Sarah Offutt Pugh, fair of skin with dark hair, medium height and weight about 140. She was a thrifty housewife who allowed her children to do their full share of the work indoors. She took an interest in livestock, and gardens, and had very definite ideas of her own on all matters of general interest which she fearlessly expressed. John and Sarah brought up their children to honor God and feel a reverence for divine things; and know that honesty is the best policy though it may not bring fame or riches.

John and Sarah both lived past three score and ten. Sarah fell lifeless frem her chair in the evening after an active day in usual health; her husband, dying from the effects of a fall. Both are buried in the Offutt family burial ground near Slanesville, W. Va. She was the daughter of Solomon and Elizabeth Roberts Offutt. Geneaology given elsewhere in this book.

Descendants of Lieut. Jonathan and Margaret Wood Pugh through John and Sarah Offutt Pugh

Effie Pugh, daughter of John N. and Sarah Offutt Pugh, was born at the old homestead on North River, December, 1828, being the oldest of eleven children. She was tall, graceful and fair, with blue eyes and brown hair. She was assistant homemaker for the large family. Effie was much like her Aunt Maria Pugh Smith whom she resembled in physical features, and like her, was an artist in handwork and could weave coverlets in elaborate designs. It was a sad day for the younger children when "Alex Monroe" came a courting to their father's house. Effie and Mr. Monroe were married soon after the Civil War and went to their home at Burning Springs, W. Va., where they lived very happily together. Mr. Monroe had a rugged, kindly manner, was a Scotchman, he died early, then his wife was prevailed upon to adopt several children, some of whom were self-willed, took advantage of her gentle disposition to sadden her later life. She had a remarkable memory and the writer owes much legendary history to her.

Effie Pugh Monroe owned the antique silver watch handed down from the first Jonathan Pugh, which she gave, at her death, to the writer who was with her at the time. She also had inherited the bird's eye maple chest, made as a gift by Arthur Tansy to his brother-in-law and sister, Capt. Johnathan Pugh and wife. This she intrusted to the writer to be handed down in the Pugh name successively. They left no children.

Alexander Monroe, son of Alex. Monroe, Baptist minister of Kentucky, and cousin to Col. Alex, was a successful business man, farmer and stockraiser, of the oil fields in Wirt County, W. Va., in which fields he also had an interest. He and his wife made several visits to the home county. He was buried at Burning Springs in the late seventies. She died at 1:30 a. m., July 31, 1913, and lies buried at the old Pugh burial grounds beside her Aunt Lucy Pugh Monroe in Hampshire County.

Descendants of Lieut. Jonathan and Margaret Wood Pugh

John James Pugh, eldest son of John N. and Sarah Offutt Pugh, born on the Pugh estate, February 20, 1831, died October 31, 1920, was largely self-educated, owing much to his grandfather perhaps, the Capt. Jonathan, who lived next door, but he had the faculty of reading everything that came into his hands and digesting the best of it, so, he was well-informed. At the age of 89 he read a library book from cover to cover.

He was five feet, eleven, broad shouldered, weight 175 to 200, fair, blue eyes, high forehead, firm set mouth. During early manhood he spent some years with his mother's uncle, Joseph Offutt, in the then small towns of Pekin and Peoria, Illinois. On the trip over the Alleghenies aboard the new B. & O. R. R. train he and some fellow passengers at one point got out and walked across, arriving ahead of the train.

On this visit he had a rich experience during the pioneer days of the Middle West. Learning of trade, travel and agriculture along the Mississippi and its tributaries. These were the

John James Pugh, Co. C., 18th Va. Cav. Capt. Guinevan's Co., under Imboden's Command, while in service about 1862. He was born February 20, 1831.

days of the Showboat and the Fishing Schooner, stories of which amused and excited our imagination as children, not so much the big fish, perhaps, as his portrayal of the personality and dialect of the "River People".

After his return and before the outset of the Civil War he married Elizabeth Milleson, daughter of Wm. and Sarah Henderson Milleson, February 21, 1860. They had just gotten started in life when the Civil War broke out. As time went on they had two children, he found he must enlist or be drafted. A Pugh is never drafted. John James enlisted as a volunteer cavalryman, Capt. Guinevan's Co., 18th Virginia Cavalry, Imboden's Command. January 1, 1863, his wife and children went to share the home of her mother who was a widow living on a farm near Slanesville, Virginia.

He and his brother-in-law, late Sheriff Geo. Milleson, the 2nd, of Co. K, Capt. Pyles Division, were ambushed and captured near Wardinsville, October 3, 1863, by Capt. Humes, and sent first to Camp Chase, Ohio, for three months, when they were removed to Rock Island in the Mississippi River, where they remained for fifteen months.

During their imprisonment at Camp Chase they suffered much from bitter feeling and treatment of prison officials. At Rock Island the guards were, for a time, colored men and they had some amusing experiences, but soon things happened that caused extreme scarcity of provision and other supplies, which meant starvation, and unsanitary, appalling conditions followed. They buried their dead comrades of smallpox, and other loathsome diseases, lived on rats caught and cabbage boiled in water only, etc. March 20, 1865, they were exchanged. When they reached home their wives did not recognize them. At home he found everything swept away. One child was gone.

John James knew milling from the "Old Burrh Mill" on his grandfather's farm. They went finally to North River Mills, a village at the base of the famous Ice Mountain where their children grew up. In the seventies they acquired a part of the Old Pugh Homestead and moved into it. There Elizabeth and one daughter died, the former in 1910, the latter in 1894.

91

John James lived to the age of 89 years, eight months and 11 days and died while on a visit to ris daughter, Mrs. Artie Pugh Shaffer, of Homer, Ohio. He was buried at Salem Cemetery, Hampshire County, West Virginia, at 2:30, p. m., Wednesday, November 3, 1920.

John James Pugh was a man of strong mind and character as his face indicated, capable of holding many positions of trust and honor in his county and state, but he inherited from his father, John N., a distaste for the struggle to displace others in order to elevate himself. He shrank from political scheming and loathed its corruption while he took a lively interest in all matters pertaining to his country's welfare.

As a miller he did a lucrative business with patrons from a large scope of country who adored him and some fondly called him "Old North River Mills". He did not save money. His generosity was well known in the season of depression that followed the Civil War. No widow's son or needy ex-Confederate soldier ever went home with an empty sack, be it food for man or beast, that they craved. There was no pension or "Bonus", no hospitalization, not even a Red Cross for them. Once a young man who had gone west to prosper came back in after life to seek him out and feelingly thank him for help to him when a child with a widowed mother in destitute circumstances.

Elizabeth Milleson, wife of John James Pugh

Elizabeth Milleson, born February 2, 1835, daughter of Wm. and Sarah Henderson Milleson and granddaughter of John and Nancy Fletcher Milleson, whose parents were pioneers to this country from the Emerald Isle, was five feet, seven inches, with dark hair and eyes. She had a dignified reserve, but was magnetic and warm hearted withal. She attracted the best people to her wherever she went. She had a sister Nancy who married and died before the Civil War, leaving Elizabeth as the only daughter of a family of five and as such was idealized by her brothers without being spoiled. This family were brought up in the same community and went to school

Elizabeth Milleson Pugh, daughter of William and Sarah Henderson Milleson, and wife of John James Pugh. This picture was taken before her marriage, which took place at her Mother's home, near Slanesville, February 21, 1860. She was born February 2, 1835.

with the Monroe brothers, Col. Alex, James, Robert and Walker, and were lifelong friends.

She was to her family of girls everything a mother ought to be — and felt deeply each flight from the home nest, be it permanent or transient.

John James and Elizabeth lived to pass their Golden Wedding milestone together, she passing away at 1 p. m., March 23, 1910. Children born to them were:

Laura E., born April 27, 1861, died 2 p. m., February 4, 1894, buried at Salem Cemetery. She married E. Miller of Pennsylvania; left one child, Myrtle Miller, who married Robt. Digmon, of Paw Paw. Their children are: Gilbert, Paul, Laura, Ruby, and Inez Maud.

Cornelia Arabelle, born April 12, 1863, died April 8, 1865, buried at Salem Cemetery.

Maud, born January 6, 1866.

Artemasia Virginia, born October 5, 1867.

Effa May, born February 1, 1870.

Edith Letitia, born November 16, 1873, died 5:15 p. m., May 5, 1894, buried in Indian Mount Cemetery, Romney, 2 p. m., May 7, 1894.

Descendants of Lieut. Jonathan and Margaret Wood Pugh, John James and Elizabeth Milleson Pugh

Laura E. Pugh, eldest daughter of John James and Elizabeth Milleson Pugh, born April 27, 1861, died 2 p. m., February 4, 1894; buried at Salem Church, near Slanesville.

Laura was maried to E. B. Miller in Cumberland, Maryland, August 25, 1886. Two children were born to this union: Myrtle Flora, May 30, 1887; Grover Cleveland, born March 5, 1893, died August 10, 1893.

On March 22, 1904, Myrtle Flora Miller married Robert Lee Dignan, born December 22, 1884. Robert was at first employed by the West Virginia Central R. R. They then lived at Elkins. When the Road changed to the Western Maryland he continued his connection with that as a "Knight of the Train and Track" and later was, for many years, baggage master on the division, Cumberland to Elkins, then conductor. Faithfull at all times he has never "lost his job" and has but once been in a serious wreck. On that occasion, with cars demolished or overturned, with some of the crew killed and others injured, Robert came out with a wounded finger. He is now retired. After some years they moved to Ridgley, then to Cumberland, just in sight, and later back to Ridgley, and again to Cumberland where they now reside. They have had some reverses in fortune, but look and seem as young as their children. They have at times engaged in the mercantile business or agriculture as a side line but Robert never left the Road. Robert and Myrtle are wholesomely devoted to each other and to their family, and with them "All's right with the world".

Robert and Myrtle are members of the Christian Church. It was always the custom for Robert to kiss the mother and babies good bye when he went out. Once when the writer was present, Laura, then three, clung to him, saying, "Daddy, don't let the engine get you." A man had been killed in the yards that day by an unseen engine.

MRS. LAURA E. MILLER,
Made while a student at Oberlin
College.

DIGMAN FAMILY

MRS. LAURA D. TURNER

PAUL DIGMAN
Lieut. in the Navy

Their children are:

Robert Gilbert, born June 17, 1905; married to Virginia Cosgrove, May 13, 1928. Children to this union: Robert Edward, born April 25, 1929; Paul Herman, born December 19, 1930; Thomas James, born May 27, 1934. They live in Cumberland, Maryland. They are Catholics, 1938 a daughter was born, Virginia Lee, Gilbert is now deceased.

Paul Elmer, born July 2, 1906, is in U. S. Navy, Honolulu, 1934, now a Lieutenant stationed at Oakland, Calif., married Esther Hendricks.

Laura Alice, born January 9, 1908, nurse, Washington, D. C., maried Sept. 27, 1935, Norman B. Turner, one son, Norman Jr. They are in business in Washington D. C.

Ruby Myrtle, born October 15, 1909, Allegheny High School graduate. Married Elmer Golden Jenkins, Feb. 13, 1927. Children: Jack Clifford, born April 1, 1928; Donald Lee, born January 14, 1931. They lived in Ridgley, now divorced, she is in business in Washington, D. C.

Inez Maude, born October 26, 1911. Married to Ralph William Mathias, April 6th, 1934. They lived in Cumberland, Md., Ralph and Inez now reside at Rockville, Md., one son, William Mathias, ("Billy").

Cornelias Arabelle and **Maud Pugh** mentioned elsewhere in this book.

Artie Virginia Pugh, daughter of John James and Elizabeth Milleson Pugh, born October 5, 1867, at North River Mills, W. Va., entered school at five and was ready for the third grade at the age of six. Her first school was at Capon Lake where she continued to teach for several terms, then went to Mt. Airy, nearby. Among those who went out from these schools taught in her youth are one graduate of Fairmont College, W. Va., who became the wife of a Lutheran minister of note; one Judge of the District Court; one State Governor; several teachers and others who are doing things worth while in the world. Artie continued teaching until her marriage.

Among her classmates as a Junior at Fairmont were James W. Horn, poet of ability; S. H. Bowman; Ann Lynn, wife of Ex-Supt. Geo. M. Ford; Dagmar Neely, sister of Sen. M. M.

Neely; Ida Amos, outstanding teacher, Hal Hall, physician, and others known over the state.

Artie was the first woman of her county to serve on an Examining Board for teachers, at a date long before woman had a vote in W. Va. The Board consisted of the following members: Chas. N. Hiett, president; Artie V. Pugh and A. C. Cowgell, Commissioners.

In 1898, while visiting in Ohio, Artie met Samuel L. Shaffer, born at Mt. Liberty, Ohio, July 2, 1859, son of Peter and Ellen Thatcher Shaffer. They were married December 27, 1899. Ellen Thatcher Shaffer was from New Jersey, the father from Pennsylvania. Samuel L. Shaffer began life as a jeweler at Mt. Vernon, Ohio, but later went to Homer as a Funeral Director. At the time of his death they were living in the beautiful farm residence bordering the town, which is still Mrs. Shaffer's home, 1936. On this farm are two gas wells, a large gas plant; also a gasoline plant.

Mr. Shaffer had the flu and died Feb. 2, 1919.

Children born to this union were: John James, Samuel Sloan, George Crawford, Mary, and Elizabeth Joy, the little girls dying in infancy, as did also the first son.

After the death of Mr. Shaffer, Artie attended the Columbus Training School for Embalmers, spending week ends at home. Graduating, she took the State Examination at Toledo, in order to sponsor the work of her sons who were continuing the business but who were too young to take the State Examination, though qualified to do the work of Embalmers and Funeral Directors.

Artie is now Librarian for Burlington-Hamilton Township, which includes the High and Graded Schools of her town (Homer). She is a Presbyterian and a Democrat, and takes a lively interest in the world, as well as local affairs.

Samuel Sloan Shaffer, elder son of S. L. and Artie V. Shaffer, born at the Shaffer home, Homer, Ohio, December 31, 1901. He graduated in Columbus Training School for Embalmers, August 1918, and in Homer High School, June 1920, after which

MRS. ARTIE SHAFFER

SLOAN SHAFFER

Crawford Shaffer and his Indian
friend from San Domingo, while
Crawford was in Albuquerque, N. M.

The Shaffer Home, Homer, Ohio

he and his brother, Crawford were funeral directors under Mrs. Shaffer, at Homer, the firm being known as Shaffer Brothers, until Crawford became ill. In 1922, Sloan pased the State Examination, obtaining his license. He then went to Newark, Ohio, where he was connected with Criss Brothers, Funeral Directors. Later he was in busines in Cumberland, Maryland; Uniontown, Pa., and is now manager for the Campbell Funeral Home, Beaver Falls, Pa., (1936). He is a charter member of the Ancient Order of Anubis, Embalmers' order of National Select Morticians. 1947, is in business in Marietta, Ohio.

S. Sloan Shaffer married Isabel Mary Hawkins, daughter of Chas. O. and Isabel G. Hawkins — the former of Tarpin Springs, Florida, and the latter of Warren, Pa., October 7, 1926, in Newark, Ohio. Isabel Mary Hawkins was graduated from Newark High School and attended Wallace School and Conservatory of Music, Columbus. She is a member of Alpha Pi Sigma Sorority. Sloan is 6 feet, 2 inches, of fine physique and an amiable disposition. He is fair with blue eyes and auburn hair.

George Crawford Shaffer, younger son of the late Samuel L. and Artie Virginia Pugh Shaffer, was born in Homer, Ohio, July 3, 1904. He went through the grades in Homer Schools and was a Sophomore in the High School when he fell a victim of the dreaded influenza so prevalent during the fall of 1919. Not fully recovering from its effects he developed tuberculosis the following year, and for three years, under the best physicans and a loving mother's care, fought a seemingly losing battle at home.

In the early fall of 1923, accompanied by his mother, he went to Albuquerque, New Mexico, in the hope that climatic conditions there would assist in effecting a cure. For more than two years hope of recovery ebbed and flowed until October 7, 1925, after three days of acute suffering he quietly passed from the life militant to the life triumphant.

Crawford's body was brought back to Newark and funeral services conducted by one who loved him, were held in the

97

First Presbyterian Church, and internment was made in the Homer cemetery — the large assemblage at both places testifying to the loving esteem in which he was held by those who knew him.

Crawford's was an attractive and choice personality. The charm of his presence, his cheerful disposition and happy smiling face made him a favorite wherever he went. In childhood he united with the Homer Presbyterian church, and the writer knew him to be a fine Christian lad who responded heartily to an unusual friendship.

Crawford's career in this life was of brief duration, but it was a beautiful life, and his unsullied spirit has gone back to God who gave it. —Dr. Calvin G. Hazlett, his pastor and friend.

Bible Record

Samuel Loyd Shaffer, born at Mt. Liberty, Ohio, July 2, 1859, died February 2, 1919.

Artie Virginia Pugh, born October 5, 1867, in Hampshire county, West Virginia. Married December 26, 1899.

Children:

John James Shaffer, born and died September 30, 1900, at Homer, Ohio.

Samuel Sloan Shaffer, born December 31, 1901, at Homer, Ohio.

George Crawford Shaffer, born July 3, 1904, at Homer, died October 7, 1925, at Albuquerque, New Mexico.

Elizabeth Joy Shaffer, born October, 1906, died January, 1907, at Homer, Ohio, eleven weeks old.

Mary Shaffer, born and died November 31, 1908, at Homer, Ohio.

Descendants of Lieut. Jonathan and Margaret Wood Pugh

Effa, daughter of John James and Elizabeth Milleson Pugh, born February 1, 1870, at North River Mills, W. Va., attended school at Fairmont and taught a few years. May 16, 1894, married John Hillbrant, farmer and business man of Homer, Ohio, who was graduated at Louisville, Ky. Children born to

MRS. EFFA HILLBRANT SCANLON

The Hillbrant Children

this union: Velma, Edythe and William Pugh Hillbrant. John Hillbrant is deceased, buried at Homer, Ohio.

After seeing her children through High School at Mt. Vernon, Ohio, Effa went with them to Oberlin, where, as Matron in the college, she remained until after their graduation, when she went into business in Cleveland, where she still resided, 1936.

December, 1931, Effa married John E. Scanlon of California, a fine man, he died February 13th, 1948 and is buried at Three Churches, W. Va.

Velma Hillbrant, born July 23, 1895, graduated in Mt. Vernon High School, June, 1914, was in school at Athens from 1915 to 1917, then at Oberlin one year, after which she took up war work at Akron, Ohio. July, 1919, she went to Cleveland and into the advertising department of The National Refining Company. She was there six months and resigned to accept a place with the Shipping Board which meant more money. In the meantime, July, 1920, she had met Loran Mathews, son of Wm. and Dorothy Jordan Mathews, of Salem, Ohio, born July 13, 1899. They were married August 14, 1920. She remained with the shipping board until its work was completed in that territory, and later took up another government position. Loran, her husband, was with the United States Coal Co., Cleveland. He had not yet finished college. He had one year at Wesleyan, Delaware, before enlisting in the Army, World War I. He saw service overseas 14 months. On his return he entered the University of Pittsburgh, took a second year, then married. January, 1922, they both entered Cleveland Law School, continuing their work and studying at night. June, 1926, they both received their L.L.B. degree from Baldwin Wallace University, Berea, Ohio, passed and were admitted to the bar in Cleveland, January, 1927. Velma is a brunette, Loran, blonde. They reside at 1988 E. 81st St., Cleveland, with office at 440, Leader Building, 1936.

Loren Mathews, member, Lambda Chi Alpha Fraternity of University of Pittsburgh, Delta Theta Phi Fraternity, Cleveland Law School, Mason, Lakewood F. & A. M., McKinley Chapter R.A.M. No. 181.

Velma, member, Eastern Star, Glenville Chapter, No., 359, Cleveland, Ohio. They now reside at 1134 E. 3rd St., Salem, Ohio, 1947. No children.

Edythe Hillbrant, born November 11, 1896, near Homer, Ohio, as a child was enchantingly beautiful and sweet, and it seems has lost none of this charm as a woman. She entered High School at Mt. Vernon, September, 1910, finishing her degree of B.A. at Oberlin College, 1919. She was for a time private secretary to the President of the Federal Reserve Board in Cleveland, then taught in the city schools for two years.

January 1, 1922, Edythe was united in marriage with Alexis Caswell, son of Alexis and ———— Caswell, born ———— Minneapolis, Minn. Alexis had been a student in the University of Minneapolis before the outbreak of World War I. He then enlisted and was called overseas. They have two children: Alexis, III, born November ————, 1924 and James Offutt, born May ————, 1927.

The Caswells reside in Minneapolis, where Mr. Caswell is in business. Edythe is fair with auburn hair.

William Pugh Hillbrant, born May 25, 1898, Homer, Ohio, entered Mt. Vernon High School, 1910, finishing there 1914. He entered Oberlin College, 1915, taking the degree of B.A., 1919. He then took up Business Management at Harvard University received his MA degree two years later, the youngest man of his class. He was a member of Lambda Chi Fraternity. (He is now a CPA).

W. P. Hillbrant is a certified accountant and auditor, was connected with Price ———— Co., New York City, also was Manager of Rockefeller interests in Colorado, later in 1926 Married, October 16, 1926, Dorothy Lavinia Loggren, born in Elizabeth, N. J., on January 13, 1901. Children: William Robert Hillbrant, born in Elizabeth, N. J., on July 24, 1930.

Descendants of Lieutenant Jonathan Pugh

Edith Letitia Pugh, youngest of the family, born at North River Mills, West Virginia, Nevember 16, 1873, died at her father's home near Pleasant Dale, May 5, 1894. She began

EDITH LETITIA PUGH
Only picture we have. She was
a beautiful woman when grown.

teaching at Capon Springs in the fall of 1892, taught two terms, the second of which she was not able to complete because of ill health. She died the following spring of complications.

Edith was fair, with wavy hair, a rich brilliant auburn, tender grey eyes, and expressive mouth. She was five feet, six inches, slender and graceful. Her faultless features indicating intelligence and an unselfish disposition. She had musical talent which she was ambitious to develop and was working and saving to that end.

Edith was buried in the Indian Mound Cemetery at Romney, W. Va., in a lot overlooking the beautiful South Branch Valley, May 7th. The loneliness that followed the passing of this sweet personality from the home can only be known by those who have suffered a like loss. Only this childhood picture of Edith exists which fails to express her youthful beauty that later developed.

Children of John and Sarah Offutt Pugh

Azberinia Pugh, born March 16, 1833, died May 4, 1911. She helped bring up her father's large family. She was industrious and frugal. It was Azberinia that cared for her father in his last illness and did most of the waiting on the blind brother. For many years this father and brother kept her steadily at home on the farm with little or no opportunity for attendance at church or other functions, or for recreation. She was for a long time housekeeper and home maker for her brother Thomas, too, as he had also remained unmarried. In youth she and Lieut. Jefferson Carter were close friends.

At an early age, Azbernia connected herself with the Southern Methodist Church. She had a wholesome pride of character, a devotion to duty and a reverence for things Godly. "She did with her might what her hands found to do. She lies buried near her parents at the Offutt Cemetery near Route No. 29, Now Route No. 45.

Jonathan Pugh, IV, of Virginia, son of John N. and Sarah Pugh, was born March 18, 1835, grew up and was educated on the Pugh estate. He was engaged most of his life in agricultural pursuits. He spent some years with his sister at Burning Springs and also with Mrs. E. Yost, another widowed sister, on her farm near Augusta, Hampshire county. During the Civil War, Jonathan IV, espoused the cause of the Confederacy, enlisting with Co. K., Capt. Sherrard of Col. A. P. Hill's Division, 13th Virginia Infantry, Stonewall Jackson's men, and more lucky than his brothers with Jackson, lived to return unharmed, though imprisoned for a time at Camp Chase. In old age he became totally blind and was tenderly cared for successively by his two sisters, Azzie Pugh and Mrs. Elizabeth Yost, at the old home. He died February 19, 1914 and lies buried at the home graveyard.

Jonathan was a Democrat and a Presbyterian. He was a bachelor and was physically the Pugh type.

Elizabeth Hester Pugh, born April 16, 1837, died October 7, 1925; married Peter S. Youst, January 28, 1868. He was born in 1843 and died in 1883.

Elizabeth spent her early childhood at her father's home on North River, and later went to live with her grandmother, Elizabeth Offutt, then a widow, whose daughters had all left the home-nest for their own, and she remained there until her marriage.

Peter and Elizabeth began housekeeping on the Potomac at Green Spring Station where Mr. Youst had a position with the B. & O. R.R., and here their six children were born:

Emma L., born December 10, 1868, Eliza E., born January 20, 1871, Albert, born May 30, 1874, Lucy M. and John W., twins, born March 30, 1876, Lucy died April 11, 1892, John died December 3, 1909. Francis M., born March 31, 1879, died 1879.

Eliza E. Youst married Charles Broome, born ————, of Fort Ashby (Alaska, W. Va.), of German descent. They had one child, Maud, born in 1896. She married Samuel Logsdon of Patterson's Creek, W. Va. Maud and her husband have two children, a boy and a girl, and reside near Keyser, W. Va.

Eliza Youst Broome was a blond, of perfect type. Slender and rather tall, amiable disposition and attractive. She died soon after the birth of her daughter, 1896, and Maud was brought up in the home of her grandparents, Mr. and Mrs. Broome, who loved her as their own.

Charles Broome is an opposite type from Eliza, with grey eyes and dark complexion, quiet and dignified in manner. He remained single many years after Eliza's death but is now married a second time. Maud is like her father.

While Lucy M., and John W., the twins, were yet small children their father, Peter S. Youst, was killed on the railroad. Elizabeth then bought a farm near Pleasant Dale. She put the children in school and she and her brothers ran the farm. When the children grew up, she rented the farm and moved to Piedmont where the sons could find employment while she and her daughter kept boarders to help out.

Emma, the oldest daughter, taught school for a time. While teaching at Springfield she met James Bryan, brother of Dr. Bryan of that place, where they were married and began life together, but, a fire destroying their home, they moved to Piedmont. Eliza was married at Piedmont. Lucy had died of pneumonia while they lived at the farm.

Not long after this Albert enlisted for the Spanish American War and John went into business for himself. Then the mother returned to the farm. John, who was single, looked after her comfort. She kept a woman companion. John's business called him to Arizona and soon after he became ill with pneumonia and died there. About this time Mrs. Youst's sister, Azzie Pugh, at the old home, then owned by Thomas Dye Pugh, needed her because of illness and she went there. After this sister's death she took her place as home-maker for her brother, Thomas D., where she died and lies buried at the Pugh burial ground near Pleasant Dale, beside the twins whom she loved so dearly.

Elizabeth Pugh Youst was about five feet, seven inches tall and well proportioned. She was of generous disposition and would have divided her last crust with the needy. She, however, was most comfortably situated in later life at the home of her brother, besides herself owning a farm of considerable worth. She was a great reader, all of her life, and well informed. At her death she was aged 88 years, 5 months and 21 days.

Bryon Family Record

James A. Bryan, born 1852 and died in 1930. On May 1, 1889 he was married to Emma L. Youst. He was the son of Caroline Alkire and Jonathan Bryan. He was of English-Irish descent. A Presbyterian. Children born to them; Georgia C., 1890; James, 1891; William Pugh, 1893; Thomas C., 1896; Elizabeth, 1897, died 1900; Emma M., 1900 died 1931; John R. 1903; Margot V., 1906; Robert E. Lee, 1910.

Georgia C., December 2, 1909, married John S. Kerr, Jr., son of Anna C. Johnson and John S. Kerr. German descent and a Methodist. Home at Apollo, Pa. Children: Anna E. L.; James L.; William S. Kerr, deceased; Thomas E.

James Finley, married Minnie E. Zoon, daughter of Maud L. and William A. Zoon. Home at Peoria, Illinois. Belief, Lutheran. Children: James W., Albert, Maggie E., Elizabeth L., Georgia C., and Emma M.

William Pugh, married Mary E. O'Brien, daughter of Mary E. Byrnes and Thomas P. O'Brien, of Scotch-Irish descent; religion, Catholic; Piedmont, W. Va. Children, Mary K., J. William, Thomas E., and Virgina L.

Emma Marie, married Clyde E. Boyce, son of Ida Brumbach and George E. Boyce. Religion, Dunkard; German descent. Moorefield, W. Va. Children: Mary V., Emma Lee, Edward G., and Eugene P.

John Russell, married Emma Lyons, daughter of Mr. and Mrs. Geo. Lyons, Scotch descent. Religion, Methodist. Children: Betty C., Virginia M., and John R., Jr.

Margot Virginia, married Wilmer M. Moberts, son of Iva M. Harris and H. B. Roberts, English descent. Religion, Methodist. Marlinton, W. Va. One child: Wilmer M., Jr., Wilmer, Sr. is now deceased, 1945.

Robert E. Lee, married Olive M. Kackley, daughter of Margaret Schell and William Kackley, of Scotch descent; religion, Presbyterian. Home at Beryle, W. Va. Children: Robert E. Lee and Marlene L.

Joseph Arthur, son of John N. and Sarah Offutt Pugh, born November 11, 1841, died April 10, 1926, was married to Martha Pepper, daughter of Jacob and Frances Alverson Pepper, August 27, 1873. To this union were born the following children:

Virginia May, August 20, 1874.; Laura, June 14, 1876, died April 24, 1947; John Arthur, October 22, 1878, died May 31, 1948; Thomas W., Infant, died October 13, 1880; Ada Margaret, May 18, 1882, died July 11, 1891; Finley T., May 2, 1886.

Martha Pepper Pugh, born March 20, 1844, died ———, 1914, was a woman of modest bearing and gentle disposition, a faithful wife and mother. Arthur Pugh was slight in build, with dark hair and eyes. He was a Confederate veteran. The letter below appeared in the Hampshire Review, of April 14, 1926:

Joseph Arthur Pugh died last week at his home in Gore District, Hampshire county, aged about 83. He was a worthy, good citizen, a member of the Old Hampshire Guards. They, with the Frontier Riflemen of this county, obeyed the call of Gov. John Letcher and reported to Gen. T. J. Jackson at Harper's Ferry, the 18th of May, 1861, and there was organized the 13th Virginia Infantry, with A. P. Hill, Colonel.

Joseph Arthur was badly wounded at Cold Harbor on the 27th of June, 1862, in one of the Seven Days' battles between Generals Lee and McClellan.

Joe was a faithful comrade and a herioc soldier.

(signed) His Old Comrade,
V. M. Poling, Clerk of the Circuit Court,
Hampshire Co., W. Va.

Joseph Arthur Pugh was a member of Co. K., Capt. J. B. Sherrard's Division. Later Felix Heiskell, known as Fick Heiskell, became captain and Frank Sherrard, brother of the former captain, who had then given his life to the cause, was made first Lieutenant.

This company was one of the first in the field and one of the last to leave the field at the close of the war. Company K carried a flag of heavy silk, elaborately embroidered, presented by the women of Hampshire county. It was used throughout the war and survives until the present day, though divided up and held by relatives of members of this company as souvenirs.

Among others, Company K took part in the following battles: Front Royal, May 23, 1862; Middletown, May 24, 1862; Winchester, May 26; June 2nd, Capon Springs Road against Fremont; and Port Republic on June 6th, when Col. Ashby was killed, and on the 8th of June against Shields near Port Republic; on the next day another battle with Fremont.

This Company went into the Battle of Cold Harbor with 26 men, seventeen of these being killed or wounded, June 27, 1862. Among the killed was Lieut. Sherrard, Owen Milleson, John Washington and Thos. O'Farrell. Isaac Gibson, Thos. Brooks and Isaac Armstrong died of wounds. It is thought by some that Owen Milleson was killed at Front Royal. Geo. Milleson, 2nd, Sheriff, told the writer that he was killed at the Battle of Seven Pines. Cold Harbor is in Hanover county, Virginia, on a railroad running into Richmond about 135 miles from the city.

Relatives and close friends of Joseph Arthur Pugh in this company included Owen Van Buren and Jonathan Pugh, brothers; Owen Milleson, cousin.. Elias and Ben Ullery, the latter of whom married J. J. Pugh's wife's sister, Nancy Milleson; and William Wills, later husband of Caroline Milleson, sister of Owen, and John Flory.

Joseph Arthur and wife owned and resided on a farm near what is No. 29, this farm, having been at one time a part of the Solomon Offutt estate near the Martinsburg Pike. They are buried at the Jacob Pepper burial ground on North River, as are also, their children, Thos. W., and Ada Margaret.

Virginia May Pugh, daughter of Joseph Arthur and Martha Pepper Pugh, born August 20, 1874, near Pleasant Dale, W. Va., has always lived in Hampshire County. She, before her marriage spent some years with her grandmother, Mrs. Frances Alverson Pepper of the same community. Mrs. Pepper was an ideal personage. To be near her was like sitting as a learner at the feet of Paul.

Joseph Arthur Pugh, seriously wounded in Jackson's Valley campaign, with his sister, Asbernia Pugh, who many years cared for a blind brother.

February 16, 1897, Virgina married Chas. Mason Pepper, the only son of Isaac and Matilda Ambler Pepper (daughter of John Ambler) born Dec. 15, 1862, at the old Fred Pepper homestead. Isaac Pepper was the only child of Frederick Pepper, brother of Henry and John Jr., Pepper, all sons of the Senior John Pepper who was a pioneer to Pennsylvania, and later settled in Virginia; German descent. Frederick Pepper married Deborah Slocum. The Slocums were also early settlers and are now extinct in name in this county. Deborah was sister of Isaac Slocum, mentioned in Vol. II of this work.

Chas. Mason and Virginia reside at Cold Stream where they are now engaged in the mecantile business, own a farm and have an attractive home. C. M. Pepper is a veterinary surgeon and Virginia has the Post Office. Virginia is a blonde and rather tall, a gracious hostess, a trusted friend, Mason is also blonde and of medium height. They are both members of the Christian Church and their home is well known to the ministry. They have one child, Frances, born October 16, 1898, who was educated at Shepherd College. Note her drawing, the Old Lieutenant Jonathan Pugh family fireplace, from a description given her by one who saw it. This fireplace was very wide and high, and had a wooden arch. Frances was a teacher for some years and a church worker and very full of life.

June 10, 1924, Frances married Chester McDonald, son of the late Alvin E. McDonald, a well-known teacher. They have a daughter, Jean Pepper McDonald, born October 27, 1925. Frances has dark hair, is slight of build, Jean is a blonde. Chester and Frances are now separated and Jean lives with her mother. Later Chas. Mason Pepper died, August 9, 1934, is buried at the Malick Cemetery.

Laura, second daughter of Joseph Arthur and Martha Pepper Pugh, born near Pleasant Dale, W. Va., June 14, 1876, has had a very busy life, largely devoted to others, and romance has been crowded out. She has the rare capacity to fit in wherever she is needed and always responds among the kin. She has ability as a nurse. Besides the care of her parents in old age, after they passed away she was home-maker for her uncle Thos. D. Pugh, and cared for him during his last long illness.

Laura has energy, enthusiasm, and personal attraction. She is fiive feet, seven, black eyes and hair. She, at present, owns a chicken farm, a car and a cottage at the village of Pleasant Dale where she lives. She is a Democrat and a member of the Christian Church. Laura died in Winchester Hospital and rests by her uncle Tom Pugh at Augusta, W. Va.

John Arthur, son of Joseph Arthur and Martha Pepper Pugh, born October 22, 1878, received his education in the common schools and by reading. He spent his early life on his father's farm where he learned not only farming but carpentry and mechanics. He can make over an automobile and mend or readjust almost anything to which he lends a hand. His business is that of artesian well borer but he is in demand in his community for work along many lines.

John has an interesting collection of ancestral relics including among others the old mahogany desk of Lieut. Jonathan Pugh and his cavalry sabre; also, the sword of Capt. Jonathan of the war of 1812, son of the Lieutenant, and great grandfather of John and the writer, whose Company roll in the 114th Regiment is given in this book.

About 1903 John Arthur Pugh maried Bertha B. Shanholtz, teacher and daughter of Bazil Shanholtz, teacher and farmer before mentioned in these pages, and who married Elizabeth Pepper, daughter of Isaac and M. A. Pepper.

John and Bertha own a farm at Hoy, W. Va., where they live. They also own about 80 acres of the old Pugh estate on North River, one-half mile south of their home. They have four children living:

Arthur Clinton, born May 14, 1905; Frances Elizabeth, born Sept. 29, 1911; Ralph Gray, born May 12, 1913, died July 2, 1913; Harry Kenneth, born March 21, 1915; Dorothy Claudine, born February 2, 1917.

Arthur Clinton married Ethel Smith, granddaughter of Jas. F. and Laura Kendall Smith. They have three children: John Arthur, II, Roger and Bernice. They live in Martinsburg, W. Va. Later, in Baltimore.

108

Frances Elizabeth, a graduate of Capon Bridge High School, married Clarence Wolford, teacher, graduate of Romney High School. Children: one son.

Harry Kenneth, a quiet boy of reserved manner, is a mechanic, at home. Harry is a veteran of World War II.

Dorothy Claudine, sophomore at Capon Bridge, 1938, leads her class in grades. Later Dorothy attended Shepherds College, and now is in government employment, Baltimore, 1947.

John and Bertha are independent in politics and members of the Christian Church. Bertha is sometimes president of her Woman's Club. John is six feet tall, weighs about 180 pounds and is of the Pugh type, physically. Later Bertha died in Baltimore, 1945, and lies buried in the Malick Cemetery, near the home, John rests beside her, 1948.

Finley Pugh, youngest of the children of Joseph Arthur and Martha Pugh, was born May 2, 1886. Self-educated, a teacher he holds a life certificate. He was, for three successive terms, principal of the graded school at Augusta, W. Va. He has been in the profession thirty years. He now owns and operates a large farm on U.S. 50, near Hanging Rock, (Blue Gap) where they reside, retired as teacher, 1947.

Early in life he met and married Margaret Mowery, born March 2, 1885, daughter of Mr. and Mrs. I. R. Mowery, of Rio, W. Va. Margaret is an artist in home-making. They have two children: Marie, born September 9, 1907, Zona, born April 21, 1910.

Marie Pugh, who is a graduate of Capon Bridge High School was a teacher of ability, on July 28, 1927, maried Delbert Brill, born December 22, 1905, son of Aljorn and Elizabeth Spaid Brill of Lehew, W. Va.

Delbert and Marie Brill were classmates at Capon Bridge, They own and reside on one of the ancestral Pugh farms on North River and are a magnetic pair of young people, who love to entertain. On Dec. 11, 1940, a daughter, Lois Margaret, was born to them, and on May 15, 1945, a son, Denny Delbert.

Zona Pugh attended school at Capon Bridge but teaching did not appeal to her. May 5, 1926, she married Oren Daugherty, (born March 7, 1911) son of John W. Daugherty. Oren's father is a prosperous farmer near Salem, W. Va. Zona has the dark hair and eyes of her father, her husband being of the opposite type. They have two fine children, Welden and Catherine Elizabeth who are also opposites. Oren is an electrician. They are now divorced, 1945.

Finley Pugh and family are Democrats and Presbyterians.

Solomon E. Pugh, born June 12, 1844, died October 30, 1923. He was a farmer, carpenter and builder, and a Confedrate Veteran, Company C., Imboden's Men. S. E. Pugh was kind hearted. He died single, buried in the Offutt Cemetery, Oct. 31, 1923, 2 p. m. The writer, then a child of ten vividly remembers his description of the Centerial Celebration at Phladelphia, 1876.

Algernon Wood Pugh, born June 28, 1847, died August 13, 1870, at 8:15 a. m., at Cambria, Missouri, a victim of typhoid from the swamps there in those days. He had a very attractive personality, and wrote a beautiful letter. He was a fine cabinet maker. He had been in the west but a short time. He lies buried in Cambria. He was with friends who had gone from this county. (The Hammicks). The writer owns a walnut corner cupboard of his handiwork.

Thomas Dye Pugh, born May 19, 1849, died August 25, 1926. He was educated in the schools of Hampshire and began the profession of teaching at an early age. He took an active interest in politics but never ran for office. T. D. Pugh was a delegate to the convention that nominated Wm. L. Wilson for Congress and was entertained by Mr. Wilson. He was also delegate to other Democratic Conventions. He attended the World's Fair at St. Louis in company with J. W. Carter and Chas. N. Hiett, life long friends.

When the time came that his presence was demanded at the old home he retired from teaching and engaged in agriculture with success, at his death owning about five or six hundred acres of what had once been the old Pugh plantation in North River Valley, besides considerable other property.

Thomas D. Pugh enjoyed the friendship and society of women but never married. He was the last of his family to

WADE HAMPTON PUGH,
Son of Robert and Virginia
Deaver Pugh.

VAN BURON PUGH
Gave his life to C.S.A., Lies in
Confederate Cemetery, Harrison-
burg, Va.

pass away.   His niece, Laura Pugh, presided in his home after the death of his sisters.   His body was interred at Augusta Cemetery on U.S. 50 at his request.

Robert Owen Pugh, born December 30, 1851, died March 30, 1908, the youngest son of John N. and Sarah, was above medium height, fair, with black hair and eyes and a smiling face.   He spent most of his early life on his father's farm. He was never very strong.   In 1880 he married Virginia Deaver, daughter of Major Geo. Deaver and Lucinda Hiett, (who was a daughter of Jeremiah and Lucinda Hiett), who owned Ice Mountain, born Nov. 25, 1854, died June 13, 1935.   Robert and Virginia spent a year after their marriage at Burning Springs, Wirt Co., W. Va.   Returning to Hampshire County they lived at South Branch Depot for a time.   On the death of the father-in-law, they inherited the Ict Mountain farm and on selling his interest in the Pugh estate to his brother, Thomas Dye Pugh, they moved there, where Virginia and her son Lamar still reside, 1934.   Virginia died about 1940 and is buried in Cold Stream church yard.

Robert and Virginia brought up two sons: Robert Lamar, born June 6, 1881, and Wade Hampton, born, 1882, died Oct. 18, 1922.   Lamar is tall with dark hair and eyes.   Wade was small, and fair like his mother. He was of a friendly disposition. Everybody liked him.   His face, not handsome, was sensitive and sympathetic.   Tourists and visitors from everywhere who went to Ice Mountain found him ready to do a favor.   He was well known, was a great reader and largely self-educated. He was a teacher besides being a farmer and stock raiser. He was the comfort and support of his mother after the death of his father but his career was suddenly cut off in the prime of life by pneumonia; and perhaps few others of his day in passing called forth so many eulogies and regrets from their associates at their early taking off.

Wade was a life member of the National Geographic Society and knew the Editors of that magazine personally.   He lies buried at the Christian Church on Sandy Ridge near Cold Stream, W. Va.   His mother has never recovered from the loss of husband and son.   Later she died in the summer of 1935 and lies buried beside Wade.

111

CHAPTER IX

Maria Pugh and Husband.

William Smith, early Postmaster at Pleasant Dale.

Mrs. Lucy Pugh Monroe; her big dog "Picket."

The Home at the Old Mill.

Children of Capt. Jonathan and Mary Ellen Tansy Pugh

Maria Pugh, born about 1802, died September 14, 1875. She lived her whole life in the Pleasant Dale community where she came into being. Maria was about five feet, six, slender, with a gentle, reserved manner and had many friends and admirers of both sexes, among whom was a manly young clerk in Jackson's store at Slanesville. Her parents, however, opposed the match on pecuniary grounds, which caused her to remain single until late in life, when she married Wm. Smith, merchant and postmaster at Pleasant Dale. Wm. Smith was the son of Wm. Smith, Middletown, Shenandoah County, Virginia, a person of standing and influence. They lived many years at the Dale on The North Western Turnpike.

Maria inherited the division of her father's estate on which the old home was located and she and her husband spent their declining years there after retiring from business. After Mr. Smith's death, her faithful colored servant, "Clarasy Madison," nursed and cared for Maria during a long illness until her death. She and her husband lie buried north of and near the gateway of the Pugh graveyard. They left no heirs.

Some of the fine needlework of Maria Pugh still exists, as do, also some of the letters from admiring friends, and it was she who preserved many of the old colonial relics of former days on the Pugh estate of her father and grandfather. The turkey plate and the platter for the roast pig, the flax wheel, the beautiful brass fireplace set, the oaken settee, the brass coffee mortar and other articles, some of which are the prized posessions of the writer, besides some valuable papers, records of the family. One of her last acts was to make provision for the care of "Aunt Clara."

Maria Pugh's life was one of rich, latent possibilities, hampered by the narrow sphere of women of her day. Her personality, restricted as it was by the conventionalities the women of her class suffered — "A rose made to blush unseen and waste its sweetness on the desert air." — an intelligence that could have been widely felt, had she lived after woman came into her own. A mind, the usefulness of which was narrowed into needle work and social entertainment. Is it any wonder that woman in some cases today has made extravagant use of the freedom too long denied her — a pent up soul suddenly relieved of its shackles.

Lucy Pugh, daughter of Capt. Jonathan and Mary Ellen Tansy Pugh, was born about 1803, and died about 1880. She spent her whole life in the community in which she was born. The colored people called her "Miss Pluty". She was rather tall, with dark hair and eyes, fair complexion, average weight, with jovial disposition and ready wit, but somewhat cynical outlook on life, partly caused perhaps by that life's loneliness and its disappointments. Her marriage with Wm. Monroe had not been a happy one and they lived together only a short time. His code of morals having fallen short of the Pugh ideal, she retired to her own home beside the old Pugh mill with the great mill wheel, where she rented her land and lived alone.

Lucy Pugh Monroe had many endearing traits of character and was much loved by those around her, among whom she was known in later life as "Aunt Lucy". "Picket", the faithful New Foundland dog, named for the great Southern General whom she admired, was her constant companion in her last days., She loved all animals and, like Johnny Appleseed, would not permit Picket to injure even a ground mouse. Her lawns testified to the innate love of beauty. There was always something blooming in Aunt Lucy's yard or window. She lies beside her brother Daniel in the old Pugh graveyard near Pleasant Dale.

113

CHAPTER X

John Pugh and wife, of Mansfield, Ohio.
The "Forty-Niner" and Family, See Chapter III for children of John.
Elverda Pugh and Rev. S. B. Doty.
Poems: Overland Trail and Frontier Shift.

John Pugh II, was born in Hampshire county, Virginia, east of Romney on September 12, 1782. After the death of his father, 1794, he remained with his mother until her death about 1810, then emigrated to Ohio.

Starting over the North Western Trail on horseback, leading a second horse, he spent his first night among strangers with an old friendly Indian named Hicks. Next morning Hicks, with a stick in the dust, drew a crude map of Ohio Trails for him, pointing and nodding at the best routes and shaking his head at others.

John finally located at Mansfield, then a settlement in the midst of a wilderness, where he established the first Inn in that city, known as the Pugh Tavern, on Main Street, occupying the site of the present Masonic Temple. He also ran a tanyard several blocks north of the Tavern on ground now occupied by the B. & O. Terminals.

Hicks later visited Mansfield where that "good Indian's hospitality was returned at the Pugh Tavern.

Soon after Mr. Pugh arrived in Mansfield he married Florinda Murphy, daughter of Asa Murphy, a Marylander, born January 12, 1797. Besides the care of a large family and her duties as hostess, Mrs. Pugh seems to have been interested in art and music and her fine samplers and bed spreads are still to be seen in the homes of her descendants. She had a humanitarian side, too, and was found at the bedside of the sick of her community and, sheltered Johnny Appleseed, the homeless. Mrs. Pugh died August 23, 1847.

The children of John and Florinda were: Hannibal H., John Wood, Jonathan Gilbert, Euphemia, Margaret Ann, Elizabeth Amanda, and Elverda Tomanis.

After the death of his wife, Mr. Pugh retired from business and spent the remainder of his life among his children. When returning from Iowa to Ohio, about 1860, he was accidentally drowned at Toledo, Ohio .

The following, largely from Howe's Historical Collections of Ohio, published in 1857, will be of interest to all of the descendants of the Lieutenant Jonathans as it relates to the home town of his son, John, one of its founders and first settlers:

Mansfield is 68 miles northesast of Columbus, 25 miles from Mt. Vernon, and 45 miles from Sandusky. It was laid out by James Hedges, Jacob Newman and Joseph H. Tarwell; the latter pitched his tent on a rise of ground above the big spring and held the first lot sale, October 8, 1808.

Mansfield was located in the midst of the agricultural garden spot of the great State of Ohio, but the country all around was a wilderness with no roads through it — only Indian trails. A village of friendly Indians, the Delawares, with 60 tepes and a Council House stood 40 miles away.

The county was organized March 1, 1813 and named from the nature of the soil, Richland. About one-half of the county is level and the rest rolling. In 1846 the area was reduced by the creation of Ashland county from it.

Mansfield derived its name from Col. Jared Mansfield of Connecticut, a graduate of Yale and professor at West Point; a man of high standing scientifically, who was appointed as a surveyor of the Northwest Territory by President Jefferson about the year 1803.

This region in these early days was frequented by the eccentric Jonathan Chapman, better known in Ohio and the Eastern States as "Johnny Appleseed", who had a passion for planting apple seeds wherever he wandered. He thought hunting morally wrong and would not injure a living creature. He sold, or gave away his seeds or trees, grown in waste places, for food or old clothes and slept in the woods by a

115

camp fire. He wore on his head a tin pan, which was both hat and mush pot and went barefoot.

An itinerant preacher, once holding forth on the public square at Mansfield, exclaimed, "Where is the barefoot Christian, traveling to Heaven?" Johnny, his back on some timber with foot aloft, vociferated, "Here I am." He was a little man with long hair, eyes black and sparkling. He was welcomed and kindly treated everywhere, even by the Indians. As the country became more settled up he wandered farther westward.

In 1817, Mansfield had twenty dwellings. In 1812, it had two block houses, which were kept garrisoned by the government until the war was over. It has much Indian history. Among the first settlers in the county were John Murphy, Geo. Coffenberry, John Pugh, J. C. Gilkenson, E. P. Sturgess, Wm. Winship, Rolen Weldon and Samuel Williams.

Among the first churches established were one each of the following: Methodist, Baptist, Presbyterian, Disciple and Congregational.

Mansfield is now a growing and important city on Lincoln Highway, and John Pugh's descendants are found in nearly every state from New York to the Golden Gate.

(COPY)

John Pugh, (who later went to Ohio) Agreement to Sell Land to John Wolford, both of Hampshire County, Virginia.

Know all men by these presents, That I, John Pugh, of Hampshire county and the State of Virginia, am held and bound unto John Wolford of the Same County and State aforesaid, for the personal sum of Eight Hundred Pounds, Current Money of Virginia, for the true payment thereof, I bind myself, my heirs, executors, Administrators, or assigns, firmly by these presents, sealed and dated, Twenty-fourth day of March, Eighteen Hundred and Three.

The Condition of the above obligation is land, that whereas the above-bound John Pugh this Day sold unto the aforesaid John Wolford, Two Tracts of Land, the one of which is His Division, whereon John Thomas now lives; the other lying

116

on the North River and Tearcoat, both in the County of Hampshire, containing Two Hundred and Fifty-Nine Acres. To which said tracts of land the said John Pugh is to make a good and sufficient deed to the said John Wolford at September Court next, by the said Wolford paying one hundred pounds in hand to the said John Pugh and giving bond and approved security to pay fifty pounds per year to the amount of Three Hundred pounds more, the first fifty to be paid 18 months after the deed is made, then the above obligation is to be void and of none effect. This is to stand and remain in full force and virtue in law, sealed and delivered in the presence of Jonathan Pugh.

( )
John Pugh, (Seal)
( )

JONATHAN GILBERT PUGH

Jonathan Gilbert Pugh, son of John and Florinda Pugh, born in Mansfield, Ohio, January 12, 1825, was the true son of his father in pioneering, a live wire, to say the least. Despite his youth he served in Taylor's Division in the Mexican War, and in 1849 he and his brother, Dr. John Wood Pugh, went to California by water, crossing by way of Panama. They returned around the Horn to Ohio. In 1852 he, in company with Jacob Beam, took a "covered wagon expedition" across the plains, to Sacramento. In this ox-drawn train were one hundred persons, men, women and children. Braving the danger of Indians, swollen streams, bad roads, burning desert sands, buffalo and other wild beasts, this train of human freight got through without the loss of a soul — see poem, "Overland Trail" by his son, A. D. Pugh. Among this party was "Jack Foulks", John Pugh Foulks, of Mansfield, aged sixteen.

The next year, 1853, a short train went through, among whom were Dr. John Wood Pugh, his sister, Mrs. Effie Pugh Foulks and family, whose husband, Alfred Foulks of Rome, Ohio, had recently died, and another sister, Elverda Tomanis Pugh, who later married Solon Moore. Jonathan Gilbert Pugh and Jack

Foulks met them at Salt Lake and saw them through. While in California Jonathan Gilbert located a ranche at Elk Grove, whose beautiful home was visited by A. D. Pugh on his return from the Hawaiian Islands, 1931, as was also that of Mrs. Josie Foulks Freeman, the last survivor (known) of this expedition. She lives at 3303 Washington Avenue, San Francisco. Mrs. Freeman has one daughter, Mabel Romine, whose husband was a prominent lawyer, now deceased.

On Jonathan Gilbert's return to Ohio again he, for a time, engaged in business at Ashland, and later pioneered in Kansas and Colorado, then located in Iowa and married Harriett Virginia Baker, who, during his adventures in the far west was teaching school and boarding with Jonathan's sister, Mrs. Elizabeth Callwell, where John Pugh spent part of his last years. He and Harriett were great friends and John planned the match before they met but on Jonathan's arrival secretly told him he was afraid she was an "abolitionist".

After the marriage of these two they settled in Muscatine county, Iowa, where they lived during the Civil War, twenty-five miles from Rock Island on which was located the famous Federal prison by that name. During the war John James Pugh, father of the writer, one of Imboden's Calvarymen, was captured and confined in this prison fifteen months.

Jonathan Gilbert Pugh was appointed by Gov. Kirkwood, a Lieutenant of Home Guards but was never called into action as the service was not needed there.

These cousins did not even know of each other's existence, much less of their proximity to each other, or their adverse position on the great matter at issue. These facts have been worked out as a matter of history by their descendants.

The family of Jonathan Gilbert and Harriett Pugh were all born in Muscatine county, Iowa. In 1875, they removed to Poweshiek county and in 1893 to Des Moines where April 13, 1894, Mr. Pugh died. A detailed account of their children is given elsewhere in this history as is also the lineage and date of death of Harriett, who outlived her husband.

118

JONATHAN PUGH, the "49er"
Atty. A. D. Pugh's father.

JONATHAN PUGH, Word War I
Banker. A. D. Pugh's eldest son.

LAWRENCE T. PUGH,
Noted Aviator, World War II,
A. D. Pugh's son.

THE OVERLAND TRAIL

By A. D. PUGH

Des Moines, Iowa

The following was conceived in outline while flying over this historic trail recently in a single day. It is intended to faithfully commemorate a typical ox-train crossing of the plains in 1852, which was conducted by my pioneer ancestors, it is affectionately and admiringly dedicated. The names and incidents are accurate, and intended to enable survivors or their descendants to identify the train; and the writer would be most happy to hear from any of them. Much of our history is tied up with the old trails whose traditions are most worthy of preservation. For instance, my Father drove oxen over this one in the fifties, I railroaded over it in the eighties, and now my son pilots an air transport over it, which doubtless is quite typical. It is hoped these lines may succeed as history if not as verse.

In "Fifty-two", they westward rode
    To the Head of the Trail, — Saint Joe,
Nine hundred miles, by the settlers' code,
    To Missouri's muddy flow.

When loving Ohio lips were press't,
    They left in the springtime, green,
Their vision set on a distant quest,
    With three thousand miles, between.

And one was tall and quick and strong,
    Who looked you straight, with steel-blue eye,
Whose brown hair — worn a trifle long,
    Fell from a brow that was wide and high.

He had been with Taylor in Mexico,
    In the "Rush" for gold, in "Forty-nine",
And now, by oxen, he planned to go
    Across the plains, by autumn time.

So, He was Captain of the Train,
    To scout and guide it thru,

119

Knowing the way of the trail and plain,
    And his name was Jonathan Pugh.

Quick of temper, but clear of head,
    He met trail issues in the ruff,
And never pack't a gun, t'is said,
    As guns, to him, were mostly bluff.

And the other partner was Jacob Beam,
    Of the Pennsylvania Dutch,
Who rationed the food, so it would seem,
    A plenty, if not, too much.

They bought their stock along the road,
    And outfit, at St. Joe,
A hundred, strong, was the human load,
    When chains were stretched, to go.

Said Jon't to Jake, "A month we'v spent,
    Then, why should we longer wait?
Tomorrow, at dawn, let's fold our tents,
    An Steer for the 'Golden Gate' ".

Loaded with grub till they nearly broke,
    The schooners were setting sail,
And swaying oxen leaned to the yoke,
    As they took the "Sunset Trail".

The Captain cantered along the line,
    And, seeing Doc. Keeler, about,
Said: " Hi There, Doc, you'r just in time,
    We need another scout."

Jack Foulks "rode herd" of truant steers,
    He was sixteen years, or so,
While "Little Josie" loosed her tears
    For the fallen buffalo.

"Dan Cupid" played a ruthless part,
    When crossing o'er the Blue,
He sent a dart, thru Ella's heart,
    Which wounded Solon's, too.

In mind we see their campfire's glow,
  Where sky and mountain meet,
Hear, coyotes' call, and cattles' low,
  The threat'nini tom-toms' beat.

Snailing o'er mountain, desert and plain,
  Fording rivers, ascending heights,
A hundred and twenty days, the train
  Creaked its way, thru the days and nights.

And then, came cherring, singing and fun,
  Tho bleached and worn was sun-baked crew,
For, SACRAMENTO, AT LAST, WAS WON,
  And, "every mother's son," came thru.

The schooner crews, foundations laid,
  Almost, without a flaw,
And now, the hum of the pilot's blade,
  Echoes, the "Gee-Woa-Haw".

We sing the heroes of bygone years,
  Their valorous deeds, admire,
We'r Bound by Faith of the Pioneers
  Who Trailed the Western Fire.

Descriptive genealogy of descendants of Jonathan Gilbert and Harriett Baker Pugh

Robert Wood Pugh, Lawyer, Williamsburg, Iowa, born Aug. 29, 1858, died, Williamsburg, Iowa, March, 1927. Graduate of Iowa University, Law Department, 1886, L.L.B., and teacher, common schools and Iowa City Academy. Married Mary Long, 1889. Children:

Helen, born 1890, Graduate, State University of Iowa, unmarried, taught successfully, high school. Abstractor, Montezuma, Iowa.

Robert L. Pugh, born about 1892, electrical engineer, Bliss Electric, Washington, D. C. World War I, overseas. Philadepphia, Pa., unmarried.

121

John Pugh, born 1895, studied law, George Washington U., invalid, Veteran's Hospital, unmarried.

Mary L. Pugh, born 1897, attended State University, and Drake University. Married Raymond Yarcho, Vice-Pres., and Auditor, Royal Union Life Insurance Co., Des Moines, Iowa.

George Howard Pugh, born March 3, 1860, mined and ranched in Colorado, since 1879. Residence, Garfield, Colo. Married Bertha Sweitzer, 1892. No children.

Clara Pugh, born 1861, attended Ashland, Ohio, High School, and State University, taught successfully 40 years, mostly in high school, examiner, State Department of Education, died August, 1932, unmarried.

Frank Edward Pugh, born March 5, 1863. (This date is correct, and so is birth date of Brother Wood, George and my own. The girls are approximately so, and whenever I have given day of month they are correct.) Studied law, never practiced, engaged in farming and business pursuits. Married Winifred E. Cash, of New York City, school-teacher about 1900. Children:

Harriet W. Pugh, born about 1902, graduate of Tacoma, Wash. High School and L.L.B. University of Southern California about 1925, and has since practiced successfully in Los Angeles, Cal. Office, I. W. Hellman Bldg., Room 571, unmarried. Medium size, rather slender blonde, very energetic and talented, and good looking. Made her way in college. Plenty of will and a good head.

Roderick and Katharine, twins, about 1904, Roderick killed in automobile accident, in San Francisco early in 1927.

Katharine, High School and College Graduate, unmarried.

Elverda Pugh, born 1865, attended Iowa City Academy, taught successfully, married Rev. S. B. Doty, about 1904. Both Presbyterian Home Missionaries, Oakes, N. D. No children.

Albert Douglas Pugh, born, Lake Township, Muscatine County, Iowa, April 5, 1868, L.L.B., Iowa College of Law, (Dep. Drake University) 1897, married Dr. Marian A. Howe, June 20, 1901, died December 31, 1911.

Parents, Lafayette and Mary Howe, of Fredericksburg, Iowa.

Children: Jonathan Howe Pugh, born June 16, 1902, and Lawrence Tisdale Pugh, born May 15, 1906.

Jonathan H. married Miss Gloria Glenn, of Philadelphia, April 5. 1923. Children, Marian, born November 14, 1925. Gloria, born 1929.

Jonathan, veteran, World War I, Air Service, Graduate West Des Moines High School, 1920. University of Penn. Wharton School B.S. in Econ., 1923, instructor, Wharton School till 1930, Co-author "Man and His World" with Bossard and others, writing first Nine Caps., Harper & Bro., N. Y., 1933. Taught Geography and Industry, and lectured on sociology at U.

Director of Education and Research, U. S. Building, Savings & Loan Institute, 1930, Chicago.
Director of Education, Illinois Building & Loan League, and Expert, Chicago, 1931, 1932.

Examiner, Regional Home Loan Bank, of Evanston, Ill., 1933. Residence: 6940 Overhill Ave., Chicago.

Lawrence T. graduated, Roosevelt High School, Des Moines, 1925, M. E. Course, Iowa State College, Ames, Iowa, 1926. Traveled, and worked Extra Movies, Hollywood, 1927. M. E. Iowa State College, Ames, 1928, and Inspector, State Highway Commission. Cadet, Air Corps, March and Kelly Fields, 1929-1930. 2d. Lt. 23rd. Bombardment Squadron, Luke Field, Honolulu, T. H., 1931-32. Co-Pilot, United Air Lines, Chicago to Oakland, Calif., 1933. Married Julia Barker, daughter of Mr. and Mrs. Andrew Barker of New York.

Effie Pugh, born 1870, attended Des Moines College, taught successfully in high school in Iowa and Chicago, last 25 years. Acting Principal, Shopan School, Chicago, Residence, 500 Diversey Parkway, Chicago. Also practices and teaches art.

Zada Pugh, born 1872, taught successfully, graduated, Des Moines Musical College, 1897, unmarried, invalid. Residence, Des Moines, Iowa.

Harriet Pugh, born 1874, died in childhood, 1881.

123

Clementine Pugh, born 1877, graduated, West D-M. High School, and science Dept., Drake University, B.S., 1897, taught successfully in high school, married Dr. Archiabald Louis Arends, M.D. Residence, 1643 Berkeley Ave., St. Paul, Minn. Children: Eleanor, born 1908, graduated, St. Paul High School, Minn. U., B.S., 1932, Chicago Dietetics 1933, unmarried.

Elverda Pugh, daughter of Jonathan Gilbert and Harriett Baker Pugh, born February 20, 1865, educated in the public schools and State Normal School for teachers with a special course in Elocution. After teaching for a time took up Home Mission work for the Presbyterian Church, U. S. A., traveling in Iowa, Wisconsin and North Dakota.

September 1, 1903, Elverda was united in marriage with Rev. S. B. Doty, one of the four North Dakota Sunday-school Missionaries. They have no chldren. Mrs. Doty thinks that God intended her to minister to the thousands of neglected ones, so together they carry the Gospel of Christ to his children. There is no greater work.

Rev. and Mrs. Doty reside at Oakes, North Dakota. Later Rev. Mr. Doty was killed in an automobile accident, 1935.

Albert Douglas Pugh, son of Jonathan Gilbert and Harriett Baker Pugh, was born near the city of Muscatine, Iowa, April 5, 1868, grew up on an Iowa farm, was educated for the profession of teaching but fate decreeing otherwise, he railroaded for nine years in Wyoming and Utah over the Old Trail whose history he was to sing in the future. He ended his railroad career as Contracting Freight Agent for Chicago Great Western in 1895. He resigned this position to study law in the office of Judge Geo. H. Carr and A. C. Parker, at the same time attending law school, Department of Law, Drake University, graduated as LLB and admitted to the bar in May, 1897, practicing generally in State and Federal Courts and in the Supreme Court of the United States.

Being independent in politics, Mr. Pugh has never held office. He ran for Judge in the campaign of 1912 as a party service for the Progressives and came near being elected. He has also been a candidate for Supreme Judge and Attorney General, but as Iowa is dominantly Republican, his candidacy was a party protest.

June 20, 1901, Mr. Pugh was united in marriage with Dr. Marian A. Howe, scientist and teacher, graduate of collegiate and medical department of the State University of Iowa. She was a daughter of LaFayette and Mary Howe, and was born at Fredericksburg, Iowa. Dr. Pugh was a member of the Bahama Expedition of the State University, sent out in 1890 to do dredging in the Caribbean in the interests of science. She was a member of Iowa Academy of Science, Professional Woman's League, Organized Science Department of West Des Moines High School, prominent in suffrage movement, successful medical practitioner and wrote and lectured on these subjects. She was a liberal Unitarian and a Free Thinker. She died December 31, 1911.

Two sons were born to them: Jonathan Howe, June 16, 1902, and Lawrence Tisdale, May 15, 1906, whose activities appear elsewhere in this book.

In 1913 Mr. Pugh married Glen Daugherty, also a teacher and a Free Thinker, whose life was sacrificed on the altar of motherhood; she with her infant son died February, 1919.

At this time Jonathan, aged 16, was overseas and Lawrence, in school.

February 4, 1920, Mr. Pugh married Harriett Hunt Magrew, daughter of Chas Elliot and Elizabeth Barstow Magrew, of British descent. He met Harriett when on a visit to his sister Clementine, the wife of Dr. A. L. Arends at their lakeside residence on White Bear Lake, near St, Paul, Minn. Harriett is an attractive woman and a Free Thinker. She likes to fly and is otherwise congenial and companionable to Mr. Pugh.

In the spring of 1932, while Lawrence as 2nd Lieutenant Air Corps Reserves 23rd Bombardment Squadron stationed at Luke Field, Honolulu, T. H., his father, A. D. Pugh, visited the Islands, making a tour of inspection for National Aeronautic Association of which he is a director, Des Moines Chapter.

He flew all the Islands and was royally received and entertained, not only by the Army officialdom but by the citizenry as well. Returning by way of California he visited the Pugh relatives in Sacramento, San Francisco, Oakland and Los Angeles, and flew home over the Old Trail, having altogether been in the air 50 hours on the trip.

On his return Mr. Pugh wrote and spoke in California and Iowa of conditions on the Islands, Massie Trial, and aviation, military and civil, and was variously interviewed. He stressed the need of air travel between the Islands and the mainland, and our need of adequate air defense as a nation, comments on which appeared in National Aeronautics, Air Corps News Letter and the Daily Press. He had shortly before entertained Clarence Darrow and they went over together on the S. S. Malolo.

Mr. Pugh has a prolific mind, capable of handling many subjects and has poetic ability. Read his "Frontier Shift", a true staging of which was given at the Chicago Fair this summer (1933) in Wings of Progress, a pageant of progress from the prairie schooner to the plane. He is also an engaging personal letter-writer, his strong points being arguments and persuasiveness, of course, and withal, he is very human and friendly, with a spice of humor that illuminates his personality.

Attorney Pugh is a member of the City and State Bar Associations, Unitarian Church, University Club, Golf and Country Clubs, pioneer lodge of Masons and several Insurance Fraternities.

Jonathan Howe Pugh, student, University of Beaune, AEF, Cote D'Or, France, spring, 1919.

THE FRONTIER SHIFT
By A. D. Pugh
Des Moines, Iowa

My thoughts trail back to the ox-team,
    the schooner and stage of the plains,
When strong men drove to the westward,
    with little but faith and brains.

To the "Pony Express" of the sixties,
    that raced across the stage,
The crisp crack of a rifle,
    a falling form in the sage.
To the railroad men that followed,
    the knight of the train and track,
Who retired the stage and schooner,
    to never again come back.
To the motor cars and busses,
    that all the records broke,
That nearly put the race on wheels,
    made distance seem a joke.
And then I think of the pilots,
    that fly us everywhere,
The "Kelly" yield, who beat the field,
    whose tracks are the trackless air.
And oft' we muse, as the frontier shifts,
    "where do we go from here?"
As we hope for good, clear heads, to think,
    and sure, strong hands, to steer.

Lawrence T. Pugh, 2nd Lt. ACR, upon graduation at Kelly Field, October 11, 1930, and assignment to 23rd Bombardment Squadron, Luke Field, Honolulu, T. H., where he served actively for two years. Since March 1933, Co-pilot, United Air Lines, Chicago to Oakland, California.

Cincinnati, Ohio, November 26, 1897.

Mr. A. D. Pugh,
    Des Moines, Iowa.

Dear Sir:

The information which I have sent you is all that I have respecting a Jonathan Pugh. I have the full descent from Ellis Pugh to the generation which would embrace any one born prior to 1750.

There were four or five families of Pughs in Philadelphia county prior to 1700, as evidenced by marriages which were a matter of records amongst the Quakers. There is no Jonathan in these early people (prior to 1700). There was an Evan who married Mary ———, but I never had it traced up.

The information you desire could probably be had by corresponding with Gilbert Cope, West Chester, Pennsylvania, who makes a specialty of this work and is better informed in these matters than anybody else in the country.

Yours very truly.

(Signed) A. H. Pugh.

CHAPTER XI

Pughs of North Carolina, Georgia, Alabama, Tennessee and Arkansas, Capon Valley Origin.

Congressman Jas. Lawrence Pugh, of Alabama.

Col. Dick Pugh, of Wisconsin.

Attorney C. R. Pugh, North Carolina, and Reno, Nevada.

THE OLD OAKEN BUCKET

SAMUEL WOODWORTH[1]

1. How dear to my heart are the scenes of my childhood,
    When fond recollection presents them to view!
The orchard, the meadow, the deep, tangled wildwood,
    And every loved spot that my infancy knew.
The wide-spreading pond, and the mill that stood by it;
    The bridge and the rock where the cataract fell;
The cot of my father, the dairy house nigh it,
    And e'en the rude bucket which hung in the well—
The old oaken bucket, the iron-bound bucket,
    The moss-covered bucket which hung in the well.

2. That moss-covered vessel I hail as a treasure;
    For oft' when at noon, I returned from the field,
I found it the source of an exquisite pleasure,
    The purest and sweetest that nature can yield.
How ardent I seized it, with hands that were glowing,
    And quick to the white-pebbled bottom it fell;
Then soon with the emblem of truth overflowing,
    And dripping with coolness it rose from the well—
The old oaken bucket, the iron-bound bucket,
    The moss-covered bucket arose from the well.

---

1. Samuel Woodward was born at Scituate, Mass., in 1785. His death occurred in 1842. He was the editor of several publications and wrote a great many short poems, some operettas and a romantic tale. All of these, however, are practically forgotten, and he is remembered only because of the little song we print here.—SYLVESTER

3. How sweet from the green mossy brim to receive it,
       As poised on the curb, it incliued to my lips!
    Not a full blushing goblet could tempt me to leave it,
       Though filled with the nectar that Jupiter sips.
    And now, far removed from the loved situation,
       The tears of regret will intrusively swell,
    As fancy reverts to my father's plantation,
       And sighs for the bucket which hangs in the well—
    The old oaken bucket, the iron-bound bucket,
       The moss-covered bucket which hangs in the well.

North Caroline Pughs, thought to be descended from John Pugh of
Frederick, now Hampshire county, West Virginia, who went to Orange
county, North Carolina about 1760 to escape Indian wars. His ancestors
were from Wales, 1698, to Pennsylvania.
Line of late George B. Pugh of Little Rock, listed in Whos Who, about
1932, died in March, 1933. Frank N. Pugh, banker, of Hamburg, Arkansas
and Robert E. Pugh of Ripley, Tennessee, and others, including Senator
Pugh of Alabama.

————— **Pugh,** North Carolina, married Ibelen Whiticon.
Their son, James R. Pugh, born in Angola county, North Caro-
lina or Burke county, Georgia, died 1817; married a second wife,
Cynthia Lester, daughter of Ezekiel Lester, English descent,
about April, 1805. They had seven children as given on page
     of this genealogy. The oldest son, Green Wood Pugh, of
Burke county, Georgia, born May 5, 1809, married Albena L.
Lowe of Georgia, daughter of Thomas Lowe and Parthenia
Stanley Lowe. They moved first to Mississippi, then to Arkansas
in 1850. Their son, John D. Pugh, born May, 1839, married
————— —————. Children:
    Frank N. Pugh, banker, Hamburg, Arkansas; Robert E. Pugh,
Ripley, Tennessee; Atty. George B. Pugh, Little Rock, Arkansas.
No record of participation in Revolution by James R. Pugh.
He was a soldier in the Creek and Seminole Wars, proving they
were not Quakers.

Pughs of North Carolina, Tennessee, Georgia, Arkansas and other states.
Thought to have been descended from John Pugh of Hampshire county,
who went to North Carolina about 1760 to esape the Indian wars, after
selling his lands on North River.—from Frank N. Pugh, banker, Hamburg,
Arkansas and others.

Thomas Lowe was the son of John Lowe, who married Charity Butler, (sister of General John Butler). He first married Parthena Stanley and had twelve children. Parthena —died about 1818. They lived in Tennessee.

Three Lester Brothers came from England to North Carolina. Ezekiel Lester married Celia Cook. They lived in Burke county, Georgia. Their daughter, Cynthia, married James R. Pugh, who had been married before and had two sons, Robert and Whit. Pugh. James R. Pugh was born in Burke county, Georgia, or Angola county, North Carolina. His mother was a Whiticon — Ibeline Whiticon.

James and Cynthia Pugh had seven children born in Burke county, Georgia, namely:

Betsy Pugh, born March 7, 1806; Lucinda Pugh, born January 25, 1808; Green W. Pugh, Born May 5, 1809; Julia Ann Pugh, born March 9, 1811; Patsey Pugh, born February 15, 1813; Eleaden L. Pugh, born April 1, 1815; James R. Jr., born April 26, 1817.

James R. Pugh died April 1, 1817, then his widow, Cynthia Lester Pugh, married Thomas Lowe above, and Cynthia Pugh Lowe, as second wife to Thomas Lowe, her second husband, had three children: Daniel Lowe, born November 12, 1822; Ezekiel E. Lowe, born August 24, 1824; John C. Lowe, born March 14, 1826.

Thomas Lowe, 15 children; James Pugh, 9; Cynthia Lester Pugh Lowe, 10.

The Lowe Family that Intermarried with Pughs of North Carolina

John Lowe lived in Randolph county, North Carolina. He married Charity Butler, sister of General Butler. Children: Martha Lowe who married Sherwood Stanley. Matilda Lowe who married Abney McCoy. John Lowe who was killed by the Indians at Nashville. William Lowe went to Kentucky, then to Illinois. He was a preacher. Daniel Lowe lived in Georgia. Aran Lowe lived in Georgia and was a member of the State Legislature. Edwin Lowe lived in Georgia and left a large family. Thomas Lowe lived and died in Tennessee. Left a large famiy. James Lowe lived and died in Georgia. Thomas Lowe of the above family married Parthena Stanley. They had twelve children as follows: Sherwood Lowe, born January 28, 1797. Parthena Lowe, born October 18, 1800. Elizabeth Lowe, born May 17, 1802. Nancy Lowe, born July 6, 1804. Susan Lowe, born February 1, 1806. Thomas B. Lowe, born January 2, 1808. Patsy Lowe, born April 4, 1810. Albena Lowe, born April 2, 1812, died August 24, 1812. Albena Lowe, the 2nd, born August 27, 1813. Francis Emeline Lowe, born April 6, 1817. Then the mother died, and Thomas Lowe married Cynthia Pugh, widow of James R. Pugh.

My dear Miss Pugh:—   March 19, 1936

Mr. Alfred Pugh, Jefferson County Circuit Court Library, Birmingham, Ala., is a grandson of James Lawrence Pugh, congressman from Alabama. James Lawrence Pugh was the son of Robert Pugh, who moved from North Carolina to Burke County, Ga., where his wife, Anne Silvia Tillman, died. After her death he removed to Pike County, Ala.

Sincerely yours,
(Mrs.) Marie B. Owen
Director.
Per M. M.

Miss Maud Pugh,
Pleasant Dale, W. Va.

The Pugh Family, probable descendants of John Pugh who went from Virginia to the Carolinas during the Indian wars.

James L. Pugh, U. S. Senator

United States Senator James Lawrence Pugh, born in Georgia, son of Robert Pugh, of Georgia, who was born in Georgia or North Carolina, held office soon after the Civil War; he married Serena Hunter of Virginia.

They lived at Eufala, Alabama, and nine children were born to them. Several died in infancy; those who reached adult age were: Serena, Edward Lawrence, James L. (now living, 1937), John C., Henry L. (now living), and Sally. Senator

Pugh was a Southern Statesman of ability, nationally known and recognized as such in that period of bitterness and reconstruction.

J L. PUGH IS DEAD; ONCE JUDGE HERE
Succumbs in Allentown, Pa., at 77— Practiced Law in D. C. Till 1933.

Wash. D. C.—July 10, 1938—James L. Pugh, 77 years old, for many years an assistant United States attorney and police judge here, died last night at Allentown, Pa.

Judge Pugh, who left the bench about 18 years ago, practiced law here until 1933, when his wife and he went to Allentown, where they made their home with a daughter, Mrs. Bernard Poland. Mrs. Pugh died about two years ago. Judge Pugh had been in ill health for some time.

Widely known in the Capital, Judge Pugh, a native of Eufala, Ala., was the son of the late United States Senator James L. Pugh of Alabama.

His first appointment in the local courts was as assistant United States attorney assigned to Police Court, and from there he went to the bench. In all, his services covered 19 years. Mrs. Pugh was the daughter of the late Representative Snowden of Pennsylvania. For many years the family resided at 3402 Mount Pleasant street, N.W.

Surviving are three daughters, Mrs. Poland, Mrs. Arthur T. Roach, of Hartford, Conn., and Mrs. Louis Hellmuth of Cleveland; a sister, Mrs. Sallie Pugh Elliott of Atlanta, and a brother, Henry L. Pugh, State's attorney for Montgomery County, is a nephew.

James Hunter Pugh, States Attorney for Montgomery county, Maryland, residing at Rockville, is a grandson of Senator Pugh, being a son of Edward Lawrence Pugh, one of six children. The above information was received, partly from him and partly from the Department of Archives and History of the State of Alabama, given on another page of this book. From Bible records of this line of Pughs it is found that the Robert Pugh

133

of Georgia was son of James R. Pugh, born in North Carolina and had a whole brother Whiticon Pugh. The mother of James R. Pugh was a Whiticon.

October 5, 1933

Miss Maud Pugh,
Pleasant Dale, W. Va.

Dear Miss Pugh:

Your letter of September 29th has been received and I recall when I was a freshman or sophomore in Trinity College (now Duke University) about 1902 that I began investigating the Pugh family, but some other interest intervened and I ceased my investigation and have long since forgotten just how far I got.

My grandfather was named John but his immediate relatives came from North Carolina from which State I came.

Personally, I have served in the North Carolina Legislature; I am a graduate of Trinity College or Durham, N. C., also from the law department of the University of Chicago and one semester at the University of Wisconsin., Have been practicing law since 1912, five years of which time in Reno, Nevada, previous to that time in Elizabeth City, N. C. I have no photographs of the Pugh family which you would be interested in. I have taken all the branches in Masonry and have been interested for years in these service clubs and organizations, principally Kiwanis, and in 1928 was District Governor in that organization in the Carolinas district. Volume 4 of Lewis' "History of North Carolina" considered me of sufficient importance at that time to place my "physiogomy" in that book with a column write-up concerning me, etc.

However, none of these things have made me rich in this world's goods but I have always managed to get along fairly well; have good health and am at peace with my fellow men.

I find the work here most interesting because it deals with human nature and human problems, for to me men and women and children are the most interesting subjects in creation and in the matters of divorce and domestic relations there are always

134

something new, something significant which challenges the best thought and sympathy which any of us may possess.

There are lots of Pughs throughout the country. I have met several of them since I came here, but I think the most of them out this way came from Ohio and Iowa. There is quite a colony of them in Fresno, California; one Charles Pugh, Goldfield, Nevada, whom I just recently met. There is an interesting name-sake, Miss Lucille Pugh, who has made quite a reputation as a criminal lawyer in New York City, she came from North Carolina.

We have one Pugh who produced a noted work on Admirality Law; I think he was from Boston. I have never heard of a rich Pugh, but in line with Sir Roger DeCoverly, the Pugh family seems to have been the embodiment of the expression: "I have never seen the righteous forsaken nor his seed begging bread".

I wish I could help you and I should be glad to hear from you at any time. Being a teacher you likely travel during vacations and should you come this way, in keeping with the Pugh hospitality, "the latch-string hangs out".

With kind regards and best wishes, I am

Yours very truly,

C. R. Pugh

C. R. Pugh, Attorney and Counselor-at-Law, Reno, Nevada.

C. R. Pugh, evidently a direct descendant of John Pugh who bought land on North River of Lord Fairfax by deed from the Proprietor, bearing the date, the 5th day of September, 1765, and on November, 1770, from the county of Orange, province of North Carolina, sold it to Bethuel Pugh of Hampshire county, Virginia, Deed Book 2, page 206, of Hampshire county records at Romney. This land joined the first home of the Lieut. Jonathan Pugh of Virginia. It has been in the Hiett family three generations, and Bethuel Pugh and wife lie buried at the foot of a large tree in the old cemetery on the farm. Legend says that they were the first persons to be buried there. Excerpts from this deed are given on another page.

Other descendants of this John Pugh, is seems, have been found in Georgia, Mississippi, Tennessee, Alabama, Louisiana, and Arkansas, including the ancestors of the late George B. Pugh, Attorney-at-Law of Little Rock, Arkansas, given in "Who's Who" and his brother, Frank N. Pugh of Hamburg, Arkansas, banker; Robert Pugh of Tennessee and others. The southern Statesman in Congress after the Civil War was of this line it seems. Capt. Dick Pugh, late of the Governor's Staff, Madison, Wisconsin. Perhaps many of the old records were lost during the Civil War which makes it impossible to positively delineate the kinship of the Pughs here in Hampshire, in this John's time, but everything seems to prove that there were the following brothers: John, Jonathan, Joseph, Evan Jr., Robert and Jacob, (Jacob is a witness on the above deed.) and that these men were all sons of an Evan, Senior, from Pennsylvania, who was here very early in the Century, but who is first found on Hampshire county records in a deed from Evan to Jonathan, Deed Book I, page 284, for 160 A. of land on a small stream that runs into Great Capon —"granted to said Evan Pugh by Deed under the hand and seal of the Right Honorable Lord Fairfax, proprietor, etc", bearing date "MDCCLij, Viiv day of April". Will Book, No. I is lost which would doubtless set this matter at rest, as mentioned elsewhere in this volume.

Colonel Dick Pugh, Wisconsin

Colonel Dick Pugh's father, John Pugh, was born in Ohio and removed with his parents when a lad to Illinois, then to Hutchenson, Minnesota, where Colonel Dick was born May 15, 1888, his mother being Eleanor Snyder, born in New York City, a descendant of General Francis Marion, the Swamp Fox. Her father was a printer on the Horace Greeley's Newspaper staff and later joined the 69th regiment in the Civil War; wounded, losing an arm.

Colonel Pugh has five brothers and one sister, all scattered over the nation doing things as are also his father's brothers' children. He himself is married to a charming woman and has

COL. DICK PUGH
McArthur's Army

a family. Col. Dick Pugh is an officer on the staff of General McArthur in Japan at this writing, 1947.

Newark, Ohio Pughs, Probably of the Capon Valley Pioneer Stock.

Nelson Pugh, wife, Lucy McLure, of Nelson county, Virginia. Children: John H., Benjamin Franklin, Sarah (Mrs. Bridgewater), and others, one of whom, William, went to Missouri and, after the death of his wife, returned to Virginia. John H. was at one time Postmaster at Greenfield, Ohio. Benjamin Franklin Pugh, born March 12, 1844, married Ella Pew, whom he met in the oil fields of West Virginia after his return from participation in the Civil War as a Confederate soldier, enlisting at the age of seventeen years. Ella's family were originally from Georgia and not related to the Pughs.

Frankiln and Ella Pugh had six children, five of whom were born in Grafton, West Virginia, one in Newark, Ohio, whence they removed in 1881. Mr. Pugh died while the children were small. Two sons are in the west, one of whom, Robert E. Pugh, Springfield, Illinois, Executive Secretary for the Illinois Council of Churches, has been a Presbyterian minister in Ohio and Illinois for thirty-five years, 1936. Miss Mabel G. Pugh and sister are teachers in the Newark High School. Other members of the Nelson Pugh family married and reside in Nelson and adjoining counties of Virginia. They and the Newark family, because of the early death of the father, have lost track of each other.

137

CHAPTER XII

Will of Joseph Edwards.

Ruins of Old Fort Edwards, built by Joseph Edwards, 1747-48

Bible Record of Robert and Mary Edwards Pugh.

Will (abridged from Will Book, No. 2, Romney's Old Records) of Joseph Edwards, father of Mary Pugh of the Robert and Mary Pugh branch and builder of the first Fort in what is now West Virginia. (Note: Five shillings bought a good farm in those days.)

The 10 Day of April, 1781

In the Name of God Amen.

I will and bequeath to Joseph Edwards, my son, Five Shillings Sterling.

I will and bequeath to Thomas Edwards, my son, Five Shillings.

I give and bequeath to Mary Pugh, wife of Robert Pugh Five pounds old money of Va.

I give and bequeath to Samuel Pugh and Jesse Pugh sons of Robert Pugh all my old tract of Plantation, 400 A., on Great Cape Capehon and that it be divided from the one side of the land to the other as the road runs, and that my will and devise is they shall cast lots which shall have the part where the dwelling house stands.

I give and bequeath to Sam'l Edwards, my grandson and son of David Edwards, all my Claim on Dillon's Run of land.

This being my last will and Testament, in witness whereof I set my Hand & Seal the day and year first above written.

Witnesses: Timothy Hiett, David Caudy, Joel Chesher.

Joseph Edwards (Seal)

Descendants of Robert and Marw Edwards Pugh, Pioneers, who built their home on Great Ca Caphon, south of where Capon Bridge is located.

Bible Record

Children of Robert and Mary Edwards Pugh: 1. Sarah Pugh, July 7, 1756. 2. Samuel Pugh, April 1, 1758. 3. Jesse Pugh, March 18, 1760. 4. Mary Pugh, January 29, 1762. 5. Lucy Pugh, Novermer 14, 1763. 6. Elizabeth Pugh, April 6, 1766. 7. Joseph Pugh, January 18, 1768. 8. Hannah Pugh, November 13, 1769. 9. Robert Pugh, Jr., January 12, 1772. 10. Eleanor Pugh, April 21, 1774. 11. Mishall Pugh, July 29, 1776. 12. Amy Pugh, September 27, 1778.

Lifelong home of Amos L. Pugh, Capon Bridge, thought to have been built by Jas. Caudy, II, late in life, about 1832. Mr. Pugh built the wing. Picture, kindness of Mrs. Russell Lovett Duncan, Winchester, Va.

CHAPTER XIII

The Descendants of Jesse and Martha Pugh — Jesse and Charity Gard Pugh.

The Lemuel Pugh Family.

The Daniel and Margaret McKee Pugh Family.

The Mary Pugh and Evan A. Nelson Family.

DESCENDANTS OF ROBERT AND MARY EDWADS PUGH,

Welsh Descent

Jesse Pugh, II, son of Jesse and Martha Pugh, born 1787, died 1868. About 1810 married Charity Gard. Resided on the old Pugh estate south of Capon Bridge. Children: six sons and two daughters.

Lemuel Pugh, born December 8, 1817, died October 28, 1877. Residence, Capon Bridge, West Virginia. On November 12, 1840, he married Margaret Hiett, daughter of Joseph and Ailsia Sutton Hiett, English descent, born November 6, 1817, died January 9, 1848. Children: 1. **Mary Ellen**, born Feb. 19, 1844, died about 1885, she married Capt. Wm. H. Powell, born 1835, son of Robt. Massie and Mary Moreland Powell, Bloomery, West Virginia. Mr. Powell was Captain of Co. A., 33rd Virginia Infantry, was wounded at Gettysburg. His Company also took part in the Battles of Winchester, around Richmond, Fredericksburg, the Wilderness and others. He was twice sheriff of Hampshire county. Mr. Powell was a man of fine physique and of high standing. Mr. and Mrs. Powell left no children. 2. **Virginia Ann**, born February 1, 1846, died in Missouri, about 1893, about 1876, married Taylor Urton, son of Mr. and Mrs. Alfred Urton of Slanesville, at North River Mills, West Virginia, and removed to Peculiar, Cass county, Missouri, where he was a farmer and stockman, where their descendants now live.

Lemuel Pugh, March 14, 1852, married Elizabeth Amelia Twiford, born in Washington, D. C., September 13, 1832, died at Capon Bridge, West Virginia, April 6, 1916. Scotch descent. Children:

Amos L. Pugh, born January 23, 1853, was married April 12, 1877 to Alma Garvin, daughter of David J. and Margaret Garvin, (born July 16, 1855, died February 2, 1924). Mrs. Pugh was a charming hostess and Christian woman.

Mr. Pugh, educated in the schools of Capon Bridge and in Eastman Business College, Poughkeepsie, N. Y., began business life as Deputy Sheriff for Willam H. Powell. In 1887 he was elected a member of the House of Delegates, serving two terms, after which he was elected Sheriff. On retiring from this office, he went into the banking business at Romney, W. Va., where the First National Bank owes its origin and largely its growth to him during his connection with it. He was one of the founders of Capon Bridge High School and donated his services to it. Mr. Pugh died August 4, 1938, buried beside his wife in Winchester.

Mr. and Mrs. Amos L. Pugh, were Democrats, members of the M. E. Church South, and residents of Capon Bridge. One child, **Robert Beall Pugh,** born September 7, 1879, was educated at Capon Bridge, W. Va. In 1904 he went to Morris, Oklahoma, where he engaged in business. On a visit to Capon Bridge, in 1908, he met and married Bertha Mae Simmons, January 28, of that year, a woman of magnetic personality.

Miss Simmons was a daughter of Rev. C. E. Simmons of the Baltimore Conference, M. E. Church, South, who was then pastor of the Capon Bridge Church. They reside in Morris Oklahoma. Mrs. Pugh, an active church and civic worker, died at her home, May 17, 1946.

Mr. and Mrs. Robert Beall Pugh have a daughter, Mary Elizabeth, born January 3, 1909. She married Clifton Campbell, December 25, 1929. Residence Ocmulgee, Oklahoma. Mrs. Campbell, a university graduate, talented in music, died of pneumonia, December 31, 1946.

The death of the daughter following so soon on the death of his wife leaving Mr. Pugh alone in the world, called forth much sympathy from his many friends everywhere. The wife and daughter are intered in the cemetery at Morris, Okla.

Margaret Catherine Pugh, born April 19, 1856, daughter of Lemuel and Elizabeth Twiford Pugh. Teacher. Married 1879 to George Taylor of Hampshire Co., W. Va., a prosperous farmer and one the the pioneer commercial orchardists of Hampshire Co. The homeplace in Hampshire Co., is still a residence of the family as is also their home in Winchester, Va. to which Mr. and Mrs. Taylor retired in 1927. Mr. Taylor died Dec. 1, 1940 and was buried in Mt. Hebron Cemetery, Winchester, Va. Children: Pauline Mabel, Georgiana, Mary Elizabeth, Edith Pugh, Catherine Twiford, Roberta Margaret. Children:

Pauline Mabel, Student Force Public School, Washington, D. C. Senior Valley Female College (Fort Loudoun) Winchester, Va. Student Randolph Macon College, Lynchburg, Va. Teacher. At home "The Woodbine", Winchester, Va.

Georgiana, student, Force Public School, Washington, D. C., graduate, Valley Female College (Fort Loudoun) Winchester, Va. Graduate, Southern Seminary, Buena Vista, Va. Student Peabody Conservatory of Music, Baltimore, Md. Head of the Music Department at the Montgomery Preparatory School, Montgomery, W. Va., just previous to her marriage to Hamil W. Thompson of Hampshire Co. 1911. Teacher.

Mary Elizabeth, student, Valley Female College (Fort Loudoun) Winchester, Va., student, West Virginia University, Morgantown, W. Va., graduate of Thomas Normal Training School, Detroit, Mich., graduate of Teachers Normal Training Class, N. C. School for the Deaf, Morgantown, N. C. Taught in public schools of West Virginia, has taught in schools for the deaf in the following states, Virginia, North Carolina, Alabama, Massachusetts and the Territory of Hawaii.

Edith Pugh, student at Fairmont Normal, Fairmont, W. Va., and West Virginia University, Morgantown, W. Va., taught a few terms of school in Hampshire Co. then entered government service, Washington, D. C.

143

Catherine Twiford, student Fort Loudoun Seminary, Winchester, Va., student, Southern Seminary, Buena Vita, Va., graduate of Washington Norman Kindergarten Institute, Washington, D. C., graduate of Teachers Normal Training Class, N. C. School for the deaf, Morganton, N. C. Has taught in schools for the deaf in the following states: Virginia, West Virginia, North Carolina, Georgia, Arizona, Lousiana, and the Territory of Hawaii.

Roberta Margaret, student Southern Seminary, Buena Vista, Va., student, Montgomery Preparatory School, Montgomery, W. Va., and Thomas Normal Training School, Detroit, Mich. Received certificate from Federal School of Commercial Art, Minneapolis, Minn., also received certificate from the Critcher School of Art, Washington, D. C., for their three-year course in Commercial Art. Employed in Washington, D. C.

Children of Hamil W. and Georgiana Thompson

Margaret Annesley, born September 13, 1913, graduate of Handley Public Schools, Winchester, Va., graduate of West Virginia University, Morgantown, W. Va. Married Francis A. O'Brien, Bramwell, W. Va. Home and business, Arlington, Va.

Katherine Rae, graduate of Handley Public Schools, Winchester, Va., senior at West Virginia University, Morgantown, W. Va. Special course at Bowling Green University, Bowling Green, Kentucky. Married David Nichol Dannert of New York and Washington, D. C. Residence: Arlington, Va.

Arthur Benton Pugh, son of Lemuel and Elizabeth A. Pugh, born March 26, 1854, died December 30, 1916; was married to Louisa Anderson, only daughter of David C. Anderson, of Franklin, West Virginia, 1885. Mrs. Pugh died in November, 1896.

Arthur B. Pugh studied law at the University of Virginia and began the practice of his profession at Petersburg, West Virginia. Here he met his wife. In 1888 he received the appointment as assistant Attorney in the Interior Department, Washington, D. C. He was there three years, then resigned and went to Salem and Roanoke, Virginia, to practice; here he met with success but in 1896 his wife's health failed and they returned to Washington where he was District Attorney until his death. Children:

Benton Anderson, born 1887, died February, 1896.

Mary Anderson, born November 3, 1890. Attorney-at-Law. Educated in Washington.

Louise Benton, born August 9, 1896, married Captain Charles Edward Riggs, Medical Corps, U. S. N., 1921; Rear Admiral and Surgeon General, U. S. N., 1929. They reside at 1802 "R" Street, N. W., Washington, D. C., and have a family of young children, 1938.

Lemuel William Pugh, son of Lemuel and Elizabeth A, Pugh, born May 17, 1865, died April, 1928. He was educated at Capon Bridge schools and Eastman College; was four years Deputy Sheriff of Hampshire county under William H. Powell, then went to Missouri where he was employed until he joined the Hope Lumber Company, and from a position as bookkeeper in a branch office rose to General Manager for the company at its office in Kansas City, which position he held at his death. Mr. Pugh remained single.

Lemuel and Elizabeth A. Pugh were also the parents of the following daughters:

Dora C., wife of Dr. C. F. Rinker, Farquer County, Virginia

Roberta A., born June 15, 1867, attended Teacher's College, Fairmont, West Virginia. Teacher, homemaker for her brother's family, Attorney Arthur Benton Pugh, after the death of his wife. Present residence, "R" Street, N. W., Washington, D. C.

Elizabeth Pugh, born July 24, 1870, deceased, buried at Winchester.

Martha Belle Pugh, born August 1, 1872.

These two sisters have spent the latter half of their lives as teachers of the middle West and Southwest, and now the West. 20,945 Gresham Street, Canoga Park, California and are retired.

The Lemuel and Elizabeth A. Pugh family are Democrats and members of the M. E. Church, South.

Daniel Pugh, son of Jesse, Jr., and Charity Gard Pugh, born June 27, 1826, died April 16, 1857, married Mary Margaret

McKee, born August 27, 1831 and resided on a farm near Capon Bridge. After Mr. Pugh's early death, Mrs. Pugh, a strong-minded woman, displayed much courage in bringing up her three children, all of whom became honored citizens. She died at the home of her son, Evan, in 1912, aged about 81 years. Children: Evan P., Martha, and Jesse W. Pugh.

Evan P. Pugh, born May 12, 1853, died March 19, 1903; married Amanda J. Loy, October 21, 1876 and began life as a merchant at Augusta, W. Va., where he, by his industry, tact and amiable disposition, built up a good busness. Their children were all born there. Later they moved to Romney where he continued the mercantile business. Mr. Pugh was elected assessor, 1888, District No. 2, and was elected to represent his County in the Legislature, 1895. He was spoken of in Charleston papers as the "Typical Old Virginia Gentleman". Despite a physical handicap from childhood he made good in life and earned the high record of his fellow man. Mrs. Pugh, too, deserves special mention, besides being a beautiful and attractive person. She was an exemplary wife and mother, and shared her husband's affections for his mother who spent her later life with them, and loved their children as her own. Mrs. Pugh is now living and resides with her oldest son at Romney. 1936. They were members of the Brethren Church and Democrats.

Bible Record

Evan Preston Pugh, son of Daniel and Margaret McKee Pugh, born May 12, 1853, died March 19, 1903; married Amanda J. Loy, December 21, 1876. She was born October 4, 1856. Children:

Daniel Elmer, born October 6, 1877; Ira Clement, born December 5, 1878, died May, 1914; Charles William, born April 8, 1881; Tamzen Abner, born June 21, 1883, died April 16, 1908; John Ellsworth and James Otto, born June 23, 1886; John Ellsworth died May 27, 1887 and James Otto died June 5, 1887; Olley May, born June 2, 1891, died January 14, 1892.

Mrs. Amanda J. Pugh, widow of E. P. Pugh, died Wednesday evening, December 14, 1938 at the home of her son, D. E. Pugh, in Romney, in her 83rd year.

Funeral services were conducted Friday afternoon at the Pugh residence by Rev. J. L. Robertson. Interment was made at Augusta.

Bible Record of Daniel Elmer Pugh

Daniel Elmer Pugh married Elizabeth May Schnibbe, June 15, 1904. Their children: Mary Elizabeth, born April 11, 1907; Evan Preston, born February 18, 1910; Margaret Louise, born March 5, 1913; Lewis Deitrich, born February 24, 1915.

Mary Elizabeth received a B.S. degree from George Peabody College, Nashville, Tennessee, in 1933. She is a teacher in Hampshire county, W. Va.

Evan Preston, received an A.B. degree from Shepherd College, Shepherdstown, West Virginia, in 1933. He married Marjorie Waddle Hazlett, July 7, 1834. Child, Margaret Hazlett Pugh, born June 24, 1935. Evan is in business with his father at this time.

Margaret Louise, received a Standard Norman Certificate through Shepherd College in 1932. She teaches in Hampshire County. Later she married J. Edward Soville, they reside in Shepherdstown, W. Va.

Lewis Deitrich, attended Marshall College at Huntington, West Virginia. They are all Democrats and Southern Methodists. Residence, Romney, West Virginia.

Daniel Elmer and Elizabeth Schnibbe Pugh are people of quiet, dignified bearing and real worth. They have a pleasant home in the heart of their little city where Mr. Pugh, assisted by his sons, enjoys a lucrative business, while the wife and daughters are leaders in church and social work. Mary Elizabeth being the outstanding 4H worker of her community and county at this time.

Marriage Announcement

Wednesday, May 12, 1937 (Coronation Day), Louis D. Pugh, son of Mr. and Mrs. D. E. Pugh of Romney, weds Miss Harper

147

Eloise Thompson, daughter of J. Bruce Thompson of Three Churches.

Mrs. Pugh is a gratuate of Cumberland Memorial Hospital School for Nurses, Class of '36, and Mr. Pugh attended Potomac State School, Keyser, and Marshall College, Huntington. They will reside in Romney. —From the Hampshire Review

Martha Pugh, daughter of Daniel and Margaret McKee Pugh, born in 1855, is still living, married Newton Flory in 1876. They lived in West Virginia some years, then moved to Maryland where they resided eleven years, then again to Washington, D. C., where they lived nineteen years. Their next move was to Sebring, Florida, 1922, where Mr. Flory died in February, 1927, and where Mrs. Flory now lives, 1933, age 78. Still living at Sebring, 1939 — living, 1948.

Mr. and Mrs. Flory were both members of the Brethren Church. These two were a model couple, physically and morally, and if to live in hearts we leave behind is not to die, then they are still both present with us in Hampshire county, where they have many friends and relatives. The Florys had no children.

The Flory Family, early settlers in Capon Valley (North River) are of our best citizenry, and leading church workers of the Brethren. Besides Newton, Frederick and James, were John, William, and Mary (known as "sister"). The name is practically extinct now in this county. The older members of this family were schoolmates of the writers mother and attended school in the famous log schoolhouse near old Salem Church, before the Civil War. "Fred Flory" died in young manhood. He was a special friend of hers.

James Flory, (Jimmy") a soldier of C.S.A., was killed in battle, (lost) and lies buried somewhere among the unknown dead. Mr. Flory was member of Co. C., 18th Cavalry, Mathias Guinevan as first Captain of this Co., he died from wounds received at Gettysburg and was succeeded by his brother Luther Guinevan.

Jesse W. Pugh, son of Daniel and Mary Margaret McKee Pugh, born on Capon River, West Virginia, 1856, was the young-

148

est of two sons in this family of three left by Daniel Pugh, who died five months after Jesse's birth. Jesse married August 31, 1876 to Lillie E. Berkeimer of Hampshire county, born 1860. In 1882 Mr. and Mrs. Pugh moved to Missouri where they resided until 1928, and where their children were born. They then moved to California and now reside on a farm at Lindsay that State. They are members of the Baptist Church. Mr. and Mrs. Pugh have seven living children, one deceased, twenty-four grand children, five great grandchildren, all living in the state of California, 1935.

Jesse, II, and Charity Gard Pugh. Children: Amos, Lemuel, Margaret (born about 1830, died about 1908) Mary, Ezra, and an infant. Mary, born 1832, died 1899, married Evan Atwell Nelson, born 1834, died 1890. Religion, Methodists; vocation, farmers; politics, Democrats. They were honored citizens of Capon Valley. Children:

Ina Forrest Nelson, born 1866. Jesse Francis Nelson, born 1868, died 1929. Harry Horn Nelson, born 1870, died 1893. Mary Elizabeth and Evan Caudy Nelson (twins) born 1872, Mary Elizabeth died 1892, Evan Caudy, died 1873.

Ina F. Nelson, precocious and talented from childhood, educated at Fairmont College for Teachers, the Roemer Class, was a teacher in the school there for a time, later attended the West Virginia University. She then decided to take up library work and went to Drexel Institute Library School for training. Miss Nelson has since done work in Brooklyn, Library of Congress, Washington, D. C., and other places, being now library cataloguer for the State Woman's College, Denton, Texas, where she has been employed for years, and is a specialist in that line of library work. She is the last of her immediate family.

J. Frank Nelson, educated at Fairmont and the West Virginia University, engaged in newspaper work; married, first Alice Boyer, of Morgantown, West Virginia; they had three children, Hugh Francis, born in Morgantown; another son who died in infancy, and Mary Elizabeth, born in California. The mother died while the children were small and seven or eight years after her death Mr. Nelson came back to Virginia and married Bessie Garvin of Millwood. They have one son, Lee Nelson, eighteen, a freshman in the Univrsity of California at Los Angeles. Mrs. Bessie Nelson, Frank's widow, lives at Pasadena, California, 1940.

Hugh Francis Nelson, graduate of the University of California, married in Los Angeles.

Mary Elizabeth married a New York man soon after her graduation at Los Angeles, and they have two small sons.

Harry Horn Nelson died at his home in early manhood, a promising young man who filled the father's place in the home.

"Mollie" Nelson, educated at Fairmont, noted for her mathematical ability in her classes, and cherished for her wit and humor, passed away in her twentieth year.

Evan Caudy Nelson died in infancy .

CHAPTER XIV

THE JOSEPH PUGH FAMILY

Robert J. Pugh and descendants, David Pugh and Children, and children of Sallie Pugh Giffin, the John Giffin Family. Descendants of Robert and Mary Edwards Pugh.

Joseph Pugh, third son of Robert and Mary Edwards Pugh, born January 18, 1768, died ———, married ———; was a farmer who lived on the east side of Capon River, opposite where his brother Robert lived, south of Capon Bridge. The deed for these lands of Joseph and Robert to their father and mother dates back to 1760, from Lord Fairfax. Children: Robert J., David, and Sally Pugh.

I. Robert J. Pugh, born ———, died April 5, 1886, married Jane Giffin; second wife, Susie Allen, 1876. They lived on the old home place. Children: Marion, Emeline, Ed ("Col.") and Margaret (Mrs. McPherson of California). Ed ("Col. Pugh"), never married. Marion, who still lived at the time of the publication of Swisher and Maxwell County History, was born in 1844. He was a Confederate veteran. Emeline, who resided with him, outlived him and spent her remaining days with relatives in California.

II. David Pugh, born ———, married "Esther" Hook, who died August 2, 1871, aged 68. Children: George, Lemuel and Malachi Pugh.

George Pugh, born 1843, died December 20, 1926; first married Alverta Carpenter. He was a Confederate veteran, member of J. Mort Lovett's Company, which was Company E, 23rd Virginia Cavalry. Residence, Capon Bridge, P. O. near Bethel Church. Children of George and Alverta Carpenter Pugh:

1. Fannie, married Henry Schafnaker, Capon Bridge, and after his death she married John Nelson, Hayfield, Virginia.

151

2. Rena, married Albert Schafnaker, of Capon Bridge.

3. Omer, married Vernie Gill, of Capon Bridge, daughter of Spencer Gill. Their children (6):

Elson, married Mollie, daughter of Sam and Anna Wolford.

Ethel, married William Wolford, cousin of Mollie and brother of Caudy who married Violet Anderson. Ethel lives in Gore, Virginia. She is telephone operator there. They have two sons and two daughters living; one son dead.

Forest Pugh, married Miss Sheets. Residence Morgantown, W. Va. He is the youngest son.

Hazel, married Kenzel Oates of Capon Bridge. They own and reside at Green Lantern, summer resort near Gore. They have three children: Phyllis Juanita, Milaine Sue, and Gary Kenzel Oates.

Wilbur, married Miss Oates, sister of Kenzel.

Ray, married Ethel Henderson, daughter of T. F. and Carrie Henderson. Residence, Slanesville. One daughter (1947).

Ruby, graduate of Capon Bridge High School; married Bruce Hahn of Winchester, Virginia.

4. Edgar, married first, Anna Oates and after her death, Fannie Johnson of Winchester, Virginia. He is now deceased.

5. Martha, married Anderson Horner, Capon Bridge. He is now deceased (1947).

6. Clinton, went West and married there.

7. Stanley, went West and married there.

8. James, died young.

9. Wilbert, married Beulah Oates, Whitacre, Virginia. They have two children, Verlis and Garland.

Children of George Pugh and his second wife, Melissa Josnson:

10. Eva, married Wade Brooks, October 22, 1896; Millbrook, West Virginia.

11. Effie, married Elmer Good, Winchester, Virginia.

12. Manard, married Hilda Larrick, Akron, Ohio.

13. Elsie, married Wilmer Nixon, Akron, Ohio.

1. Carolyn E., died quite young, (1907).

152

15. Cecil, married Velda Belford, Capon Bridge, West Virginia. Mrs. Melissa Johnson Pugh, widow of George Pugh, has the family Bible at this time, March, 1935. October 21, 1947, it is in the home of Mrs. Bruce Hahn, Winchester, Virginia.

Lemuel, second son of David and "Esther" Pugh, born 1841, married 1864, Mary E., daughter of James C. and Malinda L. Nixon. Children: James C., Florence B., Minnie V., Martha A., David W., Sarah E., Mary E., and Gertrude.

Malachi, oldest son of David and Esther Pugh, born ———, died ———, married Margery Johnson. Children: Charles Newton, Evan L., and Albert D. Pugh.

a. Charles Newton, born October 8, 1862, married Lucy Bell Largent, (born January 3, 1874), Bloomery, West Virginia. Children:

1. Ira Russell Pugh, member the County Board of Education, born December 15, 1897, married Hilda Marie Omps (born April 6, 1903). Their children:

Doris Marie, born February 9, 1925.

Grannis Virginia, born March 5, 1927.

Albert Russell, born December 25, 1930.

Monna Lou Ethel, born July 8, 1932.

2. Estella Pugh, born February 28, 1899, married Simon Adams.

3. Lilly May Pugh Hammock, born May 14, 1900.

4. Bessie Golden Pugh Omps, born September 7, 1902.

5. Frances Lavonet Pugh Whitacre, born December 1, 1904.

6. Charles Loring Pugh, born May 25, 1909.

7. Martha Virginia Pugh, born August 18, 1913.

b. Evan L., son of Malachi Pugh, born 1874, married 1891, Louise L., daughter of Elijah and Eliza Fletcher of Virginia. Farmer; residence: Bloomery, West Virginia.

c. Albert D., born 1871, married Margaret Eaton. Children: Joseph F., George L., Lucile M., Residence: Bloomery, West Virginia. Later, Akron, Ohio.

III. Sally Pugh, sister of Robert J. and David, married William Giffin, brother of Jane, Bartholomew and others.

William and Sally Pugh Giffin's Children:

153

1. Mary, married Joseph White, four sons: Charles, Iraneus, John B., William F.; all in the West.

2. Margaret V., married Elias La Follette. See La Follette Family, Volume II.

3. Joseph G., married Sallie Allerton. One son, Elmer Giffin.

4. Frank, married ————. Children: ————.

5. Charles Fenton, married Martha Moreland. No children.

6. John, died in youth.

7. Martha, married Frank White.

8. Catherine Giffin, married Spencer Gill. Children:
   Minnie, married Harris Arnold; both now deceased.
   Verne, married Omar Pugh.
   Dora, married Fred Seldon; both now dead.
   Conrad, now deceased.
   Clarence, now deceased.

9. Jennie, never married.

Four Giffin farms in the Bethel neighborhood, Capon, joined. The elder John Giffin was a slaveholder.

The Giffin Family. Winchester Records.

They at first intermarried with the McKees, a family here much earlier.

1. Jane McKee, married William Colbert, 1795.

2. Sarah McKee, married John Giffin, March 21, 1803.

3. Eliza McKee, married John Cather, February 13, 1800.

4. William McKee, married a daughter of William La Follette, September 16, 1819.

5. Anna McKee, married Thomas Davis, November 1, 1801.

The Will of John Giffin, 1850, mentions the following children:

    a. John, married Mary Brown.

    b. William, married Sally Pugh.

    c. Bartholomew, married Elizabeth Fletcher.

    d. Jane, married Robert J. Pugh.

    e. James, married Eliza Keckley. See Volume II.

    f. Sarah, married William Milleson. Not found.

    g. Margaret.

John Giffin, married Sarah McKee, (J. Robert Giffin gave this information). John Giffin took up fifteen hundred acres of land and gave each of his children a farm.

Bartholomew Giffin, married Elizabeth Fletcher. They had seven children. Virginia Giffin married William J. Oates. Children: Elizabeth Oates, married A. D. McKee. Children:

Hattie McKee, married William Moreland. They have two children.

Winford and Genevieve Moreland.

Harry McKee, married Granis Funkhouser. They have one child, Mrs. Helen Davis. Second wife was Mary Oates and they had one child who died young.

Nellie McKee married Clint Keckley. They have two chil-:lren, Jean and Charles Keckley.

Dora McKee, married Ben Lockhart. They have two children, Louise and Dorothy Lockhart.

Beulah McKee, married Harry Swisher. They have one child, Mary Lou Swisher.

Paul McKee, married Chubby Saville. They have two children.

A. J. Oates, son of William J. Oates, married Emma Oates Second wife, Beulah Hook, ???? of John Hook.

R. J. Oates and Emma Oates' children are as follows:

Corine Oates married Clatus Whitacre. They have two children, Virginia Lovett and Maxine Riley.

Jenning Oates married Irene Oates. They have two boys.

Roy Oates, married Leona McDonald. Roy Oates was killed while serving in the Armed Forces in Luxenburg.

Lena Oates, married William Norton. They have two children, Mary Lou and Patricia Norton.

Virgil Oates, married Virgie Wolum.

Max Oates, married Laverine Rosenburger. (Virgil Oates and Max Oates both served in the Armed Forces).

Fannie Oates, married Jacob Shantholtz. Children: Mrs. Rosie Schaffenaker and Mrs. Grace Crane.

Catherine Giffin, married Scott Whitacre. Children:

Lycugus Whitacre, married Ammanda Abrel.

155

Elizabeth Whitacre, married Frank Lieth. They have three children: Icy Dick, Beatrice Hawkins and Austin Leith.

Hattie Whitacre, married John Lieth. They have three children: Mrs. Herbert Parson, Mrs. Chancy Guess, and Mrs. Jennings Liller.

Laura Whitacre, married Dora Payne.

Charles Giffin, married Ella Berkheimer. They had three boys and six girls.

Asbery Giffin, married Daisy Kackley.

Herbert Giffin, married Miss Malcolm.

Thurman Giffin, married Ada Hawkins.

Daisy Giffin, married Albert Elliott.

Grace Giffin, married Charles Pool.

Hazel Giffin's husband (unknown).

Mary Giffin, married Edward Good.

Virgie Giffin (unknown).

Leota Giffin (unknown).

Frank Giffin, married Catherine Foreman, second wife was Elizabeth Smith Monroe.

Rosie Giffin, married Elmer Fletcher.

Beatrice Giffin, married Charley Farmer.

Bertie Giffin, married Dr. Katchenburger.

Conrad and Leslie Giffin died young.

Mary S. Giffin, married Edward Oates. They have three children. Walter Oates, married Ethel Jackson, Lindsey Oates Shobe and Dorothy Oates Anderson.

Conrad Oates, married Grace Lockhart. They had one son, Conrad Oates, Jr. He married Edith Adams. They have one child, Alan Oates.

Icy Oates, married Cecil Sanders. They have four children, Wanda, Mary, Helen, and Mildred.

Edmund Giffin, married in Germany, wife's name not known.

Austin Giffin (Dead), James Edward Giffin, Nita and Corine Giffin, Dorothy and Mary Elizabeth Giffin.

J. Robert Giffin married Fannie Barrett. Children:

B. A. Giffin married Myrtle Cooper, they have five children:
1. Garland Giffin married Helen Largent. They have two children, Conrad and Joyce Giffin. Garland Giffin died at the age of thirty four, September 22, 1943.
 Elizabeth Giffin, married George Price, Jr. They have three children: Janice, Miles, and Perry Price.
 Robert Giffin married Ruby Poland. They have one child, Robert Dale Giffin.
 Roy Samuel Giffin (single), Robert and Roy Giffin both served in the Armed Forces.
2. Onile Virginia Giffin died when an infant.
3. Letcher Giffin married Jessie Weatherholtz. They have two children:
 Nellie Giffin, married Edwin Shade.
 Glen Robert Giffin's wife, unknown.
 4. Caudy Giffin (dead).
5. Ira Giffin married Lillie Johnson. They have four children:
 Goldie Giffin.
 Mildred Giffin married Henry Taft.
 Evelyn Giffin, married Oddie Williamson. They have one child.
 Edsel Giffin, married Elva Shanholtz. They have one child, Ronald Edsel.
6. Arthur Giffin, married Effie Anderson. They have three children: Edward Giffin, John Giffin, and Dorothy Giffin.
 Ira Giffin is deceased.

CHAPTER XV

Robert Pugh and wife, Margaret.

McDonald Pugh and children.

Margaret Pugh and Dr. Jas. Monroe.

James Pugh and Evelyn Howard.

Benjamin Pugh and Sarah Hiett and the descendants,
Robert Pugh, of Ohio and wife, Rebecca Larne.

Descendants of Robert and Mary Edwards Pugh, through
Robert II, and Margaret McDonald Pugh.

Robert Pugh II, son of Robert and Mary Edwards Pugh,
born January 12, 1772, died on Capon, December 5, 1849 and
is buried at Capon Chapel Cemetery. He married Margaret
McDonald, daughter of Benjamin and Margaret Hiett Mc-
Donald, who resided on North River where the summer home
of Judge Kennedy is now located. Robert II and Margaret
lived on what is now known as the John J. Monroe place on
Capon River, which Robert inherited from his parents — 470
acres of that which was deeded to them by Lord Fairfax, 1760.
Children: Margaret, Benjamin, James and Robert, III.

1. **Margaret,** born ———, died ———, married November
9, 1827, Dr. James Monroe, son of Dr. John Monroe, Scotch
ancestry, physician and Baptist minister of North River. Three
children were born to this union: Jeremiah, John J., and Benjamin.

Jeremiah, born 1831, died 1875, remained single. He was a
farmer and resided on Capon. Familiarly known as "Jere"
Monroe. He was a Confederate veteran, First Lieutenant in
Captain John H. Pyles Company, which was Company K of
General John Imboden's Cavalry, Jefferson Carter being 2nd
Lieutenant. B. F. McDonald was 1st Sergeant, Benjamin Mon-

roe, 2nd Sergeant and B. F. Kump, 3rd Sergeant. Many men from Capon and North River served in this Company.

John J., born 1833, died 1892, married Lydia T., daughter of Joseph and Elizabeth Kackley, 1862. Children: James A., Joseph Turner, and John J. Jr. Mr. Monroe was elected to the County Court, 1871; was a member of the State Legislature, 1872, and sheriff of Hampshire county, 1880.

The eldest son, James A. Monroe, born 1864, married, 1890, Virginia, daughter of John W. and Mary N. Monroe, Shinnston, West Virginia, Scotch-Irish ancestry. Children: Mary L., and James W. Mr. Monroe served one term as sheriff of Hampshire county and has also been Justice of his district. They resided at Capon Bridge, Mr. and Mrs. Monroe are both deceased,1947.

Joseph Turner Monroe, born about 1866, married Fannie Horn, daughter of John Horn of Capon Bridge about 1893. She is related to the pioneer Caudys on the mother's side and is an alumnus of Fairmont Teachers' College, West Virginia. Mr. Monroe lived only a short time and Mrs. Monroe brought up the children at the home. They are: Heiskell Monroe, Councilman of Capon Bridge, now deceased. Joseph Monroe, Mrs. Thurman Riley, Mrs. Lovett Kendall, and Mrs. Frances Gardner of Capon Bridge. Turner Monroe had a fine form and a magnetic personality. See Volume II.

John J. Monroe, Jr., son of John J. and Lydia T. Monroe, born '869, cared for the widowed mother and still remains at the old home. He is a prominent agriculturist as well as a business man. The writer is indebted to Mr. Monroe for much valuable information on the Robert and Joseph Pugh line, as well as on other branches of the family — the product of a remarkable memory. He is popular in his community. Later Mr. Monroe died, 1940.

Benjamin Monroe, third son of Dr. James and Margaret Monroe, born 1837, died 1910; was married late in life to Miss Smith of Capon Bridge, who survived him. Mr. Monroe was a Confederate veteran, Campany K., Imboden's Cavalry. The Monroes are Democrats and Baptists.

2. **James Pugh,** son of Robert II, and Margaret McDonald Pugh, was born on Capon, married Evelyn Howard, also born on Capon. Children: Ann Elizabeth, Robert James, Susan Howard, and William Edward. James Pugh, after the death of his wife, went West where he died, in Ohio.

Ann Elizabeth, died without heirs about 1860.

Susan Howard, married William Russell, son of Alexander Russell. William was born June 10, 1848, in Frederick county, east of Winchester, and died in Romney, aged nearly 86. He was a merchant and banker there. Mrs. Susan Russell, at this writing, still survives and resides at the New Century Hotel, Romney. The Russells had one daughter, Francis Howard, who died March 18, 1887, aged 15 years. Father and daughter are buried in the Indian Mound Cemetery, Romney. The Russells are Democrats and Presbyterians.

Robert James Pugh, son of James and Evelyn Howard Pugh, was a Confederate veteran, "Co. I", the famous Frontier Riflemen, one of the first Companies to be formed and the last to leave the field. It is said this Company fought until the last man fell — but some of the wounded survived the war and among these was Robert James Pugh. When they began to fight Grant in 1864 in the Wildenress, there were nine men of this Company left in the field, ragged and starved, one of these being Robert J. Pugh. He was wounded in the leg at Hanover Court House, there then being five left. After the ⸱⸱ar he was many years a merchant in Romney. The firm was known as Gilkeson & Pugh. He left no descendants.

William Edward Pugh, dentist, went West during, possibly, the 80's.

3. **Benjamin Pugh,** son of Robert II, and Margaret McDonald Pugh, born on Capon, married Sarah, daughter of Joseph and Ailsia Sutton Hiett (sister to Margaret who married Lemuel Pugh, son of Jesse II, and Ellen who married Joseph Snapp). Benjamin and Sarah Pugh lived in Sherman District, Hampshire county, south of Augusta. He was a farmer, was elected assessor, 1870, District No. 1. They had one daughter, Mar-

161

garet E., who, in 1866 married Alexander W. Monroe, his second marriage. Colonel Alex, born 1817, son of Robert and Elizabeth Monroe, began life as a teacher, was militia Colonel, 114 Regiment, Virginia; was later member of the House of Delegates and County Surveyor. Children: Robert P., Sallie E., Ella G., and Annie H. The Monroe family were brought up on a Barnes Mill farm. See Volume II.

Robert P. Monroe, married Miss Kidner. They have one daughter, Margaret. Robert was a farmer and surveyor. He was killed by a truck accident. Margaret recently married Brooks Hauser, of Romney, W. Va.

Sallie E. Monroe, married C. W. Haines, teacher, later county clerk, now deceased. Children: Blair M., Lyle, Nellie (Mrs. King), Margaret (Mrs. Rev. Whedbee), Lillian (Mrs. Luttrell), secretary county Board of Education. Some of these are graduates of Romney High School and some, of West Virginia University, Law School. Residence, Romney. Blair M., is Mayor of Romney, 1948.

Anna H. Monroe died single — cared for her mother in her declining years. She had an amiable disposition and attractive personality.

Ella G. Monroe, married William Tharp, orchardist, now deceased. Residence of Monroe and Haines families, Romney, West Virginia. Religion, Baptist. One son of Tharp family survives, Earl Tharp. See Volume II.

THE PUGH FAMILY

Mrs. Susan Howard Pugh Russell died at her apartment in the New Century Hotel, Romney, Saturday evening, May 15, 1937. Born near Capon Bridge, she was brought up, after the death of her mother, by relatives, Mr. and Mrs. John Heiskell. She was daughter of James and Evelyn Howard Pugh and granddaughter of Robert Pugh II and Margaret McDonald ?ugh. In 1880 she married William Russell, also born on Capon. (See another page of this book).

162

Funeral services for Mrs. Russell were conducted in the Presbyterian Church at Romney by Rev. C. K. Pool Tuesday following her death with interment in the family lot in Indian Mound Cemetery there.

—From the Hampshire Review

4. Robert Pugh III, son of Robert and Margaret McDonald Pugh, went West. A Robert Pugh, we think was the above Robert, lived in Homer, Licking county, Ohio, and died there about 1890. He visited Artie Pugh, of this county (Hampshire) while at her Aunt Mary Willis's of Homer, Ohio in 1884. He then looked to be about 70, which would take his birth date back to about 1814. He was of medium height and the Pugh type. He married a Miss Rebecca Larne. They were called, by the younger generation, "Uncle Robert and Aunt Becky". They were highly respected. No children. Both were later deceased when Artie Pugh (Mrs. Artie Shaffer) went to Homer to live.

Mr. and Mrs. Robert Pugh are buried in Homer, Ohio. Miss Rebecca Larne was an aunt to Mrs. Kate Dunlap, respected citizen of Homer, a church worker in the Presbyterian church, known to the whiter on her visits to her sister, Mrs. Shaffer. Mr. and Mrs. Pugh lie buried in an unmarked grave at Homer Cemetery, but their lot is identified by number and ownership on Cemetery plot.

Blackwater Falls
Davis, W.Va.

CHAPTER XVI

Mishall and Margaret Pugh and children.   Malachi Pugh.

Captain David Pugh, the Statesman and the Margaret Pugh
and William Dunlap Family.

Descendants of Robert and Mary Edwards Pugh.

Mishall Pugh, son of Robert and Mary Edwards Pugh, was
born July 29, 1776; married Margaret Reese, November 16, 1796,
Winchester Records.

Captain David Pugh, second son of Mishall and Margaret
Pugh was born at Capon Bridge, February 8, 1806 and died at
his farm on Capon south of the Bridge, January 29, 1899. He
was married, 1830, to Mary W. Caniford of Baltimore (born
December 25, 1808, died April 14, 1831); and a second time,
1835, to Jane, daughter of Abraham Creswell (born December 7,
1809, died December 10, 1851). Children: Preston, John,
Mary C., Maria L., Almira V., and Martha J. He was married
again, 1852, to Elizabeth, daughter of Hugh and Annie Garvin
(born February 3, 1820, died March 14, 1900). Children: Florence M., David C., and Annie Lee, who is still living (1935).

Mr. Pugh was a member of the Convention which signed the
order of secession 1861. He was in the Virginia Legislature,
1841; was for many years a Justice when Justice meant Judge—
and after there was a County Court, elected to that, was elected
to the West Virginia Senate, 1876.

Mr. Pugh was personally known to Henry Clay and Andrew
Jackson, and was a visitor at the White House during Jackson's
presidency. See clipping from Hampshire Review of 1899.

165

We believe M. Pugh, Justice, 1831, was Mishall and again M. Pugh elected Sheriff, 1835, given in Romney Records, was Mishall, father of Malachai, Captain David Pugh, and Margaret Pugh (Mrs. William Dunlap).

The reader will note that Robert and Mary Edwards Pugh had two grandsons named Malachi, Malachi, grandson of Joseph, and Malachi, son of Mishall. It seems that Malachi, son of Mishall died single.

CAPTAIN PUGH —From the Hampshire Review, Feb. 1899

In another column will be found a notice of the death of Captain David Pugh, of this county, accompanied by a brief sketch of his life.

In the death of Mr. Pugh, this county loses, perhaps her oldest and one of her most distinguished citizens. He was in many respects a most remarkable man. His name for years has been a houhehold word in this county, and a synonym for honor and integrity.

After holding many offices of trust he has spent his declining years in the sacred precincts of his home, where he delighted to relate his checkered career and discuss the early history of this country. There he waited for the evening of life, and the closing of his days, with perfect composure and equanimity.

Line of the Husband of Margaret Ann Pugh, daughter of Mishall and Margaret

William Dunlap (Scotch descent), born 1775, died 1858, married Flora A. McMullen (Irish descent), born 1769, died 1851; came to the United States in 1788.

William Dunlap served in the war of 1812, for which he received two land warrants. Settled on Timber Ridge, one half mile north of what is now Shiloh Methodist Church. The graves of both are in the family burying ground there. Children: Abner, Archabold, William, John, and Nancy.

William Dunlap, son of William and Flora, born at the home place on Timber Ridge, 1807, died 1888; married **Margaret Ann**

Pugh, daughter of Mishall, and sister of Captain David Pugh. She was born 1810 and died 1864. William Dunlap was a miller and built the first mill, what is now known as Hook's Mill, on Capon River, five miles southwest of Capon Bridge. He sold this mill and built another on Back Creek near Rock Enon Springs, Virginià, which is still standing and owned by his son, Turner Dunlap, 1938. Children: Ferdinand J., Algernon W., Tucker, Turner A., Mary A. K. (Mrs. Garvin), Sarah, Malcena, and Elizabeth.

Ferdinand J. Dunlap was a Lieutenant in the Civil War, was wounded in Chancelorsville, died at Staunton, Virginia, and is buried in the Confederate Cemetery there.

Algernon W.

Tucker

William

Turner lives at Rock Enon Springs, Virginia.

Mary married Malon Garvin.

Sarah married Capt. H. A. Herself, Washington, D. C.

Malcena died in San Diago, California.

Elizabeth never married and lives in Washington, D. C., 1938.

Elizabeth and Turner are the only members of the William and Margaret Pugh Dunlap family now living, 1938.

Children of Malon and Mary Dunlap Garvin: Wm. Carson, 1865.

Beall Garvin, 1868, many years a teacher of Hampshire county, who married Prof. Frank Sine, a college man of Virginia, also a son of a pioneer family. He is now deceased. Mrs. Sine resides at 702 Virginia Avenue, Winchester, Virginia. See Garvin Family, Volume II of this work and Sine Family, Vol. II.

Minnie Garvin, married W. J. Muse who is now deceased. They were farmers living on Timber Ridge. Children:

1. Madaline, single.
2. Robert married Nellie Roby.
3. Wm. Carlton, married Dorothy Haines, only child of Mr. and Mrs. Lester C. Haines, merchants of Capon Bridge. She died during the last war, leaving a daughter, Ann, who lives

167

with Mr. and Mrs. Haines. Mr. Muse has since married a second time, to Dillard Hopgood. He operates a store, filling station and restaurant on U. S. 50, at the west end of town.

Mr. and Mrs. Haines have sold out to Johnson and Giffin, built a bungalow and retired to private life here in the village. (A long and happy life to them.—M. P.)

David Garvin, a native of this county, who had lived in Danville, Va., for more than forty years, died there Friday night. He was the son of the late Mahlon and Mary Garvin, of High View, and went to Danville when quite a young man.

CHAPTER XVII

Dr. William L. Pugh, Celtic Linguist.

The name Pugh and its transitions from Old Welsch to Modern.

The Columbus, Ohio, Pughs.

Dr. William L. Pugh, professor of Celtic languages, Spartanburg College, Spartanburg, South Carolina, mentioned in a late "Who's Who in America" as author and linguist, and whose father, John Pugh was born in Pottsville, Pennsylvania, 1837, was the youngest of the family of children, all the rest of whom were born in Wales. After the father's death in Pennsylvania, the mother married an Englishman and they removed to a Welsh settlement in Wisconsin where the son grew up.

Later John Pugh removed to Illinois where he met his wife. Several years after their marriage they went to Iowa, bought a farm and there spent the rest of their lives.

Dr. Pugh's father never taught him to speak Welsh, since he did not wish him to speak English with a Welsh accent, but when the son was completing his studies for a doctorate, asked him to take the Celtic Courses in order to be able to know the history and language of his native people. Therefore, Dr. Pugh took Old and Middle Welsh under Prof. F. N. Robinson, famous linguist of Harvard. He learned that the name Pugh was, in old Welsh, Mab Hugh; later it was written Ap Hugh, as you will notice in Thomas Allen Glenn's book of Welsh Genealogy, Pennsylvania Historical Society, Library, Philadelphia.

Finally came "the change of the initial h to p through the influence of the final b of the preceding word", hence Pugh, which means "son of Hugh".

Dr. Pugh regrets that his ancestors were not among the early Pugh pioneers but adds: "Far back, however, our very great grandfathers were probably of the same family in Wales".

Dr. Pugh recently suffered the loss of his wife to whom he was devoted, a companion of thirty-one years. He has one child, a daughter, "Helen", who is just finishing her college course at Spartansburg, South Carolina.

COPY

PUGH & PUGH
Attorneys at Law
Columbus, Ohio
22 West Gay Street

David F. Pugh   **Lawrence R. Pugh**

July 20, 1932.

Miss Maud Pugh,
Pleasant Dale, West Virginia.

Dear Madam:

Some time ago the postmaster sent me your letter which was addressed to any member of the family of George E. Pugh, to see whether I could give you any information in regard to the Pugh family.

There are several families in this state by that name which have no traceable relationship so far as I know. My father was a judge, whose name was D. F. Pugh. We lived in West Virginia for some years and father was a member of the constitutional convention and the legislature of West Virginia at one time. There was a family by the same name, members of the legislature about the time he was, (Captain David Pugh, Hampshire county), but there was no traceable relationship so far as the members knew. There was a United States Senator from this state by the name of George E. Pugh about the Civil War time who lived in Cincinnati but we know of no relationship. Perhaps this is the family to which you are related. There are also members of this family in Guernsey

170

county by the same name and in Harrison County and some of these people went to Cincinnati at one time.

I had hoped to get some information from a Mrs. McClure, who is a clerk for Judge Florence Allen in the Capitol but have not had a chance to talk to her. Some of her family were of that name and lived in the southern part of the state but it is still another branch which might or might not be connected with your family. We also know there was a family in Alabama by the same name and one of the members was a United States Senator.

I am sorry that I can not give you any definite information. I imagine your people are either connected with those living in Guernsey or Harrison counties, or in Cincinnati, but whether any of these are living at either place I do not know.

Very truly your,

(Signed) L. R. Pugh

CHAPTER XVIII

Dr. Evan Pugh, founder of Penn State College.

Ellis Pugh Family, Quakers.

Line of Dr. Evan Pugh, Philadelphia Records, founder of Penn State Agriculture College.

John Pugh, Welsh descent, born June 9, 1747. Son:

Jesse Pugh, born March 1, 1772, at the age of five was brought to East Nottingham, Pennsylvania; blacksmith and tanner. Married Elizabeth Hudson; had two children.

Lewis Pugh, born December 4, 1796, died 1840, eldest son of Jesse and Elizabeth Hudson Pugh; married Mary Hutton. They lived at Jordan Bank, East Nottingham township, Chester County, Pennsylvania. Son:

Dr. Evan Pugh, born February 29, 1828, died ————. At the age of sixteen was apprenticed to a blacksmith. At the age of eighteen attended Manual Labor School, White Stone, New York; taught district school one term. Established a boarding and day school called Jordan Bank Seminary, near Oxford, 1853, then went to Europe for study.

In 1859 he was president of Farmer's High School near Belleforte, Pennsylvania, later Agriculture College, now Penn State College.

William Pugh, eldest of John and Jane Pugh was a resident of London Grove, Pennsylvania, Chester county, 1771. He was married to Jane Brown, 1742 —Welsh descent — Ellis line, perhaps.

The Ellis Pugh Family

Ellis Pugh and wife, Sinah, came to Pennsylvania from Wales, 1687. Children:

Ellen, born in Wales; married David Meredith, 1699.

173

Ellis, born in Wales, married Mary Evans.

Thomas, born in Wales, married Jane Rogers.

John, born in Pennsylvania 1688, died 1760; married Jane Rees.

Elizabeth, born in Pennsylvania; married Ellis Roberts.

Job, born in Pennsylvania; married Phoebe (Miles) Evans, widow no children.

Abraham, born in Pennsylvania, 1695, died 1711.

Thomas Pugh and wife lived in Merion where he died in 1723. Children:

Jesse, married Alice Malin; removed to Hogue Creek, Va.

Roger, married Sarah Hannam; lived in Kent County, Del.

Hannanniah, married Mary Davis; lived in Philadelphia.

Mischael (Michael), married Hannah Davis; lived in Norriston Township, Philadelphia County, Pennsylvania.

Katherine, married Benjamin Rhodes; later James Travilla, York County, Pennsylvania.

Azariah, married Hannah Beals; lived in Frederick County, Virginia; Newberry County, South Carolina.

Thomas, married Jane Lewis, Frederick County, (near Gore).

Azariah and Hannah lived in Frederick County, Virginia, until the Indian Wars; removed to South Carolina. Children:

Ruth, married Peter Julian, Jr., son of Captain Peter Julian and Mary Beals.

Ellis, married Phoebe Coppock; removed to Ohio, 1802.

Jesse, married Elizabeth Grey, 1786, Winchester Records.

Mary, married Alexander Tansy, III.

David, married Rachel Wright; went to Ohio, 1804.

Hannah, married Crooks (?).

Azariah, married Sophia Wright; removed to Ohio, 1804.

William, married Joannah Pearson, later Sallie Thomas.

Thomas, married Parthena ———.

David and Rachel removed to Warren County, Ohio, 1804. Children:

Job, married Nancy Swift; then Sarah Martin.

Lott, married Rachel Anthony.

Rue.

Verlinda, married Thomas Swift.

William, married Susannah Coppock.

Hannah, married H. G. Sexton.

Bathsheba, married Samuel Jay.

Leah, married Marshall.

From a letter of Miss Sallie Pugh

Prosperity, S. C., March 2, 1937

The first one of my Pugh ancestors to come to America was Ellis Pugh, who was born, 1656, at Brithdru, near Dongelly, Merioneth Co., Wales. He was a Quaker minister, preaching in the Welsh language. With his wife, Sinah, and three little children, he arrived in Pennsylvania in 1687, bought land in Plymouth township in what is now Montgomery county, Pennsylvania. He built Merion Meeting-house, which is still in use. He died in 1718. He had seven children.

1. Ellen, born in Wales; married Davad Meredith, 1699.

2. Ellis, born in Wales, married Mary Evans, daughter of Owen Evans, 1708. (died 1711) no children.

3. Thomas, born in Wales, 1685, married Jane Rogers, 1709, died 1723. His widow married Isaac Malin, 1727.

4. John (1688-1760)

5. Elizabeth, born 1690, married Ellis Roberts.

6. Job (1693-1757), married Phoebe Ellis Evans.

7. Abraham (1695-1711).

All of these lived in Pennsylvania.

Thomas Pugh, mentioned as son of Ellis, was our ancestor. He had seven children:

1. Jesse, born 1711, married Alice Malin, 1730; removed to Hopewell, Frederick county, Virginia, 1741. His children were Job, Thomas, Jane, and "probably other daughters."

2. Roger, born 1713, married Sarah Hannum, 1740. Removed to Kent county, Delaware.

3. Hananiah, born 1715, married Mary Davis. Lived in Montgomery county, Pennsylvania.

175

4. Mishael, born 1717, married Hannah Davis. lived in Philadelphia county, Pennsylvania.

5. Katherine, born 1719, married, first, Benjamin Rhoades; second, James Travilla. Lived in York county, Pennsylvania.

6. Azariah, born 1721, married Hannah Bales. Removed to Frederick county, Virginia (date not known). Removed to Bush River, Newberry county, South Carolina, 1765. Died after 1795.

7. Thomas, born 1723, married Jane Lewis. Removed to Frederick county, Virginia. His children: Michael, Mellin, Eli, Jesse, Ellis, "probably daughters".

Azariah's children were: Thomas, Jesse, Azariah, Jr., Ellis, William, David. No daughters are mentioned but in Azariah's Will, "a child's part is left to the children of Peter Julian", so there was one daughter surely.

Azariah"s son, Thomas, and his wife, Ann, were living in Virginia in 1784, according to a land sale record at Newberry. Azariah's other children moved away from South Carolina about 1800, going to Ohio (Warren county) and elsewhere.

William, my great, great grandfather had one son, Timothy, one daughter, Katherine.

Timothy had three sons and two daughters. His sons were: Hawkins, William, Thomas, and the daughters, Katherine and Martha.

My father was William. He married Caroline Moore and their children: Robert, Griffith, and Sarah. I, Sarah, am the only one of our immediate family living. Robert was a banker and Griffith, a teacher. He was president of Columbia College, a college for girls, Columbia, South Carolina, and later, head of the Mathematics Department, Winthrop College, Rock Hill, South Carolina, the largest girls' college in the state. Sarah, teacher.

W. E. Pugh, D.D., is the son of Thomas Pugh. He is a Lutheran minister, preaching in Jacksonville, Florida.

Line of Ellis, the Quaker Minister, Winchester and Timber Ridge, Va.

Azariah Pugh, perhaps the son of Jesse (not clear) lived near High View, West Virginia; had three sons and two daughters: Jesse, Jonathan, David, Amanda and Mary Ann.

I. Jesse Pugh, married Elizabeth ———, had the following children: Vincent M., Smith, Zacariah (Jack), Thomas, and ? ? ? Mrs. Jas F. Blaker, of Blaker's factory, south of Sedan.

1. Vincent Pugh married Eva Ann Milslagle.

2. Smith Pugh went to East Virginia and married there.

3. Jack Pugh, married Miss Brooks.

4. Tom Pugh, married Miss Calvert.

5. The Blakers brough up a family and are now deceased. Children: Jettie W., and Arlie L. Blaker.

II. Jonathan Pugh, married Mary Jane Anderson, daughter of Paul Anderson; second wife was Harriet Racy Reid, daughter of Jeremiah J. Reid. Descendants given elsewhere.

III. David Pugh went west, Iowa .

IV. Amanda Pugh, married Mr. Lockhart; went to Baltimore.

V. Mary Ann married John Reid from Lehew, West Virginia; Mr. Reid's third wife.

A replica of old covered bridges over Capon River

CHAPTER XX

Descendants of Ellis Pugh, Quaker Minister, and son, Thomas Pugh.

Line of U. S. Senator George Ellis Pugh and Son.

Judge Robert C. Pugh and others.

Line of Judge Robert C. Pugh, whose father was United States Senator from Ohio, 1855-1861.

Ellis Pugh, born 1656 in Grath Gowen, Wales, joined the Quakers, became a minister, married Sinah ———, emigrated to Pennsylvania in 1687, died near Plymouth, Philadelphia county, Pennsylvania, 1718, leaving children: John: Ellis (died 1711), Abraham, Job, Thomas, Ellen and Elizabeth.

Thomas Pugh, born 1685, married Jane Rogers, June 7, 1706. Children: Jesse, Roger, Hananiah, Thomas, Micael and Azariah.

Azariah Pugh, born 1721, married Hannah Bales, grand-daughter of Alexander Tansy, 1746, removed to Virginia, then to South Carolina. Children: David, Jesse, Ellis, William, Azariah and Thomas.

David Pugh, born 1750, married Rachel Wright, removed to Ohio about 1802. Children: (Sons) Job, Rue, Lot and William.

Lot Pugh, born ———, married Rachel Anthony. Children: Jordan, Anthony, George Ellis, Mary and Willam Henry.

George Ellis, born ———, died 1876, married Theresa Chalfant, born, ———, died 1860. Children: Robert Chalfant, Nina Theresa (Mrs. Nina Pugh Smith) and Thomas.

Robert Chalfant Pugh, born September 10, 1857; died Nov. 28, 1935; married Ada Hampton, born ———, died ———. One child: Robert Hampton.

Robert H. Pugh, physician in Cincinnati, Ohio, born ———,
married ———. Child: Robert C., II, born ———.

Authorities: Memoirs of Chester county, Pennsylvania, by
Cope-Ashmead; History of Hocking Valley, Ohio; Hopewell
Records (Friends); Southern Quakers and Slavery-Weeks; and
Judge Pugh, himself.

Judge Pugh's Line of Genealogy, 1656 to 1935, in brief.

Judge Pugh's Line:
1. Ellis Pugh, Grath Gowan, Wales.
2. Thomas Pugh, Pennsylvania.
3. Azariah Pugh, Pennsylvania, Virginia and South Carolina.
4. David Pugh, South Carolina and Ohio.
5. Lot Pugh, Cincinnati, Ohio.
6. George Ellis Pugh, Cincinnati, Ohio.
7. Robert Chalfant Pugh, Cincinnati, Ohio.
8. Robert Hamplton Pugh, Cincinnati, Ohio.
9. Robert Chalfant Pugh, II, Cincinnati, Ohio.

Jordan Anthony Pugh was married twice but left no children.

Mary Pugh married Judge Samuel Hart and left five children.

William Henry Pugh left three children, all still living, and
one, Laura, is a widow with children. Jordan, the eldest, is a
widower with two children (one married) and Alice Church,
married to Dr. Frankland, Washington, D. C., with no children.

Lot Pugh and wife are buried in the family lot at Spring
Grove Cemetery, Cincinnati, Ohio, as are also, Senator George
E. Pugh and wife, and his brother, Jordan Anthony and first
wife. William Henry and wife are buried in Arlington Cemetery, Washington, D. C.

Judge Pugh is listed in a late edition of "Who's Who" and
his wife in "Principal Women of America".

In his letter to the writer, Judge Pugh says: "I am happily
married and my beloved wife is Ada Hampton Pugh who was
born in England." And again he says:

"The name Pugh is quite common in Wales. I heard of them
when in England in 1914. I know that for many years there

was a Pugh in the House of Commons and he or his people may be there yet.

"The Pugh family in Cincinnati ran to lawyers. I am the fourth member of my family to have been a member of the Cincinnati Bar."

Judge Pugh's father was City Solicitor, then Attorney General of the State of Ohio and later, for six years, 1855 to 1861, United States Senator. Date of his death, 1876.

From "Who's Who"

Robert Chalfant Pugh, Professor of Law, Parents: George Ellis and Teresa Chalfant. Born September 10, 1857. Xavier College, Cincinnati, LLB., Cin. Law College 1879, L.L.D., University of Cincinnati 1921. Married Ada H. Hampton, Ilfra Combe, Devonshire, England, Dec. 21, 1895. One son Robert Hampton. Admitted to Ohio Bar, 1878, and practiced at Cincinnati until 1912. Judge Superior Court, Cincinnati, 1912 to 1918. Professor of Law, College of Law, Cincinnati, since 1918. Professor law of contracts, formerly Asst. Dean and Acting Dean. Member American Bar Association, and Ohio State Bat Assn., and American Society of International Law, American Law Institute, American Institute of Archeology, Order of Coif., Phi Delta Phi, Democrat. Home, Senator Place Apartment, Cincinnati, Ohio.

Judge Robert C. Pugh Expires in Hotel Room
Long Illness
Active as Member of Law School Faculty

Former Judge Robert C. Pugh, widely known Cincinnati jurist and law teacher, died Friday, November 28, 1935 in his residence in the Hotel Alms, Walnut Hills. He has been in failing health for some time, but an attack of influenza, several weeks ago, hastened the end.

Arrangements for the funeral will be announced later, members of the family stated.

Judge Pugh was born in Cincinnati, 1857, the son of former Senator George E. Pugh and Mrs. Theresa Pugh. He attended Xavier University and was a graduate of the Cincinnati Law School. He was admitted to the Ohio bar in 1878 and practiced until 1912. In 1895 he married Ada M. Hampton. From 1912 until 1918 he served as judge of the Superior Court, which no longer is in existence.

In 1918 he became assistant dean of the College of Law, and the G. H. Wald professor of the law of contracts, University of Cincinnati, and had served on the faculty since that time. At one time he served as prosecutor of Hamilton County and attorney for the Board of Health.

He was a member of the American and Ohio State Bar Associations, the A.A.A.S., American Society of International Law, American Law Institute, American Institute of Archeology, Order of Coif, and Phi Delta Phi, legal fraternity.

Judge Pugh leaves a sister, Mrs. Nina Pugh Smith, music critic for the Times-Star, and a son, Dr. Robert H. Pugh.

CHAPTER XXI

Descendants of John Pugh, son of the Quaker Minister, including A. H. Pugh, Editor, of Cincinnati.

Mrs. McClure, Columbus, Ohio, Miss Georgia B. Pugh, St. Louis, Missouri.

Gilbert Cape, the Historian and Genealogist of Pennsylvania, and others.

Line of A. H. Pugh, Cincinnati, Ohio.

(Embracing a Jonathan, not the Lieut. Jonathan of my line, but the line of Ellis Pugh, Quaker Minister.—M. P.)

(COPY)

Mr. Albert D. Pugh,
    Des Moines, Iowa.

Dear Sir:

In reply to yours of 30, our emigrant ancestor was Ellis Pugh, born in Grath Gowen, Wales, in 1656, joined the Quakers, became a minister, married Sinah ———; emigrated to Pennsylvania 1687, died near Merion, 1718, leaving children: John, (Ellis, who died 1711), Abraham, Job, Thomas, Ellen and Elizabeth.

Thomas was born 1685, married Jane Rogers, June 7, 1706. They had children: Jesse, Roger, Hannanniah, Thomas, Micail, and Azariah.

Micail, born 1717, had sons: Eli, Levy, Thomas and Jonathan.

Jonathan, born 1761, had sons as follows: Eli, born 1793; Job, born 1805; Jesse, born 1807; Jonathan, born 1809; Stephen, born 1810; Levi, born 1812, Louis, born 1816.

I am descended from John Pugh, son of Ellis.

Yours truly,
(Signed) A. H. Pugh.

Lineage of Mrs. Ellie McGilivary McClure, East Town Street, Columbus, Ohio. (Mrs. S. B. McClure, Sec. to Judge Florence Allen).

Ellis Pugh, born 1656, in Grath Gowen, Wales, Quaker minister; wife, sinah, from Dongelly, Merioneth, Wales. Arrived 1687, settled in Radnor Township, Chester, county, Pennsylvania; later in Plymouth, Phylidelphia county; died 1718, near Marion. Children: John, Ellis (deceased, 1711), Abraham, Job, Thomas, Ellen and Elizabeth.

John Pugh, son of Ellis; wife, Jane Rees; settled in East Nottingham, Township, Chester county, Pennsylvania, died 1760.

William Pugh, son of John; wife (1) Mary Brown, married, 1742; (3) Patience Cosner (widow); East Nottingham, Pennsylvania; died 1775.

Ensign John Pugh, son of William Pugh, born June 9, 1747; wife, Rachel Barrett, born September 18, 1744, died before 1828. East Nottingham, Pennsylvania, until 1803, when he removed to Harrison county, Ohio, with four of his sons; died in Ohio, 1840. Sons: Thomas, James, John, Ellis, William and David, also Hannah and Mary (twins).

William Pugh, son of Ensign John Pugh, born December 4, 1775; wife, Bathsheba Johnson, who was born September 3, 1792, died December 9, 1855. Six children, four sons and two daughters; he died September 6, 1822.

Ellis B. Pugh, born October 18, 1819, died January 29, 1899. He was the son of William Pugh. Wife, Cassandra Selfridge, born June 9, 1819, died June 7, 1890. Three children: John C., Ada P. McGillivray and Helen L. Booth.

Lineage of Georgia B. Pugh, Eads Avenue, St. Louis, Missouri.

John Clarence Pugh, born December 24, 1848, died July 9, 1907; married Alice Hanning, (born October 21, 1851, died March 27, 1919) August 31, 1881.

His father, Ellis B. Pugh, born October 18, 1819, died January 29, 1899; married Cassandra Geer Selfridge (born June 9, 1819, died June 7, 1890) March 31, 1846.

His father, William Pugh, born December 4, 1775, died September 6, 1822; married Bathsheba Johnson (born September 3, 1792, died December 9, 1855) ————, 1808.

His father, Ensign John Pugh, born June 9, 1747, died 1840; married Rachel Barrett (born September 18, 1744, died before May 17, 1828, when the will was dated, not mentioned in will) May 9, 1711.

His father, William Pugh, born ————, died 1775; married Mary Brown, 1742.

His father, John Pugh, who married Jane Reese, died 1760.

His father, Ellis Pugh, born 1656, died 1718; married Sinah ————.

Authorities: Hist. of Hocking Valley, Ohio, (1883) page 1258. Genealogical and Personal Memoirs of Chester Co. Pa., Cope-Ashmead, Vol. 1, p. 887.

Children of Ensign John Pugh:

James, born March 1, 1772, married ———— Hudson.

Thomas, born November, 1773, married Esther Gatchell.

William, born December 4, 1775, married Bathsheba Johnson.

John, born October, 1778, ———— ————.

Mary and Hannah, twins, born February 16, 1781. Mary married Jacob Cope, Hannah married Wm. Howell.

Ellis, born February 25, 1785, married Anna Skelton.

David, born October 8, 1788, ———— ————.

Ellis Pugh Family — L. T. Payne Research

Hannah Baels (or Bayles) married Azariah Pugh. She was the granddaughter of John and Mary (Clayton) Bales of Pennsylvania, Chester county. Mary Clayton was the daughter of William Clayton, who presided at the first Court held in Pennsylvania under the Proprietory Government. Hannah's parents were William and Rebecca (?) Baels.

Ellis Pugh, Quaker minister, born 1656 at Grath Gowen, Wales, died 1718 Merion, Pa. married Sinah ————, of Brithdiew, Dongelly, Merioneth, Wales. Children: John, Ellis, Abraham, Job, Thomas, Ellen, Elizabeth.

Ellis Pugh and wife arrived in Philadelphia in 1687, and in 1718 they were living near Merion, Pennsylvania.

Thomas Pugh, fifth son of Ellis and Sinah Pugh, was born in Wales in 1685; married October 23, 1710, Jane Roger, daughter of Roger (Robert) — Will, 8-16-1720, died 1723 in Pennsylvania. Children: Jesse, Roger, Hananiah, Thomas, Michael, and Azariah.

Azariah, fifth son of Thomas and Jane Pugh, born 1721, married 1745, Hannah Baels, granddaughter of John and Mary Clayton, the latter a daughter of William and Rebecca Chambers Clayton. Children: David, Ellis, William, Jesse, Azariah, Thomas, Ruth, and Mary. Azariah's Will is dated 1793.

Ruth Pugh, 1771, married Peter Julien, Jr., son of Captain Peter and Mary Baels, sister of Hannah Baels. Children: Stephen, William, Azariah, Eli, Jesse, Ruth and Hannah.

William, second son of Ruth Pugh and Peter Julien, Jr., married Charlotte Tansey, daughter of Alexander Tansey III, and Mary Pugh, daughter of Azariah and Hannah Baels Pugh.

The immigrant, Alexander Tansey of Anne Arundel county, Maryland, married Mary Parsons.

Edward Tansey patented land in Frederick county, Maryland, in 1774, called "Tansey's Chance." This Edward Tansey married Lydia Nelson, daughter of John of Frederick county. Office, Annapolis.) Edward's patent, see Library B.C. and 9 S 51 (Reference Judgments, Library, 61—Folio 496—1770-1771 Land Folio 12.

Lydia Tansey, in 1790 Census, Frederick County, Maryland, as head of family (Edward having died between 1774 and 1790), three sons under sixteen and four females.

Land office, Annapolis, Maryland, list of first settlers, 1634-1680, Liler W. C., No. 2, Folio 406: Transported, 1680, Alexander Tansey. Anno. 1680, Transported in the "Charles": married Mary Parsons and also probably married a second time to Rebecca ———, for the the St. George Parish Record, Harford county, Maryland, page 195, "Rebecca Tansey, daughter of Alexander and Rebecca, baptized July 12, 1702." Alexander

Tansey I, died in eastern Maryland.

On December 24, 1741, his son, Alexander Tansey, who married Katherine ———, secured certificate from Gunpowder Meeting, Society of Friends, Baltimore, Maryland, to Monoquacy Mtg. (near Frederick, Maryland) (Minute Book A, 1739 to 1768). Children: Ann, born 1729, Mary, 1731, Abraham, 1733, Edward, Lea, Catherine, Martha, William and Alexander, Jr.

St. Paul's Parish, Baltimore, Maryland, Volume I,
Births, Deaths, Marriages, etc.

Ann, daughter of Alexander Tansey and Katherine, born January 18, 1729

Mary, daughter of Alexander Tansey and Katherine, born January 25, 1731.

Abraham, son of Alexander Tansey and Katherine, born January 18, 1733 or 1734.

Fairfax Meeting Book of Marriages, Fairfax county, Virginia,
page 2:

Marriage of William Ballenger and Casander Plummer, the third day of the 8th month, 1751; the following sign as witnesses:

Alexander Tansey (this would be II).

Edward Tansey.

Alex Tansey Jr. (this would be III).

Therefore, I woud say, in a general way, that the Tanseys moved from Gunpowder Mtg, (Monthly Meeting) in Anne Arundel county, Maryland to Monoquacy Mtg, thence to Fairfax Mtg, in Virginia, and afterwards to New Garden Mtg. in North Carolina.

Evidently the Tansey line did not meet the Julien line until they arrived in North Carolina, and possibly it could have been South Carolina.

Tansey Ancestry of Louis Tansey Payne

Alexander Tansey married Mary Parsons, January 20, 1704, at St. James Parish, Ann Arundel county, Maryland. Children:

Martha, born 1705; Alexander, III, born 1707; Samuel, born 1709; Abraham, born 1711; Mary, born 1713.

Alex. Tansey II, married Catherine, 9 children; Alex. III ????
Alexander Tansey, III, married Mary Pugh, daughter of Azariah and Hanna Baels Pugh.

Charlotte Tansey of Bush River, South Carolina, 1801, married William Julien, son of Peter Julian, Jr. and Ruth Pugh, grandson of Captain Peter Julien and Mary Baels, and great grandson of Rene D. St. Julien.

Gulielma, of Darke county, Ohio, in 1833 married William Hutchins.

Alexander Tansey Hutchins, of Jay county, Indiana, in 1857, married Sarah Jane Bickel.

Mary Ladusky Hutchins, of Dayton, Ohio, 1877, married Albert Celia Payne. Children: Myrtle May, Golden Albert, and Louis Tansey, born April 5, 1885.

Louis Tansey Payne of Columbus, Ohio, in 1913, married Perle Francis. Child: Dorothy Francis Payne, born at Morenci, Arizona, January 20, 1915. She is now professor in an eastern college.

Sources of Information of Tansey Data:

1. St. James Parish Records, A.A. Co., Md.
2. St. Paul's Paris Records, Baltimore, Md.
3. St. Georg's Parish Records, Harford Co., Md.
4. Quaker Records — Gunpowder Mtg., Md.
5. Monoquacy Mtg, Frederch Co., Md.
6. Fairfax Mtg., Fairfax Co., Virginia.
7. Cane Creek Mtg., North Carolina.
8. New Garden, Mtg., North Carolina.
9. Maryland Archives, Vol. 31.
10. Maryland His. Mag., Dec. 1914.
11. Maryland Wills, Vol. V–147; Vol. III–214.
12. Teutonic Name System (Robert Ferguson), very interesting for name 'Tansey'.
13. The Parrish Family (Scott Lee Boyd).

The Tansy Family

It is fair to assume that Alexander Tansy and family must have been Friends before going to Monoquacy and to Fairfax meetings in Frederick county, Maryland, hence were offshoots of Penn's late colony.

The Alexander Tansy of 1711 was in West River Hundred in Anne Arundel county, Maryland, and West River Meeting was near at hand to which he probably belonged.

Alexander Tansy and wife, Catherine, and family broke with the Quakers at Fairrax Monthly Meeting at Monoquacy, Frederick County, Maryland, about 1756. At least two of their children are known to have been Alexander, Jr., and Leah.

Leah Tansy married William Wright at Cane Creek Meeting in North Carolina, the 5th Month, 15th Day, 1758.

"Fairfax Monthly Meeting, 8th month, 27th day, 1757, Abraham and Edward Tansy, having abandoned the principles of Friends entirely, enlisted as soldiers and declaring themselves as such and not Friends, this meeting thinks necessary to declare against them."

These men were evidently sons of Alexander and Catherine and therefore brothers of Leah and Alexander, Jr.

Since this family of Tansys are the first to be found in Maryland, from whence Mary Ellen, wife of Captain Jonathan, and her sister, Mrs. "Betsy" Hiett, wife of John Hiett(son of Evan and Sarah Smith), and Mrs. Bethuel Pugh and their brother Arthur Tansy came, all of whom were here about the close of the Revolutionary period — it would appear conclusive that they were all one and the same family, the father of our Hampshire Tansys being perhaps named Arthur, since that name comes down in both Pugh and Hiett families.

The descendants of the family who went south to North Carolina, like many of the Quaker Pughs, removed northward and westward, and some are now found in California: witness, L. Tansy Payne (a direct descendant of Leah, 1146 McKinley Avenue, Oakland.

(Promiscuous Pughs)

From Licking county, Ohio, History:

Thomas Pugh, non-commissioned officer and musician, September to December, 1861.

Albert Pugh, Volunteer Infantry, 46th Regiment, 1861.

W. D. Pugh, IOOF Lodge, No. 363, Hebron, Ohio, Charter member, 1861. Hebron is seven miles south of Newark.

Pughs of Old Frederick County Marriage Records

I found the following Pughs on eary marriage records of Frederick county, none of whom are known to be of the line of Hampshire's family. They are of the Azariah (Ellis Pugh) line doubtless, although the earliest of these marriages took place at Hopewell meetings, and are on the old Quaker records only.

John Hastings and Sarah Pugh, November 15, 1792.

Azariah Pugh and Elizabeth Rigle, by John Tildon, February 2, 1809.

Casper Rinker and Betsy Pugh, by S. O. H., February 28, 1811.

Adam Frank and Sarah Pugh, November 28, 1815.

These Pughs probably married non-Quaker communicants.

Old Land Transactions

November 2, 1762, William Owens from Peter Lehew, Deed Book 8, page 30.

October 4, 1763, William Pickering from Jesse Pugh, Deed Book 9, page 8.

October 5, 1784, Azariah Pugh to John Dillon, Deed Book 20, page 281.

October 7, 1784, Jesse Pugh from David Bedrick, Deed Book, 21, page 1.

June, 1789. Job and Jesse Pugh, Sr., to Ann Pugh; same date, Ann Pugh to Jesse Pugh; 1790, Jane Pugh from Jesse Pugh, Sr.; April 2, 1793, Jesse Pugh to Eli Pugh, Deed Book 23, page 701.

Then follows a page or more of transactions among the following: Michael, Thomas, Job, Jesse, Ellis, James and John

Pugh, 1803- to 1808; 1804, one from Thomas Pugh's heirs, Deed Book 28, page 366.

These are valuable perhaps only to include the Pughs as in the locality at these dates, there are later Pugh transactions givn at Winchester.

1937 — I have found that the above Pughs are the descendants of Jesse Pugh, son of Thos., son of Ellis. Jessie remained near Hopewell.

Dr. W. B. Pugh will give Lenten Talk

Dr. William Barrow Pugh of Philadelphia, stated clerk of the General Assembly of the Presbyterian Church in the U. S. A., will preach at the noon Lenten service in Old Stone Church Tuesday. Dr. Robert B. Whyte, pastor of Old Stone Church and president of the Cleveland Church Federation, under whose auspices daily services are held, will conduct the worship serv. ice.

As stated clerk Dr. Pugh is executive head of the Presbyterian Church in the U. S. A., which has 1,960,000 communicant members. Dr. Pugh became stated clerk last August on the retirement of his predecessor, Dr. Lewis S. Mudge.

Dr. Pugh since 1935 has been the American secretary of the World Alliance of Presbyterian and Reformed Churches, with which he has been active for many years. He was a delegated member of the Federal Council of Churches of Christ in 1932, 1934 and 1936, and since 1932 has been a member of the council's executive committee.

PART II

CHAPTER I

OFFUTT FAMILY OF MARYLAND

William Offutt, married Mary Brock, daughter of Ed. Brock, who settled in Calvert county before 1672. William Offutt died 1748.

Samuel Offutt, born April 19, 1712, married Elizabeth Burgess, daughter of Chas. Burgess, she was born November 15, 1714, died May 10, 1773. Samuel was the seventh child and fifth son of William Offutt. Samuel died May 5, 1761.

Nathaniel Offutt, born September 20, 1737, eldest son of Samuel and Elizabeth Offutt, married before 1761 Elizabeth Owen, daughter of Lawrence and Sarah Owen of Frederick county, Md., died probably in Hampshire county, Va., after 1790.

Children:

Samuel Owen Offutt, born October 18, 1760.

Elizabeth Burgess Offutt, born February 17, 1765.

Rachael ———.

Solomon, born 1776.

Samuel Owen Offutt, married Elizabeth Hite, born 1765, died 1845.

Elizabeth Burgess Offutt, married an Austin of Montgomery county, had a daughter, Sallie Austin, who married a Locker Jefferson county, W. Va.

Rachel, married Jas. Van Vector.

Solomon, married Elizabeth Roberts.

Children of Samuel Owen Offutt and Elizabeth Hite.

Sarah H. Offutt, born May 10, 1784, died July 11, 1821.

Jas. M., born February ———.

Elizabeth, born January 13 ———.

Nathaniel, born November 18, 1792.

Ann, born March 11, 1795.

Mary, born January 15, ———.

John H., born November 22, 1802.

Thornton F., born November 24, 1805. (Thornton, named for Thornton Washington, a friend).

Sarah H. Offutt, married Gilbert Gibbons, 1805, Gilbert died, 1826, Sarah 1821.

Emma Gibbons, born 1808, married, 1830, Benjamin Tomlinson (1805-1886) Emma died, 1872.

Mary Tomlinson, born, ———, married, 1880, Luke Strider of Charles Town, W. Va.

Emma Tomlinson Strider, born ———, Charles Town, W. Va.

I presume that Ann Offutt, born in 1795 and Mary Offutt, died young and that John H. and Thornton F. Offutt did not leave issue.

I understand that all the sons had left Charlestown by the time Samuel Owen Offutt, died in 1829.

Jas. Marion Offutt, born February ———, died Cumberland, Md., 1824, married Ruth Chenowith, April 27, 1806.

John Edwin, born December 9, 1809, Cumberland, Md., married Susan Lantz.

Louisa Offutt, born March 9, 1812, died, Hillsboro, Va., 1879, married, 1838, William Hough.

Susan Ann, born December 16, 1813, Cumberland, Md., married Amos Shepherd.

Jas. Wm., born January 16, 1816, Cumberland, Md., 1854, married Sarah Shepherd.

George Harris Offutt, born January 16, 1818, died about 1825, by second marriage to Matilda Ann Cressup.

John H. died before 1824.

Henry St. Geo. Offutt, born February 5, 1821.

Thos. probably died in infancy.

Elizabeth Offutt, born January 13, ——— died March 14, 1818, married ——— Grubb.

Elizabeth Ann, born May 14, 1812.

Jas. W., born November 3, 1814.

Samuel Owen Grubb, born October 28, 1816.

Nathaniel Offutt, born Nov. 18, 1792, married Margaret Fraser.

Nathaniel ——?

John Jas. Thornton.

Elizabeth E. married —— Nixon.

Johnathan F.

Samuel H.

Children of Jas. M. Offutt and Ruth Chenoweth:

John Edwin Offutt, born December 9, 1809, married Susan Matilda Lantz, died November 6, 1842. Their children were:

Daniel Edwin Offutt, married Belle Seymour.

Susan, married —— Miller.

Julia, married —— Legge of Oakland.

Thornton, ——.

Children of Daniel Edwin Offutt and Belle Seymour:

Daniel Edward; Ellwood; William R. married Mary Eleanor Humbird of Cumberland, Md.; Nelle; Bess.

Daniel Edward, married Karin ——, 1929, died, 1943.

Daniel Edward, III.

Ellwood, married Nannie Thomasson.

Seymour, Nelson, Belle. All married and have children.

Children of William R. and Mary Eleanor Humbird.

Fanny Belle Seymour married Albert Daub.

Mary Jane married Joshua Burton.

Helen Humbird married William Johnson.

Jacob Humbird married Helen Gosnell.

Louisa L. Offutt, born March 9, 1812, died 1879, married Wm. Hough of Loudoun Co., Va., July 16, 1838. Their children

William Florence, born January 14, 1839, died Sept. 4, 1840.

Estelle Louise, born Sept. 24, 1841, died June 19, 1880.

Thos. Edwin, born August 8, 1843, died July 16, 1902.

Jas. Henry Jos. born January 20, —— died Dec. 12, 1921.

Sara Eleanor, born August 7, 1852.

Jas. Henry Jos. married Elizabeth Hewlett, Dec. 30, 1886.

Helen Hewlett, born November 4, 1880.

195

Lanette Estelle, born March 10, 1891.

Henry Hewlett, born April 24, 1898, died October 9, 1914.

Helen H. Hough, married Percy Thos. Cleghorn, November 15, 1911.

Elizabeth Louisa, born November 3, 1912.

Elenor Hewlett, born January 4, 1915.

William Lodge, born August 26, 1921.

Elizabeth Louisa married Yancey Boone Smith, Sept. 12, 1939.

Don Cleghorn, born June 23, 1940.

Hewlett Yancey, born April 12, 1942.

Harriet Elizabeth, born March 16, 1945.

Wm. Lodge Cleghorn, married Patricia Lee Skivington, Aug. 26, 1944.

William John, born September 8, 1945.

Susanna Ann, born December 13, 1813, died 1873, married Amos Palmer Shepherd (1804-1875). Their children:
Jas Moses; Mary Ross, born 1844, died 1921; Louise Virginia, born, ———, died 1900; Chas. Eugene; Henry Palmer, Juliet, married E. T. Barton; Wm. Hough born 1846, died 1923; Lucius M.

Mary Ross married 1873, Lausen B. Wilson, (1843-1928).

Palmer Shepherd, born 1875, died 1914.

Lutalie Shepherd, ———.

Lutalie Shepherd married Dr. H. M. Hodgson. Their children: Margaret; Jas. Ross; Robert Lee; Helen L, Henry; Louise Virginia.

Wm. Hough Shepherd, born 1846, died 1923, married Sally Piatt. Their children: Louise, married ——— Burrell; Sue, married W. W. Williamson. Their children: Louise, married ——— Reed; W. W. Jr.

Lucius M., born ———, died ———; married twice. Children of these marriages: George; Chas.; Mary, married K. P. Heintz; Lucius.

James Wm. Offutt, born January 16, 1816, died about 1854, married Sarah Jane Shepherd (Sister of Amos Shepherd and daughter of Moses Shepherd and Mary Ross), June 5, 1838. Their children:

Francis Montgomery, born 1839, died 1905.
Mary Louise Scott, born 1840, died 1843.
Moses Shepherd, born 1843, died February 5, 1844.
Jas. W., died February 21, 1843.
Ross Julian, born 1845, died 1869.
Francis Montgomery, married Alice V. Seymour. Their Children: Mary Shepherd; Jas. Wm.; Chas Seymour; Sarah; Francis Montgomery.
Jas. Wm., married Maria Beatty Shepherd, daughter of Thos. Champe Shepherd. Their children:
Catherine married A. M. Elam; Jas W. Jr., married Helen Brady; Francis Alice, born, 1906; Chas Seymour; Robert Eugene; Eugene Wood, born, 1902; Champe.
Sarah married Eugene Harlan.
Betty — —— married. —— ——.
Frances Alice, born 1908, married Chas. Batchelder. Their Children: Chas. Ed.; Champe; Phoebe.
Jas. Marian Offutt married second time between 1818 and 1820, Matilda Ann Cresop, born 1797, died, Lancaster Co., Ohio about 1860, daughter of Thos. Cresop and Mary Briscoe. Their children: Thos. probably died young; Henry St. George; John H. probably died young.
Henry St. George, born February 5, 1821, died 1894, married Mary Ann Singleton, 1842. Their children:
Maria Eleanor, married first —— Locke, one child, Leila. second marriage to Isaac D. Barton. No children. Maria died, New York, 1931. George Washington; Henry; Alice, married —— Condit, no children. This family has died out entirely.
The Family of Samuel Owen Offutt, as given in this book complete is the work of two intelligent and capable genealogists of his line: Miss Emma C. Strider, Rhode Island Ave., Washington, D. C., and Mrs. Helen Cleghorn, P. O. Box 468, Stockton, California. Dates left out simply do not exist today. Mrs. Cleghorn did the compilation for the book.
The Cleghorns have a California farm and sometimes spend their winters in Hawaii. Miss Strider is connected with the

197

Library of Congress but they have for years been in communication on their Offutt kinship.

Of the Capon Bridge Offutts of this line see Book II, for Offutt-Nixons.

THE OFFUTTS OF CAPON BRIDGE AND SLANESVILLE
Whole Line from the Emigrant Ancestor.
(Some disagreement on dates)

William Offutt, born in Maryland in 1689, married Mary Brock. Died in Prince George county, 1748. They had ten children. The fifth child, Samuel O. (born 1712, died 1761), married Elizabeth Burgess. They had eleven children.

Nathaniel, the oldest, born 1737, married Elizabeth Owen. Their children were: Samuel Owen, married Elizabeth Hite; Elizabeth, Sarah, who married Austin; Anne, who married Joseph Van Vecter of Jefferson county; and Solomon, who married Elizabeth Roberts.

Samuel Owen, born August 18, 1760, died January 3, 1829, married Elizabeth Hite, settled at Charles Town. Children were: Sarah, married Gilbert Gibbons, died in Charles Town, 1821.

James Marion, who married, first, Ruth Chenowith, 1806; second Matilda Cressup. Moved from Charles Town to Old Town.

Nathaniel, "Uncle Natty", married Margaret Frazier and moved from Charles Town to Hampshire, near Capon Bridge, about 1820. Children: Elizabeth, married George W. Nixon; Children: Caudy Nixon of Capon Bridge and Eldridge. See Vol. II.

John James Thornton Offutt, born August 4, 1826, married Sarah Nixon, died 1886. George W. and Sarah were children of William Nixon. Children: William Nathaniel, Margaret (Mrs. (Dr.) Keckly), Dr. J. S., Anne M. (Mrs. Marion Ward), and Gertrude (Mrs. Cooper).

Dr. J. J. T. Offutt studied medicine as a side line while clerking in Chamberlin's store which was a part of the brick

Dr. John James Thornton Offutt,
Residence Capon Bride, W. Va.
First Postmaster for the village,
and physician for a large scope
of county.

DR. J. S. OFFUTT,
Capon Bridge. Beloved Country
Doctor, never married, devoted
his whole life to other people,
if he went to church he was not
allowed to stay for the service.
He slept in his chair, only, by the
week.

house now owned by Mr. A. L. Pugh, (1935) Capon Bridge. Later he entered the medical college then at Winchester and graduated there, and began his practice at Capon Bridge where he continued to serve the whole East End of the county as a successful physician until his death. He was also postmaster from pre-Civil War days until his death, and his descendants still hold the position, 1948. Before the Wards, Mrs. Margaret Offutt Keckley, wife of Dr. Keckley, served the people in that capacity. She was many years homemaker for her brother, Dr. J. S. Offutt.

Dr. J. J. T. Offutt's son, John Samuel Offutt, from boyhood, was his father's constant companion and helper, and learned to know all his father knew of medicine, but not satisfied with this he went to Baltimore and studied under the best medical men at that time to be found in the United States, graduating with high honors as physician and surgeon, and later in Special Courses on eye, ear and throat. He became, perhaps, the most loved and trusted physician and surgeon who ever practiced medicine in Eastern Hampshire County. He spent his whole life in their service, being called in emergencies far and near. The decision of Dr. J. S. Offutt was considered final. Often he was too busy to sleep or eat and sometimes never saw his bed for a whole week at a time, stealing a nap in a chair or on a couch to keep alive. He could have gone out into the world and made himself famous. He had a most engaging personality but preferred to work among the people he loved and who loved him. He never married. At his death it was found that he seldom had had time or inclination to make charges, or collect, so that his was indeed a labor of love.

Will Carleton's Old Country Doctor, which we append, is his fitting eulogy. Born 1864, died April 2, 1928. He lies buried at Capon Chapel Cemetery near the Bridge. Dr. J. S. Offutt numbered among his friends the famous surgeon, Dr. Kelly of Baltimore, Maryland, who was his last physician and who took time to write his eulogy which appeared in the Hampshire Review and other newspapers.

199

Mrs. Anne Ward, besides having the post office at Capon Bridge, was proprietor of the Moss Rock Inn, assisted by her daughters, Gertrude and Winifred. The youngest daughter, O'nile, was chosen as a Princess for the 1931 Apple Blossom Festival at Winchester, after which she fell ill and died. Mrs. Ward's daughters were all teachers. O'nile was teaching in Romney. The son, John, is in the banking business at Gore, Virginia.

Later: Mrs. Anne Offutt Ward died in a Winchester hospital from complications, February 21, 1936. Her sister, Mrs. Gertrude Cooper of Kansas, and William Offutt, besides her son and two daughters, surviving. Mrs. Ward's body was interred at Capon Chapel, the family burial place. Gertrude Ward of the Inn is now Postmaster at the Bridge.

See Vol. II for Nixon Caudy Connection.

This poem is given here as a tribute to the following country doctors who have served the people of Capon Valley long and well — Dr. John Monroe, Dr. James Monroe, Dr. A. B. Haydin, North River; Dr. Ed Beall, Capon Bridge, Dr. J. M. McKeever, Slanesville; Dr. J. J. T. Offutt, Capon Bridge; Dr. John S. Offutt, Capon Bridge; Dr. J. W. Shull, Pleasant Dale, and others.

For the Offutt Family, Vol. II of this work.

There's a gathering in the village that has never been outdone,
Since the soldiers took their muskets to the war of 'Sixty-One;
And a lot of lumber-wagons near the church upon the hill,
And a crowd of country people Sunday-dressed and very still.
Now each window is pre-emptied by a hundred heads or more,
Now the spacious pews are crowded from the pulpit to the door:
For with coverlet of blackness, on his stately figure spread.
Lies the grim old country doctor in a massive oaken bed.
Lies the kind old country doctor, whom the populace considered
With a mingled love and dread.
Maybe half the congregation, now of great or little worth,
Found this watcher waiting for them when they came upon
    the earth.

This undecorated soldier of a hard unequal strife,
Fought in many stubborn battles with the foes that sought
their life.
In the nighttime or the daytime he would rally brave and well
Though the summer lark was piping of the frozen lances fell.
Knowing if he won the battle, they would praise their Maker's
name,
Knowing if he lost the battle, then the doctor was to blame.
'Twas the brave old virtuous doctor,
'Twas the good old faulty doctor,
'Twas the faithful country doctor
Fighting stoutly, all the same.
When so many pined in sickness, he had stood so strongly by
Half the people felt a notion that the doctor couldn't die:
They must slowly learn a lesson how to live from day to day
And have somehow lost their bearings, now this landmark is
away.
But perhaps it still is better that this busy life is done:
He has seen old friends and patients disappearing one by one.
He has learned that death is master both of science and of art;
He has done his duty fairly and has acted out his part,
And the strong old country doctor and the weakened country
doctor,
Is entitled to a furlough for his brain and for his heart.

—Will Carlton.

THE WARD FAMILY

Children of John Ward, The First:

1. Elizabeth Ward, born October 30, 1776, married John
Butler, reported April 3, 1797.

2. Rachel Ward, born April 6, 1778, married Michael Fries.

3. John Ward, born October 20, 1779, married Isobel Gan-
throp, November 3, 1806.

4. Sarah Ward, born April 26, 1781, married Benj. Barrett,
June 8, 1801.

5. Joel Ward, born December 6, 1782, married Hannah Cannon, 1808.

6. Mary Ward, born March 6, 1784, married Abraham Rinehart.

7. Hannah Ward, born February 4, 1788, married Thos. McBride, 1808 and William Carpenter, February 16, 1825.

Children of Joel Ward:

1. Lydia Ward, born September 29, 1809, married Jos. Asbury.

2. John Ward, born June 10, 1811, married Polly Shivers.

3. Simeon Cisero Ward, born May 24, 1816, married Emma Bennett, May 16, 1850.

4. Reuben Ward, born September 15, 1818, married Elizabeth Ann Lupton.

5. Harriet Ward, born December 27, 1820, married Jim Russell.

6. Joel Nimrod Ward, born March 8, 1823, married Rebecca Lupton.

7. Mary Ellen Ward, born October 3, 1825, married Isaiah Lupton.

8. Mariah Ward, born November 11, 1828, married Thos. Russell.

9. Emily Ward, born October 17, 1831, married Thos. Everheart.

Ward and Bennett Family Register

Simeon C. Ward, son of Joel and Hannah Cannon Ward, was born May 24, 1816, died August 17, 1870. He was married May 16, 1850, to Emma E. O. daughter of James and Mary Brown Bennett; born October 15, 1826, died February 22, 1900. Children:

1. Ida Malissa, born February 22, 1851, died April 18, 1862.

2. Edgar Alonza Rightman, born August 2, 1852, died March 6, 1923.

3. James Marion, born April 21, 1854, died April 21, 1929.

4. Cornelia Gertrude, born May 8, 1857, died December 13, 1945.

Simeon Ward Home and Family

Above: The ancestral Ward home in Parks Valley, W. Va. Below: Marian
Ward and brothers and sisters arranged according to birthdates. Mrs.
Dora Brotherton, the only one now living, aged 86.

5. Minnetta Moore, born April 17, 1860, died September 19, 1864.

6. and 7. Hannah Ellenora and Mary Isadora, born November 16, 1862. Hannah Ellenora died December 24, 1933.

8. Emma Floretta, born August 4, 1865, died November, 1938.

James Bennett, born June 25, 1787, died July 10, 1883, aged 96. March 23, 1815, he married Mary Brown, born October 18, 1795. Children:

1. David Brown, born December 5, 1815, died May 20, 1837.

2. James Mortimer, born September 13, 1817, died February 1, 1852, aged 65.

3. Mary Helen, born February 14, 1820.

4. John Wesley, born February 5, 1822.

5. Isaac Newton, born April 6, 1824.

6. Emma E. O., born October 13, 1826, died February 22, 1900.

7. Cornelius Baldwin, born July 8, 1829, died March 26, 1890,

8. Theodore Mansfield, born November 14, 1831, died July 13, 1832.

9. Henrietta L. C., born March 25, 1834.

10. Susan J., born August 23, 1839.

Chamberlains of the Bennett ancestry came over in the Mayflower, and the great, great grandfather fought in the Revolutionary War and his son in the War of 1812.

The Edwards ancestry, wife of John Ward the First, was evidently of the Joseph Edwards, the Fort builder line. Israel Ward may have been the father of John but no proof of it is found.

Dr. Alonza Ward married Ella Oates. Children:

Geraldine, married Lawrence La Master, now deceased; two children: Marjorie and Larry.

Edith, married Moses Robbins; one child, Virginia May who is married and has two boys.

Gladys, married Scott Rush, no children living.

James Marion Ward married Anna Offutt; children:

Mary Gertrude.

John William Edgar.

Winifred Ross.

Odell O'Nile Offutt, born May 7, 1903, died May 15, 1930. See Offutt Family, this Volume.

Cornelia Gertrude Ward Coffroth's children:

Ward, married, has four children, Leroy, James, Louise and Fred. Louise, deceased, Ward and Louise were twins. Edith drowned. Gertrude, not married.

Nora Ward, never married.

Dora Ward Brotherton; no children. Nora and Dora, twins.

Emma Ward Barrett; one daughter, Thelma, deceased.

Ida and Minnie, two sisters who died young.

Joel Ward and wife, Simeon Ward and wife, and Ida and Minnie are all buried at the Quaker graveyard, Park's Hollow.

The Wards were Quakers, but some married "out of Meeting" Likely John the First and wife lie there also but buried before the engraving of stones began to known here.   —Maud Pugh

Direct Line of Capon Bridge Wards

John Ward, born September, 1745, died 1815; wife, Mary Edwards Ward, born January 14,1759, died September 3, 1844.

Joel, son of John Ward, born December 6, 1782, died July 19, 1864; married in 1808 (out of meeting) to Hannah Cannon; born January 10, 1785, died February 15, 1862.

Simeon, son of Joel Ward, born May 24, 1816, died August 17, 1870; married to Emma E. O. Bennett, May 16, 1850. She was born October 15, 1826, died February 22, 1900.

James Marion, son of Simeon Ward, born April 21, 1854, died April 23, 1923; married April 25, 1894 to Martha Anne Elizabeth Offutt, born February 28, 1865, died February 21, 1936.

My great grandfather Joel Ward seemed to have owned a great deal of land in Park's Hollow at one time. It was willed down the line to his children including Simeon. John and I were born at the old Ward Homestead of our grandfather Simeon. That place is now owned by Sam Park.

—Submitted by Gertrude Ward.

Ward Wills

Will of Israel Ward, 1779, was presented in court by Sylvester Ward and Thomas Brown, proved by David Miles and John Hogbine. Susanna was the wife of Israel Ward.

Will of Thomas Edwards, made February 8, 1786. Children: Thomas, David, Jessie, Sarah, Naoma and Margaret. Mary Edwards and Evan Hiett, executors.

Will of John Ward, made February 24, 1807; one-third to wife, Mary, and the rest to the children:

1. Elizabeth, born 1776, wife of John Butler.
2. Rachel, born 1778, wife of Michael Freeze. Ruth, granddaughter, adopted.
3. John, born 1779.
4. Sarah, born 1781, married, June 8, 1801 to Benjamin Barrett.
5. Joel, born December 6, 1782; married (out of meeting) to Hannah Cannon.
6. Mary, born March 6, 1784, wife of Abraham Rinehart.
7. Lydia, born 1786, died 1808.
8. Hannah, born February 4, 1788, married, 1808, Thos. McBride and, 1825, William Carpenter.
9. Ruth, married Thomas Allen.

Will of Joel Ward, 1858; wife, Hannah Cannon. Children:

1. Lydia, born September 29, 1809; married Joseph Asbury.
2. John, born June 10, 1811; married Polly Shivers.
3. Simeon Cisero, born May 24, 1816; married Emma E. O. Bennett.
4. Ruben, born September 15, 1818; married Elizabeth Ann Lupton.
5. Harriet, born December 27, 1820; married Jim Russell.
6. Joel Nimrod, born March 8, 1823; married Rebecca Lupton.
7. Mary Ellen, born October 3, 1825; married Isiah Lupton.
8. Mariah, born November 11, 1828; married Thos. Russell.
9. Emily, born October 17, 1831; married Thos. Everheart.

The Lemley-Ward Family Connection

Michel Lemle and Johannes Lemle (John Lemley when Americanized) came to Philadelphia, Pa., on the 20th day of October 1752 from Rotterdam, on the ship "Duke of Wirtemburg". Michel was the progenitor of the Pennsylvania and West Virginia Lemleys, and John was the progenitor of Virginia Lemleys. John came to Winchester, Virginia, and died there in 1784. He was a cooper and Innkeeper on Cameron Street, Winchester, and was one of the founders of the Evangelical Lutheran Church in Winchester in 1764.

First Generation:

John Lemley, died 1764, and Catherine Lemley.

Second Generation:

George, son of John and Catherine Lemley, died 1835; wife, Barbara Lemley.

Third Generation, their children:

1. Michael, married Rosanna Slusher.

2. Elizabeth (Betsy), married John Crider, November 29, 1797.

3. Margaret, married Jacob Gard, May 6, 1810.

4. John, married Susan Toy, October 29, 1811.

5. Jacob (1791-1874) married Elizabeth Hotzenpiller, December 24, 1818.

6. Catherine, married Thomas Chapman, October 20, 1820.

7. Sarah (Sally) married Joseph Hansell, September 26, 1822,

8. George married Ann Carver, October 27, 1827.

9. Susan Jane, married Joseph Miller, September 19, 1833.

Jacob Lemley was a wagon maker in Stephens City. In 1857, he with his son Harvey and his daughter Margaret Jane, her husband D. W. Henning and family, migrated to Missouri, settling near Macon and removing to Paris in 1859. Three more sons, George, Joseph and Robert followed in 1864 and settled in Quincy.

Fourth Generation, children of Jacob and Elizabeth Hotzenpillar:

1. George W., born December 29, 1819, died April 9, 1910; married Susan M. Ritenour, born 1826, died 1912.

2. James, born August 14, 1821, died February 1, 1899; married Mary A. Niswagner,born July 23, 1824, died March 26, 1903.

3. Margaret Jane, born April 22, 1823, died February 19, 1905; married David Wm. Hennings, born November 17, 1818, died October 11, 1899.

4. Jacob, Jr., born February 14,1828, died May 22, 1910, married Kathryne Hepner, born December 8, 1827, died September 24, 1910.

5. Harvey Augustus, born April 18, 1831, died February 11, 1915; married Sarah Jane Wilson, born March 4, 1834, died January 2, 1909.

6. Joseph T., born 1833, died 1919; married Fanny Snell.

7. Robert Davis, born 1836, died October 1, 1920; married Delia B. Rullerford.

8. Anne Katheryne, married John L. Drake.

Fifth Generation, children of Jacob, Jr., and Katheryne Hepner Lemley:

1. Elizabeth, married Jacob Carbaugh.

2. Joseph, married Mamie Kendall.

3. Jennie, married James S. Campbell.

4. Gertrude, married Boyd Hollingsworth.

5. Robert A., married Catherine Painter.

6. Gervis Franklin, married Martha Edmundson.

7. Catherine Mae, married W. D. Parker.

8. Dr. Clarence Edwin, died young.

9. Steward Preston, born 1868, died 1870.

10. Charles Davis, died 1873.

Sixth Generation, children of Gervis Franklin and Martha Edmundson Lemley:

1. Lewis Reginald, born June 27, 1891, died December 26, 1898.

2. Marvin Eldridge, born April 9, 1893, married Ruth Fries.

3. Gervis Edmundson, born October 10, 1895, married Bessie Orndorff.

4. Garland Winifred, bachelor, born September 24, 1897.

5. Clarence Edward, born January 29, 1900, married Catherine Fishpaw.

6. Clementine Virginia Lemley, born, December 29, 1901, married John W. Ward, banker, she is a teacher of languages in High Schools.

ELIZABETH ROBERTS OFFUTT
Born 1785, widow of Solomon
Offutt.

THORNTON OFFUTT
Youngest son of Solomon and
Elizabeth Offutt.

CHAPTER II

Descendants of Nathaniel Offutt,
born 1737, married Elizabeth Owen.

Solomon Offutt and wife—Bible Record

Solomon Offutt, born 1776 in Montgomery county, Maryland, died at his home near Slanesville, Virginia, February 7, 1848; was married to Elizabeth Roberts, April 6, 1804.

Elizabeth Roberts, born 1785 in Montgomery county Maryland, died at her home on the Offutt estate near Slanesville, West Virginia, September 13, 1870.

Children of this union:

1. Nancy Offutt, born January 15, 1805, died January 2, 1872. Married Jonathan Pugh, June 14, 1827; married to John Patterson, March 3, 1836.

2. Owen Osborn Offutt, born April 5, 1807, died March 1, 1848.

3. Sarah Offutt, born December 25, 1808, died May 26, 1880; married John N. Pugh, February 18, 1827.

4. Joseph Offutt, born November 14, 1810, died in Pekin, or Peoria, Illinois, soon after the Civil War. No children.

5. Rachel Elizabeth Offutt, born June 18, 1813, died May 1, 1896; was married to George R. Dye, April 9, 1833.

6. Mary Hester Offutt, born November 29, 1815; married George Milleson, I.

7. Harriett Offutt, born 1817, died in the west about 1870; married to David Gard. One son, William, died single.

8. James Offutt, born 1820, died December 27, 1827.

9. Zephaniah Offutt, born October 20, 1821, died April 9, 1848, married Eliza Haines, daughter of Daniel H. Haines, one child, Elizabeth who married Benjamin Haines. Grandchildren of Zephaniah Offutt. Children of Benj. and Elizabeth Haines, Slanesville, West Virginia, were: Mrs. Etta Nelson, Lee, William, Albert, Ashby, Orin, Mrs. Rose Carpenter and Katie Haines.

10. Thornton W. Offutt, born April 25, 1830, died May 12, 1907.

For history of Nos. 1 and 3, see Pugh History, chapters VII and VIII.

CHAPTER III

Solomon and Elizabeth Offutt

Solomon and Elizabeth Offutt acquired a large estate in a beautiful location on the Martinsburg Pike, near what is now Slanesville on "No. 45" Hampshire county, West Virginia. Stage coaches used to ply on this road and make connection with those from West to East and vise versa, on the North Western Turnpike, now U. S. 50. The stage coach was both passenger bus and mail train of its day. This road was also a thorofare for the covered wagon, too, which was both truck and freight train of the time, as well as emigrant train.

Vast numbers of hogs, cattle and sheep raised in the east in those days before the Civil War and great droves were seen passing on this road enroute to market. Did you ever see a drove of fat cattle? It is a most interesting sight. Can you imagine an excited mass of shorthorn, or Herefords, hundreds together with a colored man, pail in hand in front tolling the lead steer?

The owners, on prancing steeds with their colored boys and shepherd dogs, alert to every movement of the animals, careful that not a single one trespasses, goes astray, or is lost in forest through which the drove passes. Solomon and Elizabeth entertained the herdsmen and many a drove was fed and watered, and shut in for the night on the Offutt farm.

The coaches changed horses here too, perhaps. Besides the family help, the Offutts had colored servants. Theirs was a large house built of logs, part of which still stands today in good repair. The immense stone chimney with the great fireplaces are in perfect state of preservation and the one in the living room still open for use. The writer visited the place during the summer of 1934, and looked up this chimney, spreading her arms out on either side to get the width of the old fireplace. Mr. William Saville owns the nucleus of the

211

farm, and the house now. What a thrill was felt on entering this house after visiting the old cemetery and standing by the graves of Solomon and Elizabeth and that of their daughters, Nancy and Sarah, (the writers grandmother), their sons, Owen, Zepheniah and Thornton, and reading the epitaphs of their children's children and grandchildren and even great grandchildren, for the cemetery is filled with the kin only, and all the graves but two there, have engraved stones.

This plot, however, has but a handful of the descendants of Solomon and Elizabeth. They are scattered to the North and South, to the East and West, to many States, some have crossed the Pacific.

Will of Solomon Offutt

The Will of Solomon Offutt, among Romney Records, is dated September 25, 1834, probated March 27, 1848.

Wife, Elizabeth, first mentioned in the will. The farm to be divided into four sections, one to each of the following sons: Owen, one-fourth; Joseph, one-fourth; Zepheniah, one-fourth; Thornton, youngest son, one-fourth.

Daughters mentioned in the Will were Nancy Pugh (wife of Jonathan, 3rd), Sarah Pugh (wife of John N. Pugh), Rachel Dye (wife of George R. Dye), Hester Offutt (Mary Hester, later wife of George Milleson, I), Harriett Offutt (later wife of David Gard).

Executors, his sons, Owen and Joseph.

Witnesses: Nathaniel Offutt, (father of Dr. J. J. T. Offutt), Martin Fultz, Reuben Fultz (neighbors).

Owen Offutt died soon after his father.

Distribution and account from June 2, 1848 to October 17, 1849.

Heirs: John Pugh, George Milleson, George R. Dye.

Nationality of the Offutts

Miss Emma Strider, great, great granddaughter of Samuel Owen Offutt, brother of Solomon, says, "It is certainly interesting that you have the tradition that the Offutts came from Wales. An Offutt descended from James, son of William Offutt, the emigrant ancestor, also the descendants of Willam, son of William, have the same story. So wide a distribution among branches who have never known each other seems to make the truth evident, although there is no proof." Miss Strider is National Historian for D.A.R.

Ancestry of Elizabeth Owen, mother of Solomon Offutt and Others, and wife of Nathaniel Offutt.

The parents were Lawrence and Sarah Owen. The proof is in the Will of Lawrence Owen, probated in Frederick county, Maryland, May 5, 1761. Back of these we cannot go. Lawrence Owen was a vestryman in Prince George Parish, Frederick county, Maryland, from 1758 to 1761. This is from Emma Strider who says she has read about all the early Maryland Wills, in Offutt research.

Will of Elizabeth Roberts Offutt, Widow of Solomon.

Will Book 22, page 706, Romney, West Virginia:

To her son, Thornton, with whom she lived, or rather, who lived with his mother, at the time the Will was made, she gives one-third of her estate — others mentioned as follows:

Nancy Patterson (wife of John Patterson, (her second husband), Sarah Pugh, Rachel Dye, Mary H. Milleson, Harriett E. Gard.

To her granddaughter, Nancy Elizabeth Offutt, daugther of Zepheniah (deceased), ten cents.

To the widow of her son Joseph, ten cents.

She appointed her son-in-law, John Patterson, executor of her Will, which was dated April 2, 1866, probated October 4, 1870.

Children of Thomas and Rosana Pepper Dye
Solomon and Elizabeth Offutt—Rachel Offutt Dye Descendants

Don Charles, born in Taswell county, Illinois, July 27, 1862, died, 1927. Married Mary Hoover, February 28, 1888; religion, no church connection; politics, Democrat, changed to Republican; vocation, farmer and merchant; retired before he died. Residence: Oskaloosa, Iowa; Stockville, Nebraska, and Whittier,

California. Children: Adopted and raised four girls and one boy. Girls all went to college.

Mary Hoover, born 1864, died 1926; religion, Friend.

George Henry, born in Mahaska county, Iowa, August 24, 1864, died March 1, 1885. At the time of his death he was a junior in Penn College, Osakaloosa, Iowa. Single. Religion, Friend; vocation, student.

Laura Emma, born in Mahaska county, Iowa, December 21, 1866, died February 28, 1867.

Thomas Robert, born September 3, 1868, in Mahaska county, Iowa. Married Ida May Farmer, September 3, 1896. Religion, no church affiliation; politics, Republican; vocation, farmer, banker; residence, Sparta, Missouri. Ida May Farmer, born November 3, 1875; father, James Farmer; religion, Baptist. Children:

George W. Dye, born February 5, 1898, at Sparta, Missouri. Married Evelyn Monger, April 3, 1929; vocation, farmer; education, graduated Springfield High School; residence, Sparta, Missouri. Evelyn Monger, born March 29, 1907. Born to George W. and Evelyn Dye: Tommy Jo, February 20, 1932.

Mamie Dye, born April 30, 1900, at Sparta, Missouri; married Wayne W. Burrow, November 25, 1920. Residence, Springfield, Missouri. Education, Commercial School and graduate of Springfield High School. Wayne Burrow, born November 22, 1894; vocation, railway engineer. Born to Wayne and Mamie Burrow, Emma Lou Burrow, June 6, 1923 and Carrol Jean Burrow, July 28, 1928. Residence, Springfield, Missouri.

Fred R. Dye, born —— 11, 1902, at Sparta, Missouri; married Agnes Workman, March 23, 1931; residence, Sparta, Missouri; education, graduate Springfield High School; vocation, farmer. Agnes Workman, born July 12, 1904. Born to Fred and Agnes Dye, Roberta Mary, January 12, 1934.

Cora Alta Dye, born in Mahaska county, Iowa, January 1, 1871; married to Edward Lyman Anderson, February 18, 1890; religion, Methodist; politics, Republican; residence, Oskaloosa, Iowa. Edward Lyman Anderson; religion, Methodist; politics,

Republican; vocation, farmer, Truck Line; residence, Oskaloosa, Iowa; father William G. W. Anderson. Children:

Vida Rose Anderson, born April 25, 1893; married Othello A. Davis, Feb. 7, 1911, residence, Sheds, New York; education, Penn academy, Oskaloosa, Iowa; vocation, farmer; religion, Friend. Born to Vida and Othello Davis, Mildred Marie Davis, November 28, 1917.

Thomas W. Anderson, born November 11, 1896, in Mahaska county, Iowa; married Cleo Martin, July 1933; vocation, Truck Line; residence, Oskaloosa, Iowa.

Rose Jane Dye, born February 3, 1873 in Mahaska county, Iowa; married William A. Piersel, September 8, 1896; religion, Friend, politics, Republican; vocation, farmer's wife; education, A.B. Penn College, Oskaloosa, Iowa; residence, Grinnell, Iowa. William A. Piersel, politics, Republican; vocation, farmer; residence, Grinnell, Iowa; father, Eli Piersel. Children:

Roy Dye Piersel, born June 6, 1897, married Mabel Mitchell, November 1923; vocation, teacher; education, A.B. Penn College, Oskaloosa, Iowa. Graduate work, University of Iowa. Children: Tom Henry, born August 15, 1924 and Jene Ellen, born February 20, 1927.

Cora Alverda Piersel, born October 26, 1898, at Indianapolis, Iowa; married Joseph Franklin Lee, September 15, 1926; religion, Friend; residence, Grinnel, Iowa; education, B.A. Penn College, Oskaloosa, Iowa. Joseph Franklin Lee; vocation, farmer; residence, Grinnel, Iowa. Born to Joseph and Alverda Lee: Barbara Jo, May 10, 1934.

Zella Cope Piersel, born August 1, 1900; married Franklin Garfield Axmear, February 26, 1924; residence, What Cheer, Iowa; education, Oskaloosa High School graduate. Attended Penn College. Franklin Garfield Axmear, residence, What Cheer, Iowa; vocation, farmer. Born to Franklin and Zella Axmear: Roberta Rose, August 11, 1927.

Don Homer Piersel, born November 14, 1908; married Sarah I. Alberson, April 29, 1934; vocation, Auditor's departmental employee, Standard Oil Co., Des Moines, Iowa; education,

Oskaloosa High School graduate; attended Illinois University and Iowa University; residence, Des Moines, Iowa.

Maud Virginia Dye, born May 11, 1876, in Mahaska county, Iowa; married June 25, 1896, to William Smith; died October 21, 1903; religion, Friend; education, A.B. Penn College, Oskaloosa, Iowa; residence, Ackworth, Iowa. William Smith, born October 5, 1873, died February 14, 1908; religion, Friend; education, A.B., Penn College, Oskaloosa; politics, Republican; vocation, farmer; residence, Ackworth, Iowa. No children.

Homer Edgar Dye, born October 15, 1878, in Mahaska county, Iowa; married Florence Roe, November 4, 1903; religion, Friend; politics, Republican; vocation, farmer; education, Penn College Academy, New Sharon, Iowa. Florence Roe, born August 18, -1879; father, Abraham Roe; religion, Friend; politics, Republican; education, attended Penn College Academy, Oskaloosa, Iowa; residence, New Sharon, Iowa. Children:

Maxine M. Dye, born April 10, 1906, in Mahaska county, Iowa; religion, Friend; politics, Republican; vocation, University professor; education, A.B., Penn College, Oskaloosa, Iowa; M.A., University of Wisconsin and one year at Western Reserve University Law School; Cleveland, Ohio; residence, Akron, Ohio.

Martha Lois Dye, born February 15, 1908; married Emmett J. Thorp, November 1, 1930; religion, Friend; education, A.B., Penn College, Oskaloosa, Iowa; politics, Republican; residence, Grand River, Iowa. Emmett J. Thorp; father, Ulysses David Thorp; politics, Republican; vocation, farmer; residence, Grand River, Iowa. Born to Emmett and Lois Thorp, Jack Leigh, September 5, 1931.

James William Dye, a farmer, but later, lumber dealer at Wolcott, Indiana. Second son of George R. and Rachel Elizabeth Dye. Married Nancy Taylor, December 19, 1860. Three children were born of this marriage as follows: Edward Russell Dye, Charles Taylor Dye and George Dye. They adopted a daughter who took the name, Allie Dye.

James William Dye died January 24, 1905. Edward Russell Dye, now retired coal mine operator, living at Monticelo, Indiana, married Maud Britton and two daughters were born of them. Lou Eudora Dye and Edna Dye.

Lou Eudora married Russell Gardner and lives at 3236 Illinois Street, Indianapolis, Indiana. One daughter was born to this union. Her name is Susanne and is now living at home.

Edna Dye married Everett Gardner, brother to Russell Gardner, and they have no children. Home at Monticelo, Indiana.

Charles Taylor Dye, now retired, living at Lafayette, Indiana, second son of James William Dye, married Alice Johnson, and three children were born of this union as follows: James Dye, Charles Dye, and Lucile Dye.

James Dye, son of Charles T. Dye married Eudora Dye (daughter of Wilbur W. Dye) and have three small children, two boys and one girl. He is a lumber dealer at Hammond, Indiana.

Charles Dye, second son of Charles T. Dye, married ——, and from this union three children were born. (He is a lumber dealer at Lyde, Indiana).

Lucile Dye married a lawyer named Elmo Sturgess. Practicing law at Bluffton, Indiana. They have two children, one boy and one girl.

George Dye, third son of James William Dye, is a lumber dealer in Wolcott, Indiana. Married Mintie Irons and from that union five chidren were born; two boys and three girls:

Robert Dye, in lumber business at Wolcott, Indiana, with his father. Married Mary Jackson and has one son and one daughter.

Russell Dye, in lumber business at Monon, Indiana. Married Emma Hinkle and has one small child, a girl.

Letha Dye, teaching. Helen Dye, also teaching, Janett Dye, in college.

Offutt Descendants — Offutt-Dye

Sarah Elizabeth Dye, second daughter of George and Rachel Elizabeth Dye, born June 10, 1844, married November 28, 1866, to William H. Pepper (born April 21, 1839, died ——), member County Court — farmer, son of Henry and Rachel Pepper of North River, West Virginia. They were Democrats and Methodists. From that union there were the following children:

Edna Rachel Pepper, born August 21, 1867, died aged 14.

Hattie Jane Pepper, born January 28, 1869.

Rosella Viriginia Pepper, born April 19, 1870, died ———.

Henry Dye Pepper, born June 13, 1875, died ———.

Hattie J. Pepper, ———, 1892 married R. Lee Frye, of an early pioneer family, son of Benjamin and Mary I. Frye of Rio, West Virginia. To this union were born two daughters and one son as follows:

Inice, who married Reverend Strickler, pastor of a Lutheran Church, Norfolk, Virginia. They have two children, a boy and a girl.

Mary Frye, second daughter of Lee and Hattie, married Lloyd Foster, an orchardist at Waynesboro, Virginia, and they also have two children, and son and daughter.

Byran, Lee and Hattie's only son and the youngest, is a pharmacist, at home.

Rosella Virginia Pepper, July 20, 1885, married George William Billmyre at Cumberland, Maryand, Rev. P. N. Meade, rector of Emanuel Church, officiating. To this union two children were born: George William Billmyre and Ethel Billmyre.

George William Billmyre, son of George W., Sr., and Rosa V. Billmyre, was born June 27, 1888. He married Charlotte Cofad at Keyser, West Virginia, September 2, 1914, Rev. H. E. Baughman, the officiating minister. They reside in Cumberland, Maryland, where he is engaged in Business. They have two sons, Charles William Billmyre, born December 28, 1916, and Robert Blake Billmyre, born May 14, 1921. Rosa died, 1946.

Ethel, daughter of George and Rosella Virginia Billmyre was born April 11, 1892, died June 23, 1914, after a long illness, during which time the parents and friends gave full measure of their love to save her, but to no avail. She was a beautiful and charming girl who passed away at the age of 22.

George William Billmyre, the husband and father, died at their home in Romney, April 23, 1930, and he and the daughter,

Ethel, are buried in the family lot in Indian Mound Cemetery. George was amiable in disposition and thrifty in business. He loved the soil and owned a farm north of town. The Billmyre family were natural musicians. George W. was a violinist and as such, often participated in social function of his town.

Henry Dye Pepper, while away at school, married Rosa Richards, ———, daughter of Benjamin F. and Mollie E. Spangler Richards of Strasburg, Virginia. They began housekeeping at the ancestral Henry Pepper farm where they had one daughter, Ruth, the young wife suddenly died. The grandparents took the child. Several years later Henry married Allie Oats. Henry and Allie have the following children: Blanche, Lena, Russell, Ersul, Ruby and Rodney, twins. He died, 1948.

Allie, adopted daughter of James William Dye, married Ed Dibell. Had one girl who is a teacher. One son married, lives at Gary, Indiana.

George Russell Dye, third son of George R. and Rachel Elizabeth Dye. A farmer. Married Elizabeth Davis and to that union one son William and one daughter Mona were born. William married Mary Homan, daughter of H. C. Homan, and from that union two daughters and one son were born as follows:

Mary Elizabeth, George and Rosalea. All three now in college. They live at Renssalier, Indiana. William is retired.

Mona married Dr. C. P. Taylor, who is practicing medicine at Clarksburg, W. Va. They have no children. He is dead.

John Owen Dye, fourth son of George R. and Rachel Elizabeth Dye, married Mariah Millison, daughter of George and Mary Offutt Milleson. Had no children. Both dead.

Harriet Ann Dye, oldest daughter of George R. and Rachel Elizabeth Dye, married Enoch Bales, November 27, 1867, and from this union one son George O. Bales was born and married Ella Greggs. George was a very successful lumber dealer and at his death April 15, 1934, had controlling interest in fifteen large lumber yards. Had no children. At time of his death resided at Rensslaer, Indiana, at which place his widow lives.

Robert Wilson Dye, fifth son of George R. and Rachel Elizabeth Dye, married Lena Baughman, February 19, 1873. From this union three daughters were born as follows: Gertie, Edna and Mabel.

Gertie married Thomas Ritchie, have one son who is married but no children. Edna, second daughter of Robert Wilson and Lena Dye, married I. A. Weaver, who is a very successful inventor and manufacturer in Springfield, Illinois. Have one daughter, Cleo, who married John Carroll of Springfield, Illinois. Two small children born of this marriage, boy and girl.

Mabel, third daughter of Robert Wilson and Lena Dye, married G. A. Weaver, brother of I. A. Weaver, and is a partner in the very large manufacturing business, selling their products to every country in the world. They have no children. Robert Wilson and Lena Dye both dead.

Mary Hester Dye, third daughter of George R. and Rachel Elizabeth Dye, was not married and died at the age of twenty-seven.

Thornton Cass Dye, sixth son of George R. and Rachel Elizabeth Dye, reared on the farm until he was twenty-one, then engaged in the retail mercantile business, March 28, 1873, and was very successful in this business until April 1st, 1903, when he entered the wholesale grocery business, founding the Piedmont Grocery Company at Piedmont, W. Va., having branches part time at Moorefield, W. Va., and Petersburg, W. Va., at present have one branch at Oakland, Md. He married Sue Eudora Davis, February 26, 1878, and from this marriage five boys were born as follows:

Herbert Alroy Dye, born February 6, 1879.

Wilbur Wilson Dye, born February 26, 1881.

Robert Cass Dye, born March 18, 1883.

Thornton Charles Dye, born June 23, 1885.

David Vanse Dye, born September 18, 1891.

Herbert Alroy Dye, married Elizabeth G. Bernard, June 11, 1902, and five children were born to them as follows.

Herbert Alroy Dye, Jr., born May 8, 1903.

James Dye, born November 1904.

Ella Louise Dye, born May 11, 1906.

Margaret Elizabeth Dye, born May 9, 1908.

Thornton Cass Dye, born March 25, 1910.

Herbert Alroy Dye, Sr., married Jane Bowen. Two boys were born to them. Live at Winona Lake, Indiana.

James Dye, second son of Herbert Alroy Dye, Sr., died at the age of eight months.

Ella Louise Dye, eldest daughter of Herbert Alroy Dye, married Edward Hanley and have one baby girl.

Margaret and Cass both single at home with parents in Cumberland, Md. Wilbur Wilson Dye, second son of Thornton Cass and Sue Eudora Dye, married Veda Constable, October 26, 1904. Reside at Rockford, Ohio. Born to this union, Eudora Dye, born August 19, 1905. Married James Dye June, 1926. Have two boys and one girl.

Irene Dye, second daughter of Wilbur Wilson Dye is a teacher at Gibsonburg, Ohio. Robert Cass Dye, third son of Thornton Cass and Eudora Dye, single and at home with father, Piedmont, W. Va.

Thornton Charles Dye, fourth son of Thornton Cass and Sue Dye, married Hazel Bibie and have one son and one daughter as follows: Thornton Charles, Jr., and daughter Marjarie Dye, both at home with parents, Detroit Michigan.

David Dye, fifth son of Thornton Cass and Sue Eudora Dye, married Cora Hennicy. Three children were born to this marriage, one girl, Lauretta Dye, single and stenographer in an office in Detroit, one boy eighteen. The youngest boy in school, his name is Harold Dye. The father, David Dye, died on January 7, 1925.

Emma Frances Dye, fourth daughter of George R. and Rachel Elizabeth Dye, died single at the age of nineteen.

On April 1st, 1901, the mother of the five boys and beloved wife of Thornton Cass Dye, departed this life after having lived a consistent Christian life for thirty-one years in loving companionship with her husband.

On April 25, 1911, Thornton Cass Dye and Lottie Baldwin Cox Gumpf were married. Both died in 1948 at Piedmont, W. Va.

T. C. Dye, 89, Resigns as Head of Piedmont Grocery Company Was Oldest and Best Known Wholesaler in Tri-State Area

One of the oldest and best known men in the wholesale grocery business in the tri-state area retired this week with the resignation of T. C. Dye as manager and treasurer of the Piedmont Grocery Company, of Piedmont, W. Va.

Grocery Company, which applied for its charter in August, 1901,

Dye, now 89 years old, was a charter member of the Piedmont and was the first president of the company, of which Col. T B. Davis was vice president. At this time Mr. Dye was engaged in the general retail merchandise business at New Creek, W. Va., from which business he retired April 1, 1903, and became assistant manager of the Piedmont Company.

Following the retirement of Mr. Crooks in 1907, Mr. Dye was made general manager which position he held until August, 1919 when he resigned and accepted a position as city clerk and treasurer at Piedmont. In 1929 he was called back as general manager and treasurer of the Piedmont Grocery Company, which position he held until his recent resignation.

During the many years in the grocery business Mr. Dye made a host of friends and was well known among the wholesale grocers, canners and manufacturers.

—Reprinted from the Piedmont Times-News.

Bible Record of George R. and Rachel Elizabeth Dye

Thomas Wooten Dye, born May 14, 1834.
James William Dye, born March 28, 1836.
George Russel Dye, born August 10, 1838.
John Owen Dye, born March 25, 1840.
Harriet Ann Dye, born January 26, 1842.
Sarah Elizabeth Dye, born June 10, 1844.
Robert Wilson Dye, born September 5, 1846.
Mary Hester Dye, born October 19, 1848.
Thornton Cass Dye, born January 7, 1852.
Emma Francis Dye, born September 22, 1857.

Descendants of Solomon and Elizabeth Roberts Offutt.
Offutt-Milleson Family.

Mary Hester Offutt, daughter of Solomon and Elizabeth Roberts Offutt, was born November 29, 1815, at the Offutt

THE DYE BROTHERS

Front Row: Russell, James, Robert. *Back Row:* Jack, Thornton Cass

George R. and Rachel Elizabeth
Offutt Dye, married in Hamp-
shire, lived in Mineral County,
W. Va.

estate near Slanesville. She was of the blonde type, but more slight in build than her sisters. About 1837 she married George Milleson, son of John and Nancy Fletcher Milleson, both full blood Irish of near Slanesville. "Old Johnie Milleson" was known among the early settlers for his honesty and integrity, and his unflinching stand for what he considered right. Their sons, the Milleson Brothers, George and William, were large-boned and tall, and of the true Celtic type.

George and Mary began housekeeping and spent their whole lives at the ancestral Milleson home but in later years rebuilt the house. He was a prosperous farmer and stock raiser.

In 1856 before the county was divided, this George Milleson (his nephew, George Milleson, was later Sheriff) was a candidate for sheriff. In some parts of the county remote from him the inquiry was made, "Who is he?" The answer was, "A son of old Johnie Milleson" which seemed to settle the matter of his election, and following out his Milleson ancestry's notion of fairness, he appointed a deputy of the opposite political party for a district where the sentiment seemed to call for such action. This so incensed his own party at home that a mob of excited politicians "burned him in effigy". It seems that he did not recind his appointment but the writer has heard it stated that he was so disturbed over the matter that his hair turned prematurely grey in an nubelievably short time. Political sentiment ran high in those pre-Civil War days.

Children of George and Mary Milleson were:

Elizabeth and Ellen, who died in young womanhood, un-married. Owen, killed in the Seven Days' Battle around Richmond, 1863. Maria, who married John Owen ("Jack") Dye and also died without children.

Benjamin, who married "Fayme Young", relative of Mr. Young, county clerk, Allegheny county, Maryland. They had one son, Ernest Milleson, soon after whose birth the wife died, and not long after her decease, the husband also. Ernest, an attorney-at-law, resides in Baltimore, Cathedral St.

Caroline, married William Wills, son of Deacon and Ann Wills, as his second wife, the first having been a Miss Alkire, mother of Sude Largent, wife of Stump Largent. Caroline and William Wills had several daughters; the only survivors are Mayme Wills, unmarried; and Mrs. Bertha Dalton who resides in the Middle West — Later Mrs. Dalton died, 1948. J. M. on the home place is now deceased.

Mary Offutt Milleson outlived her husband several years. They both lie buried in the Old Milleson Family burying ground near the house, as do also William and Sarah Milleson, the parents, John and Nancy Fletcher Milleson, and the single daughters of Mary and George, and perhaps others whose stones are not engraved.

Descendants of Solomon and Elizabeth Roberts Offutt.

Thornton W. Offutt, youngest son of Solomon and Elizabeth Roberts Offutt, was born and grew to manhood on the Offutt farm known as the old plantation, surrounded by influences of the average home of a slave holder, but was taught to work and when left to his own resources to obtain a livelihood was entirely equal to the occasion. He and his wife, Sarah Snapp Offutt, who was daughter of John and Hannah Milleson Snapp, (sister of Silas Milleson), were both brought up on large farms and though opposites in temperament were one in intelligence and home-making. They reared a most interesting family, all of whom were a fine citizenry.

By the early death of Mrs. Offutt, the daughters, Virginia and Augusta fell heir to a large responsibility, but in a few years Virginia married leaving Augusta, aged twelve, as home-maker which she continued to be for some years and it is not strange that the father spent his last years in her home, he having, when left alone, sold his part of the old place.

Thornton Offutt died very suddenly in 1907, aged 77 years.

Thornton W. Offutt Bible

Marriages:

Thornton W. Offutt was married to Sarah C. Snapp on the 19th day of November, 1850.

Births:

Thornton W. Offutt was born April 25, A. D., 1830.
Sarah Catherine Snapp Offutt was born May 31, A. D., 1832.

Virginia Caroline Offutt was born May 27, A. D., 1852.
Robert James Offutt was born June 27, A. D., 1854.
John Patterson Offutt was born May 5, A. D., 1857.
Joseph McKeever Offutt was born March 20, 1859.
Augusta Isabel Offutt was born August 2, 1862.
Margaret Ellen Offutt was born October 30, 1867.
Henry Leonidas Offutt was born August 13, 1871.
Deaths:
Solomon Offutt departed this life February 7, A. D., 1848.
Elizabeth Offutt, wife of Solomon Offutt, departed this life
September 13, A. D., 1870.
John Patterson Offutt departed this life March 16, A. D.,
1875.
Thornton W. Offutt, Sr., departed this life May 12, 1907,
aged 77 years, 17 days.

John Patterson Offutt, named for the second husband of
his aunt Nancy and who was a promising young man was
suddenly taken by death, aged 18.

Virginia Caroline Offutt, eldest daughter of Thornton W.
and Sarah Snapp Offutt, born at the old home near Slanesville,
May 27, 1852, married, 1874, Asa Moreland, son of David
and Priscena Spaid Moreland (born on Capon, September 24,
1851, died December 21, 1903). They removed to Kansas
City and Mr. Moreland was a "Knight of the Train and Track"
passenger conductor for nearly forty years. In a railroad
accident he lost a foot, then bought a farm in Missouri, near
Kansas City and later, while traveling, was killed in a railroad accident, 1903. After his death, Virginia moved back to
Kansas City where her children lived. Children:

Cora Maryland Moreland, born January 3, 1875.
Pearl Edith Moreland, born August 6, 1877.
Osceola K. Moreland, born September 16, 1879.
Floyd Emory Moreland, born January 16, 1882, died June
11, 1911.
Edna L. Moreland born, May 2, 1886.
Roy Spangler Moreland, born January 5, 1891.
Cora M. Moreland married Clarence Been, salesman, Kansas
City. Children:

Fred Been, June 22, 1900, printer.

Floyd Been, September 5, 1902, Postal Department, Union Station.

Pearl Edith Moreland married Reed Storms, a foreman of iron works, Kansas City. Three children:

Flora, born September 3, 1897.

Pearl, born August 11, 1902.

Claud, born July 19, 1911.

Osceola K. Moreland married Theresa Whalen. He is yardmaster for Kansas Railroad; lost an arm by accident; no children.

Edna L. Moreland married Lester Bolton, farmer. They live on a ranch in Delhart, Texas; no children.

Roy S. Moreland married Gertrude Hughs of Kansas City where they reside. He is a salesman. They have one son: Roy S., Jr., born July 2, 1914.

Robert Offutt, the oldest son of Thornton and Sarah, married Mary Elizabeth (Lizzie), daughter of Thomas F. and Sarah Loy Largent of Slanesville. They lived on a farm near Romney and four children were born to them, two daughters and two sons. A sudden illness siezed Robert and this happy home was broken up. The writer visited them while the children were small, and it was in this home that Ex-Governor Cornwell passed his first term as a teacher in a country school near by. He crossed the run with the children on a log but this was not new to him. He had gotten his education in a country school and had crossed many a stream on a log. When Robert's granddaughter excelled in 4-H and High School work he was the first to congratulate her and recount his early friendship for the family.

After the death of Robert Offutt, his wife, resourceful and energetic, removed to Slanesville where she went in as telephone exchange operator, making herself useful and popular. She still lives at Slanesville, and has been a valuable helper in this work, — urges me to hasten. She desires to live to see it in print. Mrs. Offutt is now eighty-five but mentally sound and alert. Robert Offutt died November 1, 1891, aged 37 years, 4 months and 4 days; buried at the Offutt Cemetery.

Family Record

Mary Elizabeth Largent, born November 16, 1851. Married to Robert Offutt, November 23, 1875. Children:

Bertha Selma Offutt, born September 11, 1876 and married C. W. Alkire, June 20, 1897. They have nine children.

Mary Pearl, born February 1, 1898, and married Forest W. Harrison, December 19, 1920. One Child, James Cecil.

Hetzel H. born December 20, 1899, and died May 31, 1900.

Cecil Edward, born April 15, 1901, and married Elsie M. Robey, November 19, 1922.

Forest William, born July 25, 1903, and married Myrtle Eye, November 19, 1934.

Harry Lynn, born April 17, 1906.

Theodore Alfred, born May 13, 1908.

Virginia Josephine, born October 20, 1910, married Harold F. Wills, February 28, 1931 and again married James Riley, April 15, 1933.

Golda Evelyn, born December 19, 1915.

Mabel Elizabeth, born October 27, 1918.

Edith May Offutt, born August 12, 1878, married T. D. Bloom, January 20, 1895. There are ten children.

Alta Elizabeth, born March 23, 1897, and married Fred Snyder, June 30, 1931.

Beulah Beatrice, born February 26, 1899.

Elbert Clyde, born August 14, 1900.

Zelda Iola, born September 23, 1902, and married H. W. Kidwell, July 20, 1922. Two children, Edwin Lyle, and Xyla Inez.

Gail Offutt, born September 28, 1904, and married Vara Sneathen in 1928. One child, Kyle Keith.

Kester Dent, born December 15, 1906, and married Gertrude Snyder, February 24, 1926. Two children, Kester Dent, Jr., and Ralph Kenneth.

Lovell Loy, born May 31, 1908.

Orville Lloyd, born August 21, 1911, and married Juanita Saville, December 26, 1929. One child, Elmo Lloyd.

Thomas Xen, born December 8, 1915.

Dennis Boyce, born August 3, 1919.

Howard Gilbert Offutt, born August 26, 1888, and died June 9, 1889.

Harley Thornton Offutt, born March 5, 1890, and married Ella Rhodes, July 17, 1912. Three children, Wallace Harley, Wanetia Elizabeth, and baby.

Mrs. Mary Elizabeth Offutt Expires at Slanesville

In the early morning of January 23, 1941, at Slanesville, an all-wise Father called to her reward our dear grandmother, Mrs. Mary Elizabeth (Largent) Offutt,. Her husband, Robert Offutt, preceded her in death more than fifty years. She was the daughter of Thomas Largent and Sally (Loy) Largent and the last survivor of a large family. One brother, Stump Largent, of Slanesville, passed away August 28, and about two weeks later her last brother, Alfred Largent, of South Solon, Ohio, died. She was a life-long resident of Hampshire county. She was eighty-nine years of age.

A short but impressive service was conducted at the home by Rev. J. O. Patterson. Interment was in Salem Cemetery by the side of a brother. The floral offerings were many and beautiful. The following grandsons were pall bearers: Forrest, Harry and Theodore Alkire, Clyde Gail and Kester Bloom.

Survivng are two daughters, Mrs. Bertha Alkire, Petersburg, and Mrs. Edith Bloom, Slanesville, and one son, Harley Offutt, Akron, Ohio. Twenty grandchidren, sixteen great grandchildren and many other relatives and friends also survive.

Children of Thornton and Sarah Snapp Offutt:

Joseph McKeever Offutt, known to his friends as "Mac", son of Thornton and Sarah, was educated for a teacher and was later teacher, farmer and fruit grower. Present residence No. 12, Bolton Street, Romney, West Virginia. He owns a farm and apple orchard on the State Road, near Augusta. With this and the supervision of the welfare and education of a large family he has found time for church work and sometimes supplies for the minister in charge in the pulpit. He is a Methodist and a Republican.

In 1879, J. M. Offutt and Eliza Shorb united their fortunes. Besides being a charming person she has been a worthy partner. They have a most remarkable family whose intelligence and ability have reached out to many professions. Later: J. M. Offutt died December 23, 1932 and was buried in the family lot at Salem Church Cemetery near Slanesville, West Virginia. Mrs. Offutt continues to reside at Romney.

Joseph McKeever Offutt Family

Ethel Evangeline Offutt, married Clarence W. Woolford; living at Alaska, West Virginia. Their children were educated in Allegheny High School, Cumberland, Maryland.

Edna Verona Offutt; education, Shepherd College State Normal, graduate; West Virginia University, A.B. Graduate; University of Boulder, Boulder, Colorado; George Washington University, Washington, D. C.; occupation, teacher.

Beulah Viola Offutt; education, Shepherd College State Normal; Catherman's Business College, Cumberland, Maryland; Strayer's Business College, Washington, D. C.; Montefiore Hospital Training School for Nurses, Graduate Nurse; occupation, Supervisor, Fifth Avenue Hospital, New York City.

Hobart McKinley Offutt, Romney High School; occupation, American Tea Company, Winchester, Virginia.

Nellie Fern Offutt, Romney High School graduate; Marshall College, A.B.; Graduate Columbia University; member Kappa Delta Phi, Honorary Education Fraternity; occupation, teacher of commercial subjects, Martinsburg High School.

Vernon Delmas Offutt, Romney High School; graduate West Virginia University, B.S.; graduate Medical College of Virginia at Richmond Virginia; member Tau Kappa Epsilon, Social Fraternity, and Phi Beta Pi, National Medical Fraternity. Later: Now practicing medicine in Richmond.

Ennis died at the age of eight years and lies in the family lot at Salem Cemetery near Slanesville.

Augusta Isabelle Offutt, second daughter of Thornton and Sarah Offutt, married Jethro S. Watson, of Three Churches, West Virginia, where they lived during Mr. Watson's life time on a farm. The Watsons are descendants of early pioneers and among the most substantial of our citizens.

These proud parents of sons, started them in life as teachers, knowing that that profession is the best foundation for life's work. It is in every way disciplinary.

When war broke out James Watson was principal of a graded school in McDowell county, West Virginia. Anticipating the draft he resigned and took Naval employment at Norfolk Navy Yard where he remained until the war was over. He fell ill and was operated upon, after which sleeping sickness set in. He returned home but died from the disease.

Edgar B. Watson married Ethel Johnson of Greensburg, Pa., September 27, 1924. They have one daughter, Ethelyn Lucille, born May 19, 1928. Edgar and wife live at Greensburg and the mother, Mrs. Watson, who is not in good health, is with them at this time.

Paul V. Watson married Catherine Radcliffe of Ridgeley, West Virginia, June 1, 1933. Their one son is named James Hubert, born March 22, 1934.

Watson Offutt Family Record.

Marriages

Jethro Scott Watson and Augusta Isabelle Offutt were married September 7, 1886.

Births

Jethro Scott Watson was born November 28, 1853.

Augusta Isabelle Watson was born August 2, 1862.

Infant son of Jethro S. and Augusta I. Watson was born July 23, 1890.

James Offutt Watson, Jr., was born October 19, 1891,

Jethro Scott Watson, Jr., was born February 19, 1896.

Edgar Bell Watson was born July 19, 1897.

Paul irgil Watson was born June 7, 1904.

Deaths

Infant son of Jethro S. and Augusta I. Watson departed this life July 23, 1890.

Jethro Scott Watson departed this life July 8, 1919.
James Offutt Watson departed this life December 23, 1921.
Augusta Isabelle Watson died 1944, at the home of a son.
Margaret Ellen Offutt, third daughter of Thornton W. and
Sarah Snapp Offutt, born at the old Offutt home, October 30,
1867; married about 1895, Edward P. Hiett, second son of
Jonathan and Mary Arnold Hiett. Margaret's life has been
one of anxiety and serious responsibility. One son was born
to them, Roy Hiett, intelligent and of fine physique, aged about
forty, with whom Mrs. Hiett now resides, 316 N. Negley Avenue,
Pittsburgh, Pennsylvania, she died October 11, 1938, at Pittsburgh, buried at Salem Cemetery, October 16.

H. "Leon" Offutt, the youngest son of Thornton W. and
Sarah Snapp Offutt, after his mother's death, was brought up
by Mrs. Phoebe Snapp Haines, an aunt residing near Wardensville. Reaching young manhood he became a B & O R. R.
employee in the Passenger Department, Cumberland and
Baltimore, and is now retired. He married Miss Mamie Bissett
of Baltimore. They have three children: Ethel, Thelma and
Marvin, all married and living in that city. Leon resides in
a suburban residential section of Baltimore, Maryland.

In closing the Offutt History, I wish to say the Offutts are of
Welsh descent and have intermarried with Welsh, Irish, German
and English and other peoples of the very best families. They
are not a military people nor a people who seek political office but they are religious, intelligent, industrious and thrifty.
Some of them are Democrats and some are Republicans, some
Friends.

THE MILLESON FAMILY
County Meath (?) Ireland

John Milleson, born in Ireland, came to America soon after
the Revolution or about that period, bought land from William
Reeder and wife, and others, and settled near a big spring at
the foot of Spring Gap Mountain, northwest of what is now
Slanesville. This tract of land remained in the possession of the
family as a whole until about the close of the 19th century, at

the death of the great-great-grandson John, the part owned by him was sold and went out of the family.

John Milleson, Sr., we are told, was a man of high standing among the early settlers, as was also his wife whose name we have been unable to learn, but he evidently married her in the Emerald Isle and the older sons were likely born there. The sons were: John, Jr., Benjamin Taylor, Isaac, and Jesse. (Romney Records.)

John, II, the oldest son married Nancy Fletcher, daughter of George Fletcher and sister to Elijah Fletcher, who, January 30, 1826, married Elizabeth Queen (daughter of John Queen), and sister of Mary Fletcher who married Jacob Ullery, the Ullerys were parents of Mrs. Nancy Michael, mother of Squire G. T. Michael, now of Winchester, 1936. Elijah Fletcher died, aged 101 years, 1 month and one day. John and Nancy lived at the Big Spring.

They had two children, George and William Milleson, and the parents divided the old Spring Gap farm of several tracts between them, George taking the northwest division and Willian, the home tract at the spring. John, II, died December 23, and was buried Christmas day, 1848, and Nancy died, 1863. He was about 68 and she was 81.

George Milleson married Mary Offutt, daughter of Solomon and Elizabeth Roberts Offutt. They built a new house and lived and died at this farm. George was a prosperous farmer and stock raiser, and acquired considerable wealth. He also took an interest in politics and was elected Sheriff for Hampshire county prior to the Civil War. This was before Mineral county was cut off from Hampshire and several deputies were required; as the western section was largely of a different political faith he appointed a deputy for that section who was not a Democrat. As feelings ran high at that period his own section of the county being Democratic was highly incensed at this action, even to the point of burning him in effigy. Nevertheless, he went on on with his duties and completed his term. His nephew, George Milleson, was one of his deputies and received his first political and official experience under his uncle George. Aunt Mary was

232

Mrs. Nancy Fletcher Milleson
Wife of John Milleson II, and great
grandmother of the author.

thrifty and out-spoken, and they were hospitable. Old Salem Church was built on an adjoining farm to the Millesons, 1839. Children born to George and Mary Offutt Milleson were:

1. Elizabeth Milleson, died early without heirs.

2. Owen Milleson, single; was killed in the Battle of Seven Pines; Civil War, in Confederate service.

3. Ellen Milleson, died in the bloom of young girlhood, single.

4. Benjamin Milleson, married Fayme Young of Cumberland, Maryland, a handsome and magnetic pair who died young. They left a son, Ernest Milleson, of Baltimore, an attorney-at-law.

5. Caroline Milleson, married William Wills, second wife; Children: Mayme, and Mrs. Bertha Dalton, survivors.

6. Maria Milleson, married John Owen Dye, first cousin, late in life. No children. They were prosperous farmers, living in Mineral county. Both tall, fair, brown hair, and blue eyes.

7. James M. Milleson, never married.

Nancy Fletcher Milleson, outliving her husband many years, spent her declining period of life with George, and took a lively interest in their family welfare. She is buried near the house in the graveyard on that farm, as are her husband, her children and their wives and others; perhaps the first John Milleson and wife and maybe the Reeders, who were among the first owners of this colonial tract according to an old deed on record at Romney.

William Milleson, second son of John, II, and Nancy Fletcher Milleson, grew up at the old home and married Sallie Henderson, daughter of Elizabeth and George (?) Henderson, born in Ohio. She had one whole sister also born in the state of Ohio, who married a man named Bratton and lived in, or near, Cambridge, Ohio. The mother married, for her second husband, Joseph Stern, Homer, Ohio.

William and Sarah Henderson Milleson had the following children: Nancy, John III, Benjamin, Elizabeth, George, and Elias. While the children were yet small, William Milleson, the father, was injured by a fall on ice that brought on his untimely death, and the mother managed with the assistance of her son,

John, to bring them all up and to educate them in the rudiments of learning supplied in the early schools before the Civil War. For Nancy Milleson, see Ullery Family, Vol. II.

The Milleson Family

Relatives in Ohio—Joseph and Elizabeth Stern

Elzabeth, born April 8, 1787, married George (?) Henderson, Ohio; died at Homer, Ohio, February 8, 1869. Children: Mrs. Bratton of Cambridge, Ohio, and Sarah, who married William Milleson, son of John and Nancy Fletcher Milleson (See descendants of John and Nancy Fletcher Milleson.)

Second marriage, Joseph Stern, Homer, Ohio. Their children: John, James, Frank, Eleanor, and Mary Stern.

John married and went to California where they brought up a family.

James, who visited Mrs. Milleson twice in West Virginia, married Ellen and lived in Ohio, Delaware county, good citizens, prosperous framer.

Frank married and went to Montana where his descendants live.

Eleanor married Thomas P. Larimore whose ancestors were from Hampshire county, Virginia. She was his first wife. She died February 12, 1862, aged 39 years, 10 months and 9 days. He was a leading citizen of his community. Residence, Homer. Thomas P. Larimore, born July 19, 1819, died September 20, 1883, Licking county, Ohio. Their children were: Sarah, Gill, Frank, Joe, and Newlon.

Sarah Larimore, born 1855, died 1923; married Thomas Patton, born 1884, died 1909.

Sade Patton, as she was fondly known to her friends, was full of the joy of living. She traveled much and saw most of the worth-while places in America; also, some of its World's Fairs. Her fine needlework and painting on china took premiums at the Columbus State Fairs, but so did her cookery, and she could use a hay fork at the barn if need be, or drive a team.

Mrs. Patton was a Presbyterian and an active church and social worker, not for society's sake but because she was intensely interested in religion and her fellow beings. Her influence as a prohibitionist was felt throughout the community where she lived. On one occasion when she had entertained the Larimore-Hawkins Reunion, an organization of several hundred people of all ages from many states besides her own, a friend called in by wire next day to sympathize, knowing the work such a meeting would make. Mrs. Patton's magnetic, cheerful voice was heard to respond, "You were the nicest people I ever saw! We just burned a few papers this morning and swept, and everything is all right."

The writer, a distant cousin, knew and loved her as of the same family. She was one of the rare, fine people we meet in a lifetime, and left deserving children, Reese, Cliff, and Ruth, all of Licking County, Ohio.

Bible Record of Thomas and Sarah Larimore Patton, and their descendants.

Born to them:

Reese Lee, February 28, 1883.

Clifford Carson, April 6, 1885.

Hazel Ruth, September 26, 1887.

Reese L., married Edith I. Hawkins, November 6, 1912. Children: Gerald Verner, born January 21, 1915. Graduated at Homer, Ohio, then attended college in Cleveland two years.

Harold Kenneth, born May 1, 1917. Graduated at Homer, Ohio, 1935.

Leo Clifford, born April 6, 1919. Graduated at Homer, Ohio, 1936.

Joseph Alton, born November 8, 1921. Second year High School.

Sara Anne, born November 30, 1924. Eighth grade (1936).

Clifford C. Patton married Dorothy Smoots, 1915. Born to them: Jean Clifford, April 14, 1920. Clifford C., died February 9, 1920.

Hazel Ruth Patton married Guy L. Shrider, November, 1905.

Born to them: Willard Eugene, July 30, 1914. He graduated at Ohio Wesleyan, Delaware, Ohio, June, 1936.

This family, Independent in politics — Prohibitionists and Presbyterians.

MARY STERN WILLIS

Mary Stern, born 1827, died 1912; was of the type that lives for others. She remained single until late in life to care for her parents, one of whom became totally blind, and both lived to be old. She was born and spent her entire 85 years as a citizen of Homer, and everybody there called her "Aunt Mary." She was a tailor by trade. Aunt Mary was not beautiful of face but beautiful in character and held a very high position among her townspeople. She had been sobered by the cares of life and had a dignified bearing, beneath which all rcognized a warm heart.

At the Larimore-Hawkins Reunion of the kin, Aunt Mary occupied a seat of honor, but her modesty, equalled her other good qualities.

After the death of her parents, when she had passed middle life, she married Jenkins Willis, who died after a few years. She was again alone but Sade Patton and "Newl" Larimore tenderly nursed her in her last days. She was their mother's full sister and seemed nearer because their mother was long since deceased, she lies in the same lot with her parents at Homer.

John Milleson, oldest son of William and Sarah Milleson, married, March 20, 1866, Sarah C. Moreland, daughter of Bazil Moreland, born February 18, 1839, died March 6, 1905. Mr. Milleson died several years later. He had married rather late in life, having assisted his widowed mother on the farm in bringing up the younger members of the family and stayed with her during the ravages of Civil War, no better people than this pair and Sallie Milleson with brown eyes and black hair was the soul of kindness.

John and Sallie remained on the old farm at the big Spring, brought up their family there and are buried at the Salem Cemetery. She was a member of the Salem M. E. Church, South.

MARY STERN WILLIS
The beloved "Aunt Mary" of
Homer, Ohio. Great Aunt of the
writer.

At the death of John Milleson the old farm went out of the Milleson family, having been held by them to the fifth generation. Children:

1. William Milleson, born 1867, married Sallie Haines. See Milleson-Snapp Family. William, quiet and dignified, a favored cousin of the writer, they have a daughter, Mabel, Mrs. Browning — infant son died; William died, 1943.

2. Carrie, born September 12, 1868, died August 8, 1913; married John Kidwell; lived near Paw Paw, then near Martinsburg. Children: David, a graduate of Yale, and Christian minister; and Belmont, orchardist and church worker at Martinsburg. "Carrie was a beautiful woman of fine character with children worthy of parents." (See the Kidwell Family.)

3. Susie, born July 2, 1871, married, July 22, 1914, George Seeders. They are good citizens living near Green Spring. Susie cared for her parents in their last illness. No children, but she loves Carl Seeder's foster son as her own, they have also his daughter Mayme Banksdale and charming family.

4. Charlie Milleson, born September 7, 1873, married Nannie Power, daughter of Rev. Power of the Baptist ministry. He is a carpenter. They reside in Cumberland, Maryland. Children: Forest married Lorena Yergin, Beall married Florence Parish; Grantha married Wm. Rollin, the youngest is at home. — 1937.

5. Bettie Milleson, born September 28, 1875, died July 18, 1935; married Joseph Milleson, son of Benjamin and Elizabeth Engle Milleson. See another page of this book.

Nora M. Milleson, daughter of John and Sallie C. Moreland Milleson, born April 12, 1878, married Asa H. Easter, son of Wesley J. and Margaret Alderton Easter.

They lived for many years at Shenandoah Junction, West Virginia, where Mr. Easter was an employee of the B. & O. R. R.; later they removed to Martinsburg where he and the children are employed, all three as yet unmarried, an interesting family. Children:

1. Homer W. Easter, born January 14, 1909.

2. Letha Easter, born August 8, 1912.

3. Elvy Easter, born August 24, 1917.

Wesley J. Easter, born August 16, 1812, died 1894.

Margaret Alderton was born February 7, 1828, died 1870; they were married June 10, 1856. Asa H. Easter was born February 7, 1870.

Benjamin Milleson, born 1832, son of William and Sarah Henderson Milleson, married Elizabeth E., daughter of John and Sarah Cooper Engle, 1863. He was a confederate Veteran, Company F, 7th Virginia Cavalry, known as Capt. Sheet's Company.

Captain George F. Sheets was killed, May 23, 1862 and was succeeded in command by Isaac Kuydenhall of Springfield, also a brave officer. This Company has gone down into history as one of the bravest and most daring in the whole struggle.

Mr. Milleson was one of the few who came out of the war unhurt, but his wife lost two of her brothers, Samuel C. and J. Holland Engle, both of whom enlisted with this Company. Mr. Milleson died, aged about 65, but Mrs. Milleson lived many years longer, till 1923. Their home was a farm near Slanesville, West Virginia, and they both lie buried at Salem Church Cemetery, one of the most beautiful in the county. Children: Sallie B., William, George Benjamin, Joseph M., and Mary M. (Mamie), Charles C., and Samuel H. The last two died in infancy.

1. Sallie B., began life as a teacher. She was tall and had all the Milleson characteristics and an attractive personality. She married John Portmess whom she met in school work, but the dread disease, T.B., cut short their happiness. Their residence was near Three Churches. Children: Faye Marie married John Hill, merchant and business man of Charles Town, Roger and Ira Portmess, Vienna, Va.

Portmess-Hill Record

John Portmess married for his first wife Sallie Milleson, daughter of Benjamin and Elizabeth Engle Milleson, she was a teacher, and lived only a few years. Their children were: Fay, — Marie, Ira, and Roger, still living.

Fay Portmess, born August 11, 1896, married May 5, 1917, John W. Hill, born December 18, 1881. Children:

Josephine Lenore Hill, born March 5, 1919, married Harry E. Ott.

John Wm. Hill, born August 21, 1921, was killed in action, October 16, 1943. His body was returned, 1948.

Robert Portmess Hill, born October 3, 1924.

Miriam Irene Hill, born November 16, 1926, died, December 10, 1926.

Hill family residence is Vienna, Va., 1949.

2. William T., known as "Bud", a successful business man of Winchester and Berryville, was the mainstay of the home after the father's death, and in sickness and misfortune. He married Josephine Lupton, an attractive daughter of Jonathan Lupton of near Capon Bridge, who died in Winchester, 1923. Mr. Milleson is still living 1937, and has seen all of his children married and settled in their own homes; a brood of whom he is justly proud — Edith, Lillian, Mildred, and John.

DEATH REMOVES WM. T. MILLESON
Funeral Rites Are To Be Held Friday, With Interment at Berryville

William Taylor Milleson, resident of Winchester and Clarke county for many years, died at 4 o'clock this morning at the home of his son-in-law and daughter, Mr. and Mrs. Dudley C. Lichliter, on the Valley pike, aged 73 years. He sustained a stroke last Saturday and failed to rally.

Mr. Milleson was a native of Springfield, W. Va., and was a son of the late Benjamin and Elizabeth Cooper Engle Milleson. He was born in the year 1866.

The funeral services held at the home of Mr. and Mrs. Lichliter on the Valley pike at 3 o'clock Friday afternoon by the Rev. T. M. Swann, pastor of Braddock Stheet Methodist Church. Interment made in Green Hill Cemetery at Berryville.

3. George B., a promising young man of fine physique, went on a fishing trip in early spring and was seized by rheumatism of a malignant type, after a long siege, succumbed to this disease.

4. Joseph M., farmer and orchardist, married Elizabeth Lou Milleson, daughter of John and Sallie. They lived on the home farm near Slanesville and brough up a large family of children as follows:

Norma Louella married Claude Haven Haines, son of Elmer and Leota Haines, and grandson of Noah Haines, on July 27, 1947. Claude is a teacher by profession, and they reside at Slanesville, West Virginia.

Carrie Lillian married Merle C. Eaton, of Gore, Virginia, now, at this date they are divorced and Merle is re-married to Mildred Collier of Martinsburg, West Virginia. Merle and Lillian are both graduates of Shepherd College and teachers by profession. Lillian and Merle have two children:

Noreen Rosemary, born May 14, 1928.

Waldo Merle, born July 19, 1931.

Noreen graduated from Capon Bridge High School, class of '44, and completed three years at Shepherd College. She married Robert L. Kave, Jr., son of Robert L. and Margaret H. Kave of Shepherdstown, W. Va., on September 21, 1946. They reside at Engle, W. Va.

Waldo is attending Capon Bridge High School.

Catherine Elizabeth married George Fearnow, of Berkeley Springs, W. Va., in 1936. He is a truck driver by occupation. They are living at Berkeley Springs, W. Va., no children.

Mina Josephine married Bernard Kimmel Smith, son of Lewis Smith of Round Top, W. Va., on February 8, 1932. Kimmel was born June 19, 1912. In 1939 Mina and Kimmel bought 19 acres of land on Route 40 about twenty-one miles east of Cumberland, Md. On this plot they built a home where they now reside. Kimmel is employed by the Kelley Springfield Tire Company, in Cumberland, Md. They have three children as follows:

Vernon Kimmel, born August 14, 1933.

Vianna Grace, born May 14, 1935.

Arnold Lewis, born July 19, 1937.

Charles Carroll married Nellie Lorraine Hall of Washington, D. C. Carroll is a truck driver. They own a home in Arlington, Va. They have two children as follows:

Charles Carroll, Jr., born April 10, 1942.

George William, born June 2, 1945.

Alice Ruth died at the age of nineteen.

Joseph Watson married Daisy Elizabeth Ward, March 29, 1933. They live at Fort Ashby, W. Va. Born to them were six children as follows:

Glenn Watson, born January 13, 1934.

Wilson Erward, born April 29, 1935.

Rosalyn Elizabeth, born November 16, 1936.

Kay Jean, born July 15, 1939.

Donald Earl, born October 28, 1940.

Gary Paul, born April 9, 1946.

Georgiana Engle married James Vandiver Wirgman on May 9, 1941. They are living at Tangerine, Florida. Two children as follows:

James Vandiver, Jr., born January 27, 1942.

Betty Jean, born September 18, 1944.

John Benjamin married Edna Louise Wagoner of Fort Ashby, W. Va., on December 22, 1934. He is employed as a machinist at the Baltimore and Ohio Shops in Cumberland, Md. They live near Fort Ashby, W. Va., no children.

Anna Marie married Colin Frank Page, born January 13, 1897 at Kent County, England. He is employed by the Federal Government as a Guard. They own a home at Dunn Loring, Virginia. Four children as follows:

Elizabeth Josephine, born October 31, 1936.

Colin Frank, Jr., born July 13, 1939.

George Clarke, born January 19, 1941.

Marjorie Ann, born July 26, 1946.

Margaret Susan married John Wilber Haines, son of Wilbur M. Haines of Romney, W. Va., Margaret is a graduate of Romney High School, class of '38. John is a carpenter by trade. They have five children as follows:

John Russel, born July 4, 1939.

Stanley Eugene, born March 2, 1941.

Elizabeth Ann, born March 13, 1943.

Sandra Jane, born December 20, 1944.

Mary Susan, born July 16, 1946.

Children of Joe and Betty Milleson.

John Benjamin Milleson, born September 12, 1912.

Anna Marie Milleson, born May 11, 1915.

Margaret Susan Milleson, born September 13, 1916.

Grace Irene Milleson, born June 14, 1919.

Lulu L., student at Shepherd College and teacher, on July 30, 1925 married Garland Edward Moreland, oldest son of William P. and Caroline Largent Moreland, of Spring Gap, Hampshire County, West Virginia. Garland and Lulu Moreland own and operate a farm on Little Capon River about five miles from Okonoko or eight miles from Paw Paw, West Virginia.

Born to them were ten children as follows:

Ruth Caroline, born July 18, 1926.

Glenna Marie, born January 23, 1928.

Norma Louella, born December 27, 1929.

Carroll Garland, born February 16, 1932.

Helen Elizabeth, born February 7, 1934.

Naomi Mae, born February 16, 1936.

Irene Rosalea, born July 14, 1939.

Josephine Loretta, born May 28, 1942.

Giles Roger, born June 18, 1944.

David Russell, born June 19, 1945.

The three oldest daughters are married at this date in 1947.

Ruth Caroline graduated from Capon Bridge High School, Class of '44, and on August 19, 1944, married Giles Henry Spaid, oldest son of Mary A. and Hilery Spaid of Lehew, W. Va. (They are at present living in Washington). Giles is a graduate of Capon Bridge High School, class of '39. He served in the U. S. Navy from July 1942 to November 1945. He is employed by the Naval Research Laboratory in Washington, D. C., while attending night classes at the George Washington University. He is an Electrical Engineer. Ruth is employed by the Federal Government also, since January, 1945.

Glenna Marie Moreland married Howard A. Strother, son of William and Bessie Strother of Paw Paw, West Virginia, on June 25, 1947.

Grace Irene is a graduate of Romney High School, class of '38. She married Luther Franklin Collins, son of John and Della Collins of Somerset, Va., on August 23, 1941. Luther was born October 11, 1913. They are living near Culpepper, Virginia. Two children:

Richard Franklin Collins, born August 23, 1941.

Daughter (name not shown) born June 30, 1946.

5. Mary M., daughter of Benjamin and Elizabeth Milleson, after the death of her sister, married John Partmess, as his second wife. Children:

Robt. Roy Partmess, residence, Baltimore, and Dewey Partmess, residence, Paw Paw, W. Va.

Dewey Partmess married Gladys King, they have four small children.

John Partmess born August 19, 1859, died March 28, 1936.

Mamie Milleson Partmess lived only a few years and some years later Mr. Partmess married Emma A. Streiby who survives.

For Elizabeth Milleson, see John James Pugh Family.

The Milleson Family

George Milleson, II, the third son of William and Sarah Milleson, born August, 1836, died March 14, 1921; married September 28, 1858, Kate Coffman, daughter of George Coffman of Wardensville, born February 9, 1838, died April 10, 1912. Mrs. Milleson was a brunette and in every sense a high type of woman, who held the devotion of her husband through a long wedded life. George Milleson, reared on the ancestral farm at the big Spring, went to school with the Florys and Monroes at the now famous log school house on the Run near the old Salem Church.

At the age of eighteen he was clerking for James R. Jackson at Slanesville; there 18 months, then, "rode deputy sheriff" for his uncle, George Milleson, 6 months, later for two years, at North River Mills, clerked for Squire Carmichael, when he was made constable until he answered the call of the Confederacy, enlisting in Imboden's 18th Virginia Volunteer Cavalry, Company K, Captain Pyles, the summer of 1863.

He and his brother-in-law, James Pugh, in an attempt to visit their wives, were captured and taken prisoners at the home of William Baker near Wardensville, October 3rd of the same year. They were sent to Camp Chase where they received brutal treatment at the hands of the guards, 3 months; then sent to Rock Island in the Mississippi River, where they languished and starved fifteen months longer. While there, they, amid squalor and disease, buried their dead comrades stricken with smallpox, caught and roasted rats, which, with cabbage boiled in water, made them a rare feast.

These men were not recognized by their wives on reaching home after being exchanged, March 26, 1865, before the surrender of April 9.

Mr. Milleson was again made Constable until elected assessor of the then Second District of Hampshire county, a place he held for fourteen consecutive years. He was elected Sheriff in 1888. On completing this office, Mr. Milleson went into the mercantile business at Slanesville. Retiring from business at an advanced age he spent the remainder of his life with his only child, "Mirtie", Mrs. Jacob D. Grace, of Springfield, West Virginia.

George Milleson was a man strong in integrity and natural gifts, possessing a memory that could locate and delineate most of the farms in his county, and give their successive occupants for more than half a century.

Physically he was six feet, and broad shouldered, of blond complexion with grey eyes and auburn hair, an aquiline nose, high forehead, an expressive mouth.

He rests beside his beloved wife in Salem Cemetery. Mirtie, (Lorena Denis Milleson), born at Slanesville, June 3, 1863, married Jacob D. Grace, (son of John W. and Catherine Daniels Grace), merchant and Post Master at the village of Springfield. She died a. m., March 7, 1934, buried 3 p. m., March 8. He was a Presbyterian, she a member of the M. E. Church, South, at Salem where they are buried on the George Milleson lot. Mr. Grace died, 1936. They left no children.

Elias Milleson, son of William and Sarah Henderson Milleson, was born in 1840, entered militia service in command of Colonel Alex Monroe, 1862; was sent from Camp to the Hospital at Woodstock, having contracted typhoid fever, and because of the fall back of the Confederates, was later removed to Harrisonburg, Virginia, where he died April, 1862, aged twenty-two years, and lies buried in the Confederate Cemetery there.

SEEDERS

The children of George H. Seeders, who was married to Susan M. Hodges of Edina, Missouri, in March, 1898, are:

1. Sylvester Pearl Seeders, born September 9, 1900. Passed away April 4, 1938. He married Blanch P. Wagoner of Springfield, West Virginia, on March 9, 1927. Their children are:

   a. George Sylvester Seeders, born October 5, 1928.

   b. Ronald Parker Seeders, born February 27, 1937.

2. Mamie Ellen Seeders, born October 11, 1901. Was married to John Lawson Barksdale of Paces, Virginia, on December 30, 1930. Children:

   a. George Lawson, born August 19, 1933.

   b. James Manning, born August 2, 1934.

   c. Nancy Mae, born July 17, 1942.

   d. Janice Faye, born September 6, 1945.

   They reside on a farm.

3. James Carl Seeders, born August 20, 1910. Married to M. Ireland, Lothian, Maryland, on May 4, 1936. Their children are:

   a. James Earl Seeders, born January 5, 1939.

   b. Dorothy Ann Seeders, born September 12, 1940.

Children of Bettie and Joseph Milleson:

Lulu Lorretta Milleson, born August 29, 1900.

Carrie Lillian Milleson, born April 26, 1902.

Catherine Elizabeth Milleson, born August 2, 1903.

Mina Josephine Milleson, born November 8, 1904.

Charles Carroll Milleson, born April 21, 1906.

Alice Ruth Milleson, born August 11, 1907.

Joseph Watson Milleson, born October 30, 1908.

Georgiana Engle Milleson, born April 2, 1910.

THE CAUDY FAMILY

James Caudy II, son of David and Martha Hiett Caudy and grandson of the pioneer, married Elizabeth McPherson, daughter of William McPherson. Some say he built the brick house, later the home of Amos L. Pugh, pictured in this book, but the brick house was not his first house as his children were born elsewhere earlier. They brought up their family at what is now known as Capon Bridge. Children:

1. Elizabeth (not Margaret) married William Nixon, prominent citizen of Capon — See Volume II.

2. Margaret married Eli Beall, son of Elisha and Ann Beall, January, 1817. They built the Beall Tavern, now known as Frye's Inn and among a large family of children was Dr. (Col) Ed. Beall, born July 25, 1836 and died 1880 — see Volume II.

3. Rebecca, born December 20, 1811, married Tillberry Reid, son of John Reid, born near what is now Lehew. Their first child was born on Capon, 1834, but they soon moved to Ohio and then to Indiana, perhaps in a covered wagon or by pack horses, as the North Western Turnpike was not yet completed through. See Reid Family.

4. Sarah Ann, married Willam Odell when she was aged 17. They lived at "Capon Bridge" until after four of their children were born. One of these, a son, the Father of Mrs. Henrietta Caldwell, Cleveland Avenue, Columbus, Ohio, was 12 years old. About 1841 they moved by covered wagon to Ohio, Mr. and Mrs. Odell rode hoseback all the way, they bought 1200 acres of land near what is now Piketon and built a store and established a post office. Three more daughters were born to them in Ohio. Their children moved westward, like the Reids, and are scattered to Missouri and other states.

The road now "U. S. 50" was a dirt road that crossed "Capon" down at old Fort Edwards about a mile below the present village where there was a ferry, the settlement grew up around the ferry and was known as the "Ferry." Joseph Edwards, James Caudy and Evan Pugh were here before Court records.

Caudy's Castle, on Capon, near the Forks

Miss Maud Pugh
Capon Bridge
West Virginia

Dear Miss Pugh:

You asked me to furnish you with a history of our branch of Jeremiah James Reid, the first descendants.

Most of this was compiled by my late sister, Mabel F. Reid. Like yourself, she was a veteran school teacher and an author. She was educated for a teacher in Indiana and later graduated from the University of California. Like many teachers she was always reaching for additional education so attended special short courses in other American Universities and in Europe. Most of her teaching was done in San Francisco.

My sister spent some money and considerable time in checking family history so it is probably close to correct. For the information my relatives desire, the best bargain I ever bought is your Capon Valley, Vol. Two. I am sending a copy of this to Indiana and one to California.

The Carriers, Lehew, West Virginia, own the original Jeremiah James Reid's home place. One of the L. F. Carrier family, (Capon Valley, Vol. 2 — Page 287) married a daughter of Azariah P. Reid. He was a brother of Dorsey Reid. In his will of 1853 John Reid names fifteen living children, also three who were dead.

Living children of John Reid named in his will, 1853
Elizabeth Ann, William, James, Josiah Tilberry (died in the Federal Army, a Captain), George, Morgan, Dorsey (a Confederate veteran), Theopholes, Martin (died in the Confederate Army. His name in on the Confederate Monument at Romney, West Virginia), Frances, Smith, Austin, Azriah P., Amildo.

The Will states that Amildo is the youngest. That the last six named are minors (1853). That three children named Lovina, John and Mariah are dead and that his wife is Mary Ann Reid.

Capon Valley

Jeremiah James Reid the first, was the father of Jeremiah James Reid (2) the father of John Reid, his son, Tilberry, born December 15, 1810, married Rebecca Caudy, born December 20, 1811. She was the daughter of James Caudy (2) (Capon Valley, Vol. II, Page 156) who married Elizabeth McPherson, the daughter of William McPherson.

The first child of Tilberry and Rebecca Caudy Reid was John Francis Reid, born in Hampshire County, Virginia, in 1834, but they soon moved to Ohio and then to Indiana as the other children were born in Ohio and Indiana.

Tilberry Reid had two brothers in the Confederate Army — Martin and Dorsey. Tilberry Reid and two of his sons were in the Union Army. Tilberry Reid also died in the war, January 1, 1863, at Holly Springs, Mississippi. He was a Captain in the 99th Reg. Ind. Vol. His youngest son, Lt. Benton Reid, was in the same Reg., and he also died in the war at Moscow, Tenn., April 25, 1863. The G.A.R. Post at Clayton, Indiana, was named for this Lt. Benton Reid.

Tilberry Reid, his wife, Rebecca Caudy Reid and their son, Benton Reid are all buried at Center Valley Cemetery, Hendricks County, Indiana.

Richard E. Reid, (my father) was the son and brother of the above. He was also in the Union Army, 55th Reg. Ind. Vol. He married about 1867 (no records with me, they are in Indiana and California.) All Reids in our immediate branch of the family are his descendants. His wife was Eliza J. Hunt, Indiana born, but of the Guilford Court House, North Carolina Hunt family (Quaker Stock). Their surviving descendants are:

Lee C. Reid, San Francisco, Veteran, Spanish American War. His son:

1. Richard F. Reid, San Francisco. Granddaughter, Kenyon Reid, San Francisco.

2. Robert E. Reid (Single) San Francisco.

3. Maurice L. Reid, Tuscon, Arizona. Son, Gene C. Reid, Tuscon, Arizona. Grandson, Robert Lee Reid, Tuscon, Arizona. The above Maurice L. Reid, has another son Robert L. Reid, San Francisco, (Major in the last war).

"Dr. Ed Beall," Capon Bridge, W. Va., great great grandson of the pioneer, Jas. Caudy, Col. in C.S.A. (Picture, kindness of Robert E. Reid, of San Francisco, a cousin.)

Lee C. and Kenyon Lee Reid, granddaughter, nearest of kin to pioneer
Lee C., born in Indiana.

ROBERT L. REID
Officer in the Navy, cousin of
Robert E. Reid.

4. A grandson of Richard E. Reid (His father, Benton Reid (2) is dead). Donald M. Reid (Veteran, World War I) Clayton, Indiana, who has a son Donald Robert Reid and a daughter Margaret Reid.

This Benton Reid (2) also has two grandsons, Robert Millis and Benton Millis, both veterans of last war, Crawfordsville, Indiana.

5. The only other descendants that I know about are the children, grandchildren, etc., of Tilberry Reid's daughter, Minerva. She married a Craven of the Center Valley Indiana Craven family. Before my memory, they moved to Kansas and I never knew any of them. Lee C. Reid of San Francisco and our late sister Mabel both visited and knew some of these Cravens.

6. Mabel F. Reid, San Francisco (but Indiana born).

7. and Mary Reid Mott, San Francisco, (but Indiana born) were my sisters. Both are dead.

My grandmother, Rebecca Caudy Reid (Hampshire County born of the James Caudy Family) died before I can remember. I knew that some of her relatives died in the Confederate Army and that several were in this army. Your book, "Capon Valley" lists many more of these than I realized.

Losing her husband, her youngest son and many of her relatives on both sides of the 1861-1865 war, it would seem that the last years of my grandmother must have been sad. All she had left any place near was one son (my father) and his two small sons.

My mother told me that she lived next door to us, no fence between the yards. That she enjoyed life with these two grandsons. That these smallboys were much inclined to prefer Virginia cooking over the Hoosier Tar-Heel brand in their own home.

The later senior surviving grandson is:

1. Lee C. Reid, San Francisco, a veteran of the Spanish-American War and World War I with his granddaughter Kenyon Lee Reid of San Francisco.

2. Robert L. Reid, San Francisco, (California born) a nephew of Lee C. Reid. This picture taken in Osaka, 1945. Then he

was — Cheif, Military Government, Southwest half of Japan. He is a great grandson of Tilberry and Rebecca, is well educated, a university graduate, married to a Virginia girl.

3. Benton Reid Millis, U. S. Navy, taken in the Philippine Islands, 1946. He is a great, great grandson. Home, Crawfordsville, Ind. His father is an M.D., and army Medical Officer during the late war. His time in the Navy will be up soon, and he intends to study medicine.

4. Mary Margaret Reid and Donald Reid, Clayton, Ind., great, great granchildren, and their home is only about five miles from where Tilberry and Rebecca Settled in Indiana about one hundred years ago. (These are the two children who called on you a few weeks ago.)

5. Robert Lee Reid, Tuscon, Arizona. Arizona born and the youngest member of our tribe of Reids. He also is a great, great grandson of Tilberry and Rebecca Caudy Reid.

October 14, 1947

Miss Maud Pugh,
Capon Bridge, W. Va.

Dear Miss Pugh:

Robert E. Reid, Indiana, born ——; a grandson of Tilberry and Rebecca Caudy Reid (both of them dead before I can remember.)

"Home", San Francisco for more than forty years. Never married, so, in other places much more than at home.

Have lived and worked and traveled in many parts of the world. In the Orient for a long time. Three trips to Europe, and about a year and one-half there.

Not so bad as it sounds, as twenty-five years with one commercial firm and fifteen years with another. Most of the traveling for business reasons and in the interests of above two houses.

Enclosed picture taken in Seattle about 1915, is sent in reply to your request.

Yours truly,
(Signed) Robert E. Reid,

250

ROBERT E. REID
Pine St., San Francisco. Great
grandson of Jas. Caudy, II.

Family of Robert Edwards, Sr.

Robert Edwards, Sr., son of William Edwards, was son of Joseph Edwards, who owned land and built Edwards Fort, near Capon Bridge, West Va., near route No. 50. Robert Edwards married Eva Hawkins, and moved to North River where they bought one of the Deaver farms (1 mile north of the Ice Mountain farm) where they lived and raised a large family. Shortly after the Civil War, about 1867, they sold the farm to their son-in-law and daughter Peter and Jane Edwards Largent, and moved to; I think, Peoria, Ill., where they died and are buried .

Their children were: John, who married Susan ————, lived and died in Keyser, West, Va. They had one daughter who married Henry Montgomery, an engineer on B. & O. R. R. Their children are: Erston, Ethil, Fay and Clem Montgomery, all living in Keyser, West Va., 1947.

Anna married a Carmichael, and moved to some of the western states.

Nancy married M. Hare, and moved to the west.

James married Harriot ————. killed in the Civil War. One child, James Jr., living in Marysville, Ohio.

Mary married John Ely, moved to Iowa, (see John and Mary Edwards Ely family, written by her nephew, H. E. Ely), Des Moines, Iowa, 1947.

Albert and George moved west, and the writer (E. F. Largent) their nephew, can find no trace of them, 1947.

Elizabeth married Isaac Grapes, (see their family sketch in Volume II.

Robert Jr. married Susan Funk, and moved to Iowa. His children are living in and near Stockport, Iowa, 1947.

Jane married Peter Largent, (see Volume II for family sketch.) They rode horseback to Stanton, Va., in 1863, where they were married. They started housekeeping on the Margaret Slonaker farm near Cold Stream, Va., just across the river where their son, the writer of this sketch, now has his home, 1947.

Later research shows that Grandfather and Grandmother Robert Edwards Sr., and Eva Edwards are buried at Lacross, Hancock Co., Ill., also their son Albert is buried there.

Mary Edwards and John W. Ely Family.

Mary Edwards was the daughter of Robert Edwards 1st., born February 9, 1831, died October 27, 1906. Married John W. Ely, October 24, 1850. Born June 5, 1831 in Hampshire county, West Va., died April 15, 1891, in Van Burin Co. Iowa. Moved, 1856, to Knox Co. Ill., September, 1869, moved to Van Burin Co., Iowa. Mr. and Mrs. Ely and most of their descendants were Democrats, and Methodists. Their children were: Robert E. Ely, born October 14, 1852, in Virginia., died at Mt. Pleasant, Iowa, December 16, 1937. Benjamin F. Ely, born August 27, 1854, in Virginia, died at Stockport, Iowa, 1933. Annie Catherine Ely, born March 8, 1856, in Virginia, died in Stockport, Iowa. James Albert Ely, born June 6, 1859, in Illinois, died at Fairfield, Iowa.

Robert E. married Catherine Bell Keck, October 14, 1875. Their children were: Harold Elsworth, born March 16, 1881. Raymond E., born June 18, 1882. Marie I., born November 1, 1884. All were born in Vanburen Co., Iowa. Benjamin F. Ely married Ida Stedman, March 26, 1884, died March 23, 1915. Their children: Julia May, born May 26, 1885. Lester Franklin, born April 14, 1888. Zella Maud, born May 8, 1890. Donovan S., born September 2, 1899. Josephine K. born July 1, 1901. Harry William, born January 24, 1903. Charles J., born June 23, 1905. All were born in Van Buren Co., Iowa.

Anna Catherine Ely married A. W. Warner, March 2, 1875. Their children: John W. and Lilly Jane Warner. James Albert Ely married Clara Mort, September 4, 1883. Their children: George F. and Iva F. Ely. Harold Elsworth Ely (son of Robert E. Ely and grandson of Mary Edwards and John W. Ely and great grandson of Robert Edwards, 1st, married Stella Maud Johnston, July 10, 1901, she was born December 6, 1880. Children: Alice Catherine, born June 7, 1905; Harold E. Jr., born

Ruins of Old Fort Edwards. Furnished by Frances McDonald.

The oldest house in Capon Bridge, built by Evan Caudy, grandson of
the pioneer, Jas. Caudy. Kindness of Gertrude Ward.

December 26, 1909; Frances Evelyn, born October 25, 1917; Ruth Elizabeth, born August 24, 1919, died December 27, 1923; Dorothy Anna, born September 23, 1921; all five born in Des Moines, Iowa. Mr. H. E. Ely is president of Banker's Printing Co., Des Moines, Iowa.

Zella Maud Ely, daughter of Benjamin F. Ely, married Pro. Elliott, living in Monrovia, California, where they have an orange grove. Their children are: Joe, living in Santa Monica, California; Elizabeth, married Robert Jochimson, they live at La Verne, California, and are also orange growers. Children: Don, Harry, Josephine, and Charles. Mae Ely, daughter of Benjamin F. Ely, married Justin Smith, Riverside, California; children: Florence, Keith, Ellis, Marjory, and Jennie Mae. Marjory, married Verl Hart, children: Reita, Della, Don, Doris, and Robert Hart. Jennie Mae, married Max Reswick, one child, William.

The above genealogies, are descendants of the late John Edwards, who first settled in the Capon Valley. Compiled and written by Edward Largent, who has history and genealogies connecting 14 generations of the Edwards family. From the first pioneer to settle in Connecticut, 1639, to present time, 1947.

Family of Robert F. Edwards, Jr.

Robert F. Edwards, Jr., born August 18, 1843, died August 17, 1929. Married to Susan R. Funk, born August 28, 1845, died May 26, 1930. Originally from Virginia, they lived in Illinois, Missouri, and Iowa consecutively. Descendants are as follows:

I. Minnie I. Edwards, born May 5, 1867, in Illinois, died March 1, 1868.

II. Joseph E. Edwards, born June 22, 1868, in Illinois, died February 24, 1945, at Ft. Madison, Iowa. Married to Mary Strutgill, residing at Ft. Madison. No children.

III. Mary Cornelia Edwards, born March 17, 1871. Married to William Stout. Residing at Birmingham, Iowa. Children and grandchildren:

253

A. Ralph Stout, born May 4, 1895. Married to May Carter. Residing near Birmingham, Iowa. Descendants:

1. Ralph Stout, Jr., born June 9, 1916, married Mignon Hardesty of Hedrick, Iowa. Born to them:

a. Marta Kay Stout, born June 14, 1944.

b. Steven Kent Stout, born December 3, 1946.

IV. Leonard F. Edwards, born Octiber 1, 1875, died January 17, 1940. Married to Pink Teal, died March 24, 1929. Born to them:

A. Glenn Edwards, born September 21, 1904, died June 30, 1947. Married to Esther ————. Born to them:

1. Marie Edwards, born September 13, 1927, married to Edward Weibler. Residing in Ft. Madison, Iowa.

2. Melvin Edwards, born January, 1932.

B. Dale Edwards, born March 11, 1908, married to Ruth Boone. Residing near Stockport, Iowa. Born to them:

1. Maynard Edwards, born June 19, 1938.

2. Carol Sue Edwards, born March 8, 1941.

V. Jettie Maude Edwards, born October 6, 1877, died October 18, 1879.

VI. Myrtle E. Edwards, born October 29, 1879, married to Lafe E. Knowles. Residing in Stockport, Iowa, Born to them:

A. Edward Knowles, Newton, Iowa, born March 25, 1901, married Margaret Brokaw. No children.

B. LeMar Knowles, born November 6, 1903, married to Wilma Haney. Residing at Bonaparte. Born to them:

1. Jack Knowles.

2. Robert Knowles.

3. Romelda Knowles.

C. Beatrice Knowles, born April 13, 1905, married to Charley White. Residing at Newton. Born to them:

1. Donald White.

2. Joanna White.

D. Ray Wnowles, born April 7, 1907, married Ruth Gregory. Residing at Los Angeles, California. Born to them:

1. Ronald Knowles.

2. Lora Lee Knowles.

E. Juanita Knowles, born April 15, 1918, married to Al De-Camp. Residing at Miami, Florida. No Children.

VII. Claude Olen Edwards, born April 12, 1881, married Clara Smith. Residing near Stockport, Iowa. Born to them:

A. Elvin Edwards, born June 4, 1904, married Rosetta Nelson. Residing near Fairfield, Iowa. Born to them:

1. Maxine Edwards, born March 7, 1924, married to George Volmert. Residing at Kirksville, Missouri. Born to them:

a. Karen Elizabeth Volmert, born November 24, 1946.

2. Darlene Edwards, born June 25, 1926, unmarried, residing in Ottumwa, Iowa.

3. Beverly Ann Edwards, born March 25, 1935.

B. Opal Edwards, born October 22, 1907, married Leslie Johnston. Residing in Hedrick, Iowa. No children.

VIII. George Wesley Edwards, born December 15, 1882, married to Jennie C. Wise, born May 24, 1890, died February 20, 1941. Born to them:

A. Pauline E. Edwards, born March 12, 1912, married to Lyle Crawford. Residing near Stockport, Iowa. Born to them:

1. Lanny Joe Crawford, born October 6, 1941.

B. Betty Lou Edwards, born November 21, 1919, married to James Silver. Residing in Stockport, Iowa. No children.

Family of Sallie Largent Kidwell

Robert S. Kidwell, son or Samuel and Nancy Kidwell, was born September 27, 1858; died July 20, 1924. He married Sarah Elizabeth Largent, daughter of Peter and Jane Largent, November 30, 1882. Children:

1. Osea, born April 17, 1885, married Nettie Grapes, daughter Robert and Elizabeth Grapes.

2. Omar C., born June 10, 1887, married twice. His first wife was Nora Wolford. She died December 11, 1912. He then married Inez Arnold and they are now living in Kinsman, Ohio.

3. Daily Edward, born April 29, 1889, married Nettie Croston,

daughter of Charley and Hannah Croston of North River Mills. He died May 16, 1940. His widow resides with her son Leonard at Levels, West Virginia.

4. Nannie Jane, born September 12, 1891, married Garda L. Fultz, son of William and Elizabeth Fultz, of North River Mills. They live near Romney, West Virginia.

5. William Clark, born 1897, married Christina Wink, of Frostburg, Maryland. They now reside in Pittsburgh, Pa.

6. John Wessley, born January 2, 1899, married Iva Merritt, daughter of George and Buena Merritt, of Purgittsville, West Virginia. They now live at Three Churches, West Virginia.

7. Marvin S., born April 9, 1901, married Lulu Dean, daughter of Strite and Minnie Dean of Glebe, W. Va. They are living at Higginsville, West Virginia.

8. Sarah Cordelia, born February 4, 1904, was twice married. Her first husband was Richard Kasecamp of Rowelsburg, W. Va. He died June 24, 1925. Her second husband is Clyde B. Rogers of Davis, W. Va. They are now living at Ridgeley, W. Va.

9. Mary V., born November 10, 1910, married Norman Robins of Baltimore, where they now reside.

10. Nellie P., born April 24, 1907, is single and lives with her mother.

(Robert and Sallie, both known to the author, were for many years efficient keepers of the County Infirmary, which work she and her sons continued after Robert's death, until age necessitated her retirement. She then removed from Glebe to Romney, where she now resides, November, 1947.

Family of Mrs. Mary Louisa Largent Bennett

Daughter of Eliza Jane Largent and Peter Largent, March 20, 1867, married to James Arthur Bennett, son of Luther Bennett, March 1, 1887. Son: Otis Edward Bennett, born April 28, 1889, Slanesville. Bethany Alumnus, now, minister at Monessen, Pennsylvania., Daughter, Fannie Marie Bennett, born March 21, 1904, at Slanesville, W. Va., now teaching religious education in public schools of Indianapolis, Indiana.

Grandchildren of Mary L. Bennett, children of O. E. Bennett: Arthur J. Bennett, Minister at Rogersville, Pennsylvania, five children.

Ralph Eugene Bennett, Minister at Charleroi Pennsylvania, one child.

Marian Bennett Wolfe, wife of ex-army air corps man, student in DePaw University, at Green Castle, Indiana, two children.

Arlene Bennett, finishing high school at Monessen, Pennsylvania, entering college, fall of 1947.

Great grandchildren of Mary L. Bennett (8) Byron, Val Jean, Suzanne, Rio Rey and Christy Ann, children of Rev. Arthur Bennett. Joyce Arlene, daughter of Rev. Ralph Bennett. Warren and Charles, sons of Marian Bennett Wolfe.

Brothers and Sisters of Jane Edwards Largent: Lizzie Grapes, Annie Edwards, Mary Ely, Nancy Hare, Bob Edwards, George Edwards, John Edwards, Al Edwards.

Family of Lutie C. Largent Kidwell

Lutie C. Largent, daughter of Peter and Jane Edwards Largent, married Arthur Lee Kidwell, son of Evan and Sarah Kidwell. (Their children) Mamie E. Kidwell, married Irl L. Omps. (Their children) Melvin Omps and Loyd Omps, who married Gertrude Main??, (Their children) Voyne Omps and Joan Omps. Lester Kidwell who married Edna Nixon (Their children) Onile Kidwell, who married Wade Wilfong (Their children) Jay, Kay, and Jan Wilfong. Second wife of Lester Kidwell, Florence Maley (Their children) Glenna and Lester, Jr. Kidwell, who married Grace Null (Their children) Tommy Kidwell. Etta J. Kidwell, who married Wycliffe T. Moreland. Edward F. Kidwell, who married Catherine Lippencott (Their children) Edward Kidwell, II.

Edward F. Largent Family

Edward F. Largent, (son of Peter and Jane Edwards-Largent) born September 21, 1879. A Spanish war veteran. Enlisted at Cumberland, Md., November, 1901, discharged 1904, at

Angle Island, California. Served 33 months in Philippines. Married December 20, 1905 to Ella M. Willison, (daughter of Henry Willison and Rebecca Doffit Willison.

Their children are: Wenona R., married Alvia Barney, Washington, Pa. They, at this date, 1947, own a nice home on route No. 18, eight miles from Washington, Pa. No children.

Marcellus S. married Julia Provost of Burkestown, Pa. She was born near the French and Belgium border, and came to America with her parents at the age of eight years. Their children are: Florence, Marceline, Audley, and Alvin Lee. At this date, 1947, they live near Linville, Pa., where the own a nice home.

Benjamin R., married, and has five children, all residing near Washington, Pa.

Eva M., married Earl Harris, no children. They own their home in Washington, Pa., at this date, 1947.

Donna M., married Ralph Meyers, they own their home in Washington, Pa. Their children are: Joyce, Darlene, and Ralph David, 1947.

Irene R., married Eugene Cox, of Washington, Pa., their children are: Constance Sharmayne, and Eugene Dale.

William E., not married, Washington, Pa., 1947.

Fayen W., died 1917.

Evelyn, and Vera, died in infancy.

The Edwards-Largent Family, reported by E. T. Largent and given in his language.

Hietts

Al G. Hopkins died on October 21, 1932, from injuries received in an automobile accident on Route 50, three miles west of Winchester, Virginia. He died at the Walter Reed Hospital, Washington, D. C., and was buried in Arlington Cemetery. He was a veteran of World War I.

Orion Hiett Hopkins remarried March 12, 1938, to Hugh S. Carpenter, born in Winchester, Virginia, a veteran of World War II, served three years, one of which was in Germany.

He was a Sergeant in the First Army under General Hodges, 69th Division, 880th Field Artillery, was awarded three bronze stars for services rendered in the battle of the Bulge, Central Europe, and the battle of the Rhineland.

Powell Family

William French Williamson, born May 2, 1887; married Marie A. Logan in New York City. She was a native of Ireland. To them was born George Logan Williamson, April 3, 1915. She died when he was born. William later married Lottie L. Shanholtzer, daughter of Frank and Almedia Shanholtzer of Levels, West Virginia. To them three children were born.

1. Roy French Williamson, March 7, 1918.
2. Milland Franklin Williamson, May 16, 1920.
3. Margaret Almedia Williamson, R. N., August 30, 1924.

Laura L. Dudley Line

John Cale, private soldier, Va. Militia, 1777 Capt. Wm. Croghan's Co., 8th Va. Reg't, Col. Abraham Bowmans, from 1st day of March to last of April.

John Cale, born April 19, 1726, died July 26, 1797; married July 25, 1751 to Elizabeth Pugh, born December 13, 1730 in Frederick Co., Va., died September 14, 1796.

Daughter, Elizabeth Cale, born 1759, died 1821. Was married, 1782, to George Nicholas Spaid, born Dec. 22, 1759, died June 15, 1833.

Their daughter, Mary Spaid, born December 6, 1792, died April 6, 1870; married 1813 or 14 to George Hellyer, born October 22, 1787, died October 12, 1865.

Their daughter, Isabel Hellyer, born October 10, 1818, died January 2, 1888; married September 28, 1842, to Jacob Dudley, born April 26, 1821, died March 23, 1865.

Their son, Daniel David Dudley, born June 28, 1858, died December 18, 1834; married August 24, 1882, Emma Van Dyke, born May 10, 1863, died August 25, 1905.

Emma Van Dyke, mother of Laura L. Dudley, was the youngest daughter of Arthur Van Dyke, born February 2, 1829, died August 25, 1864; married January 3, 1854 to Anne La Follette, born March 11, 1833, died March 21, 1916. Anne was the daughter of William La Follette, born December 28, 1796, died September 2, 1865; married Harriette Gill, born January 1, 1800, died May 3, 1893.

William's father was Isaac La Follette.

Jacob Hull— See Capt. Jonathan Pugh

Principle Assessor for the Sixth District, State of Virginia.
To all who shall see these presents, Greetings:

Know ye that reposing confidence in the abilty, integrity and diligence of Jonathan Pugh of Hampshire County, the said Jonathan Pugh hath been and is hereby constituted and appointed assistant assessor for all that part of Hampshire County now composing the assessment district of John Slane under the State law within the aforesaid Sixth District of the State of Virginia with full authority to exercise, discharge and fulfill the powers and duties of said office and to have and to hold the same with the privileges and emoluments thereto appertaining according to law until this commission shall be duly and legally revoked or annulled.

Given under my hand in Hampshire
County on the 8th day of May, 1815.
(Signed) Jacob Hull.

Family of Henry and Phoebe Snapp Haines

Capon Valley

Children:

Sons, John T., Bruce; daughters: Mrs. Clara Knu, Mrs. Maggie Harper (Ohio), Mrs. Florence McKeever, Xenia, Ohio, (mother of Miss Madge McKeever). Mrs. Isadore Liggett, Mrs. Sallie Heinning, Nebraska, Mrs. Lizzie Slonaker, Capon Valley.

A DIVERSION

How to Keep the Doctor Away and Live to be Old.

1. If you are taking cold, use camphor on forhead and in nostrils and on temples.

2. For throat irritation get Dr. Flower's spray at Corbetts, use twice daily.

3. If threatened with pneumonia use spray and make a big oily, hot onion poultice, cover chest to keep poultice hot, go to bed, stay there until better; reheat, or have a new poultice made if needed; use mild laxative.

4. If threatened with arthritis, **stop eating,** live on milk for a week, bathe parts with alcohol camphor and vaseline. Don't use **lemonade** or any other acid fruits. **Quit coffee** forever. Take Sal Hepatica until better.

5. If you strangle easily, empty mouth quickly and swallow.

6. In bitter weather and no bath room, take a dry rub down and bathe feet often.

7. If you have a troublesome wart, bathe it twice, or oftener, daily with castor oil. If it gets sore that is part of the cure. Persevere until it goes.

8. If threatened with heart **ailment,** eat no rich food but **eat** and **walk** in the **air.** Don't worry.

9. Beware of alcoholics, tobacco and doped canned goods — but even bread is doped now.

10. He who sends for the doctor every time he stubs a toe will die early.

11. Sleep late all your life if you can; keep active in body and mind, and work, walk.

12. Be careful of body and soul at all times, and don't forget to ask the Lord for protection when you travel.

13. Live and let live; pray and read your Bible each day.

—Maud Pugh

261

The Borderland

By Esther Wirgman in Book of the Royal Blue.

Friend, do you know the Borderland?
The fairest, flowering Borderland!
Where, rising in their greenness, stand
The lovely hills of Maryland,
As emeralds set in golden band,
From Hagerstown to Cumberland?

Friend, have you seen the Borderland?
The high, historic Borderland!
Where rolls the Shenandoah grand,
Whose valley is a wonderland
Of old Virginia's saraband
From Winchester to Cumberland?
Come dwell within that Borderland!
That richest, ripest Borderland!
Fine farms abound on every hand,
Fat cattle for your deodand
In Pennsylvania's richest land

From Pittsburgh down to Cumberland.
Oh! how we love that Borderland!
Where rise the Alleghenies grand,
The watch towers of this lovely strand,
Of valley green and mountain grand,
Of summers cool and winters bland,
On West Virginia's eastern rand,
From Romney down to Cumberland!

Company "F". 18th Virginia Cavalry, Imboden's Brigade
Officers

R. Bruce Muse, Captain, Josah Seibert, 1st Lt., John Good,
2nd Lt., (Silas?) La Fayette La Follette, 3rd Lt., Beverly Lockhart, Ord. Sgt., Arsker Bywater, 1st Corp., Robert Chamberlain,
2nd Corp., Thomas Morrison, 3rd Corp.

Roll of Privates

Anderson, D.H.
Anderson, Zebulon
Anderson, Bruce
Anderson, Alfred
Arnold, Tilberry (#29 Spaid H)
Arnold, Harvey
Arnold, Lemuel
Anderson, Snowden
Braithwaite, John
Cline, Strother
Cline, Snowden
Crim, William
De Haven, Andrew
De Haven, James
Duffy, John
Evan, Robert
Fletcher, Jacob
Giffin, Joseph
Giffin, Edward
Giffin, David
Griffin, James
Garrett, Samuel
Johnson, James
Johnson, Sabe
Johnson, John
Johnson, Richard
Johnson, Lemuel
Kern, Washington
Kern, Robert
Kern, Benjamin
Kelso, John
Luttrell, Robert
Luttrell, Joseph
La Follette, Caney
Loy, Chas

Loy, John
Larrick, Benj. (Went to Iowa. Related to Reuben Russell La Follette through his mother.)
Mills, ————
Nidon, John
Nidon, William
Martin, Pope
McIntyre, Lige
McKee, Wood
McCoy, John (1149 Spaid History)
Mounts, Joseph
Oliver, Joseph
Popkins, Addison
Payne, Richard
Pool, John
Pugh, V.S.
Pugh, George
Pugh, Francis
Reid, Dorsey
Reid, Frank
Reid, David
Rogers, Hamilton
Smith, William
Siler, John
Stickley, Benj.
Sherman, Isiah
Strother, French
Spade, Lemuel
Strottler, John
Triplett, Wm.
Ward, Evan
West, Frank
White, Frank

Aunt Emma says the old Kackley home stood, a log cabin back of Calverts and they used to play. One of the girls used to laughingly say "lets go see Mrs. Oats". Oats were stored on second floor. These homes were in Virginia somewhere near Bethel cemetery.

Calvert Israel married Marie Kackley, niece of Elizabeth K. Giffin. Children:

1. Mary, went to Nebraska, took up a claim, married a Scott.
2. Addie, died single.
3. Emma married Thos. Pugh, no children.
4. Fannie married ———— ————, lived near Keyser.
5. Meda married ———— ————, lived at Astabula, Ohio.
6. Rene married ———— ————, lived at Wardensville.
7. Martha, youngest daughter, married her first cousin, Arthur Kackley, son of Wm. B. Kackley, Princeville, Ill., no children.

1. LaFayette Calvert married ———— ———— used to live at Princeville, Ill.
2. Lee Calvert.
3. John Lot Calvert, No. 1474 Spaid, born January 20, 1859.
4. "Doc" Calvert, the yongest son.

Both Mafia, wife of Israel Calvert, Wm. B. Kackley, Joseph Kackley, were cousins of my grandfather, Ed. R. Giffin.

From Mrs. Coggins

Deaths

The author of this book has lost three dear friends recently, vital assistants in this work.

Miss Fannie Hiett, born genealogist, died at Paw Paw, W. Va., 1948, buried at Romney.

A. D. Pugh, Attorney-at-Law, writer and poet of ability, 1948, at Des Moines, Iowa.

Mrs. Elizabeth Poland, Missionary wife of Dr. M. E. Poland, who typed both volumes of the book. We first met while she was secretary for the Christian Woman's Board of Missions, stationed at Bethany, W. Va., twenty-five years ago. Mrs. Poland had been Court Stenographer, Teacher, Assistant Medical Missionary to China and Magazine Editor. She was an expert letter writer. Her death occurred in Orlando Hospital, Florida, February 20, 1949.

Deaths — from the Hampshire Review
Into The Next Room

"Where bide they all?
Dear friends of yesterday, last year and long ago,
Who walked with us when life was all aglow
And rainbows spanned the gloom?
Not far away we know,
They've only gone, we know,
Into the next room.
"How sweet and strange!
We hear their tender voices as in olden days,
While we drift backward into sunny bays
With lilies all abloom—
In murmurs low they say;
'Love lights in the mystic way
Into the next room'.
"Years wear apace,
Dark days with heavy mist now deep'ning into rain,
Close down upon us, and we view with pain
The spectral shadows loom
A mournful gleam; and lo,
We too lift latch and go
Into the next room."

In memory of Miss Margaret Taylor. —By Mrs. J. B. Rannells.
Back of God's commands He puts omnipotence.

Mrs. Nancy Alkire Taken by Death

Mrs. Nancy M. Alkire, 73 of Slanesville, died Saturday in Memorial Hospital, Cumberland, where she had been a patient for eight weeks. She was the widow of Truman Alkire, who died in 1939.

She is survived by the following children: William K. Moreland, Cold Stream; Dorie Moreland, Slanesville; Robert Z.

Alkire, Paw Paw; Wycliffe T. Moreland, Winchester; Mayo Moreland, Baltimore, and Lloyd W. Alkire, Canton, Ohio; three daughters, Mrs. Gwendolyn Warder, Cumberland; Mrs. Margaret Hinds, Canton, Ohio, and Mrs. Louise Schoolcraft, Yuma, Arizona; also one sister, Mrs. Orra Chapman, Cumberland; and two brothers, Robert K. Taylor, Holloway, Ohio, and Dr. R. E. S. Taylor, Paw Paw.

Funeral services were held Monday at Mount Union Church near Slanesville and burial was in the cemetery adjoining the church. 1947.

Wade G. Emmett Dies from Heart Attack

Wade Gordon Emmett, son of the late Jacob Emmett, of Hanging Rock, died at his home at Belle Haven, Va., July 5, of a heart attack, aged about seventy-five years.

Mr. Emmett was a teacher in the public schools of Hampshire county for a time and later taught at Shenandoah Normal College. For thirty years he was cashier of a bank at Belle Haven, where he taught the men's Bible class in the Methodist Church for twenty-five years. In 1945 he retired from active business.

Deceased, who was buried at Belle Haven on July 7, is survived by a daughter, Mrs. Griffin C. Martin, of Belle Haven, and one son, Wade G. Emmett, Jr., of Baltimore, and five grandchildren. In addition he is survived by one sister, Mrs. Lee A. McKee, of Shanks, and by seven brothers, W. W. Emmett, of Sebring, Fla., James S. Clifton and Jacob Emmett, of Greybull, Wyoming; M. F. Emmett, of Fromberg, Mont.; Frank I. Emmett, of Bellevue, Michigan, and Hill Emmett, of Spokane, Washington.

Mrs. Gertrude Brill Dies Near Capon Springs

A lifelong resident of the Capon Springs section, Mrs. Gertrude Brill, 80, died Thursday afternoon at ther home after an illness of several months.

She was a daughter of the late Benjamin and Rachel Good Anderson and is the last surviving member of her immediate family. She is survived by one daughter, Mrs. Clarence Bland, Capon Springs, and by a grandson, Keith Bland, of Wardensville.

Funeral services were conducted Sunday morning in the Hebron Lutheran church on Capon with interment in the adjoining cemetery.

The Rev. C. H. Anderson, of Winchester, officiated.

Miss Fanny Hiett Dies at Paw Paw

Sarah Frances Hiatt, known to her many friend as "Miss Fanny", died after an illness of three weeks at her home in Paw Paw, Thursday, July 15. She was the youngest daughter of the late James Walter and Margaret Largent Hiett and was born February 24, 1865, at Sandy Ridge.

For many years Miss Fanny was active in the millinery business in Romney. She was a life-long and loyal member of the Christian Church.

Surviving are one sister, Miss Kizzie Hiett, three nieces, Mrs. H. H. Cookus, of Arlington, Va.; Mrs. H. N. Van Voorhis, of Bowling Green, Ohio, and Mrs. John M. Snarr, of Romney, and one nephew, James P. Shull, of Ft. Lauderdale, Florida.

The funeral services were held at the McKee Funeral Home, at Augusta, Saturday at 11 o'clock, conducted by her pastor, the Rev. Don Spangler, assisted by Rev. Mr. Ritz, pastor of the Augusta Church. Interment was in Indian Mound cemetery here.

Out-of-town relatives attending the funeral services were: Mrs. H. H. Cookus, Arlington, Va.; Mrs. H. N. Van Voorhis, of Bowling Green, Ohio; Mrs. W. F. Brown, Baltimore, and a number of relatives from nearby towns.

Richard McLain Billmyer

Richard McLain Billmyer, 53, of Points, farmer and veteran of World War I, died Thursday, January 21, 1948 at Newton D. Baker Hospital, Martinsburg, where he had been taken for treatment several days before.

A son of the late Richard D. and Clara E. Billmyer, he was born at Rio. He served in World War I enlisting at the beginning of the conflict. He was a member of the Hampshire County Court, the Presbyterian Church, Clinton Lodge No. 86 AF&AM and the American Legion.

In January, 1947, he married Miss Charlotte Rannells, daughter of Mrs. Edith Rannells and the late Samuel F. Rannells, of Points.

The survivors are the widow, two sisters, Mrs. Blanche Coffman, Rio, and Mrs. Bess Coffman, Winchester; and eight brothers, Brent, Loring and George Billmeyer, Rio; Eugene, Winchester; Bentley, Marietta, Ohio; Otis, Hamburg, Pa.; William, Xenia, Ohio, and Therman, Washington State.

Funeral services were held Sunday at the Presbyterian Church at Three Churches, conducted by Rev. Allen Jones, assisted by Rev. Taylor O. Bird, and interment was in the Baptist cemetery at that place. The service at the grave was in charge of Clinton Lodge. Active pallbearers were C. J. Powell, Guy Hannas, Clarence Wolford, Heber Parsons, Estes Stewart, and John Pancake.

In Memory

Of Mrs. Olive E. Slonaker Hiett, born in August, 1875, at Cold Stream, and died on April 20, 1947, at her home. She was the youngest child of Christopher and Sarah Jane Leith Slonaker and married Samuel Lee Hiett, of Cold Stream, November 30, 1892.

Surviving are her husband, one brother, Evan J. C. Slonaker, of Winchester, and six daughters, Charlotte Geraldine Haines, Winchester; Iliff Vuenna Loy, Paw Paw ;Orion Leith Carpenter, Capon Bridge; Vivian Little Shanholtz, Augusta; Fern Mavis Clarke, Moorefield, and Ruth Hilda Riley, Augusta. Eight grandchildren, Douglas Bruce Haines, Ivan Fearing Shanholtz, Morris Hiett Clarke, Carroll Lee Clarke, Wendell Hiett Shanholtz, Presley Wilmott Clarke, Jr., Sammy Lee Riley and Linda Louise Riley, and two great granddaughters, Jayanne Haines and Sharon Leigh Shanholtz, also survive.

Mrs. Hiett was a member of the Christian Church for a period of over fifty years. She and her husband were baptized in Capon river soon after their marriage. She was a noble devout Christian mother, with the highest standards and ideals of life. She possesed a courageous determination to succeed in all her undertakings. No deed was too difficult for her to perform if she felt it was her duty. Her health was impaired for fourteen years, and during the past four years she had been greatly afflicted. She carried her cross all those years uncomplainingly and most bravely. It was the height of her ambition to be of service to her church, family, relatives and many friends until the end.

Officiating minister at the last rites was Rev. S. J. Goode, pastor of the Christian Church at Capon Bridge, who was a most faithful visitor during the years of her affliction.

Pallbearers were her six oldest grandsons.

I cannot say, and I will not say
That she is dead—she is just away—
With a cheery smile and a wave of the hand
She has wandered into an unknown land
And left us dreaming how very fair
It needs must be since she lingers there
And you, O you, who the wildest yearn
For the old-time step and the glad return.
Think of her faring on as dear
In the love of there, as the love of here.
Think of her still as the same.
She is not dead—she is just away.
                    —James Whitcomb Riley.

E. O. Coffman Dies in Winchester Hospital

E. O. Coffman, a native of this county, died eary Monday, October 13, 1947, at the Winchester Hospital, after an indisposition of several years. He was 62 years of age.

Mr. Coffman was a son of the late Mr. and Mrs. Julius Coffman and was born in the North River section of the county and had lived in that neighborhood his entire life until going to Winchester several years ago.

Among the survivors are his widow, the former Miss Bessie Billmyer, and several brothers and sisters, one of whom is Ira Coffman, of Augusta.

The funeral services will be held tomorrow afternoon at 2 o'clock in the Lutheran Church at Rio and burial in the cemetery there.

William D. Haines Passes Away

After a critical illness of two weeks William D. Haines passed away at his home on Rosemary Lane early Friday Morning. About two years ago Mr. Haines suffered a stroke but became critically ill only two weeks before his death. He was 83 years of age.

Mr. Haines was a native of Hampshire county, a son of the late William and Caroline Snapp Haines, and had lived in the county his entire life. About two-score years ago he moved to Romney from his farm near Hoy. His wife died ten years ago. Mr. Haines was the last member of his immediate family.

The survivors are two daughters, Miss Glenna Haines, Romney and Mrs. Hazel Smith; one son, Carl Haines, St. Louis, Mo., and two granddaughters, Miss Maxine Smith, at home, and Mrs. Emory Turner, of Cumberland.

Funeral services were conducted from the Methodist Church, Sunday afternoon by the Rev. E. S. Wilson and the body was taken to Salem cemetery, near Slanesville, for interment.

David Lee Larrick Dies in Winchester

David Lee Larrick, 79, died Monday afternoon at Maplewood Nursing Home, Winchester. Mr. Larrick was the son of the late John and Margaret (Murphy) Larrick. He was born at High View, this county, November 14, 1868, and was the last survivor of a family of thirteen children.

Deceased was a retired merchant, postmaster and farmer of High View, and joined the Timber Ridge Christian Church in early manhood. On moving to Winchester in the early '20's he transferred his membership to the Congregational Christian Church there.

He is survived by his widow, Mrs. Retta (Oates) Larrick; two sons, Roy A. Larrick and Albert Larrick, of Winchester, and two daughters, Mrs. Nellie B. Cline, Petersburg, and Mrs. Lewis G. Dinkle, Romney; also six grandchildren and five great grandchildren.

Funeral services will be conducted from the Jones funeral home, Winchester, this afternoon at two o'clock, Rev. Roy D. Coulter and Rev. Robert Whitten officiating. Interment will be in the family lot in Mt. Hebron cemetery, Winchester.

Lemuel H, Larrick Dies at High View

Lemuel Howard Larrick, of High View, died Friday after an extended illness. He would have been 80 years of age in September. A native of Hampshire county, he was a son of the late John and Margaret Larrick, of High View.

The deceased was a retired farmer and a member of the Timber Ridge Christian Church where services were held Sunday with interment in the adjacent cemetery.

Mr. Larrick leaves his widow, the former Miss Letitia Arnold; five children, Guy Larrick, Capon Bridge; John Larrick, Lehew; Mrs. Ethel Johnson and Edgar Larrick, at home, and Harry Larrick, Cumberland; also one brother, D. L. Larrick, Winchester, survives.

William C. LaFollette Taken by Death

William C. LaFollette, retired farmer of Lehew, died Sunday, October 12, 1947, at the home of his son, Roy LaFollette, in Winchester. He had been ill for some time. Mr. LaFollette, a son of the late Silas and Jane Johnson LeFollette, was 81 years of age.

Surviving are his widow, the former Miss Mary Kline, of Yellow Springs, and four children.

Funeral services were held yesterday at the Timber Ridge Christian Church by the Rev. Francis Eldridge.

271

World War I Veteran Dies Very Suddenly

Chas. B. Henderson, a successfull merchant of Slanesville, died very suddenly of a heart attack Friday evening of last week. He was 52 years of age.

Mr. Henderson, a son of the late T. F. Henderson and Carrie W. Henderson, was born at Slanesville. He was a World War I veteran and a member of the Loyal Order of Moose. He received his education in the public schools of Hampshire county and did graduate work at Marshall College.

The deceased was never married and is survived by one brother, William Harold Henderson, one sister, Mrs. Ethel Henderson Pugh, and a niece, Fraya Jean Pugh, all of Slanesville.

Funeral services were held at the home at Slanesville Sunday afternoon and the burial was in the family burying ground at Slanesville.

Funeral Rites for Mrs. Bertha W. Dalton

Funeral Services for Mrs. Bertha Wills Dalton, who died in Tulsa, Oklahoma, Hospital Monday, August 18, were held at 2 p. m. Friday in Salem Methodist Church, Rev. J. O. Patterson officiating. The interment was in Salem cemetery.

Mrs. Dalton leaves one son, Frank Dalton, of Okmulgee, Oklahoma, and one sister, Mayme Wills, of Slanesville. The pallbearers were Charles Love Miller, Bernard Nixon, Marshall Nixon, Finley Largent, Lorenza Robinson and Bruce Miller.

Funeral Services for Samuel B. Lyons

Funeral services were held Thursday for Samuel B. Lyons at his home in Paw Paw. Mr. Lyons, a retired foreman for the Union Tanning Company, died Monday June 14, at the home of his daughter, Mrs. Maude L. Flora, after a lingering illness. He was 90 years of age.

The survivors are three daughtors, Mrs. Flora, Mrs. C. E. Frye and Miss Ada Lyons, all of Paw Paw, and two sons, Samuel B. Lyons, Jr., Paw Paw, and Tony B. Lyons, Green Spring.

Mrs. Laura E. Oates Dies at Capon Bridge

Mrs. Laura E. Oates, 76, widow of L. C. Oates, died Saturday at the home of her daughter, Mrs. Wilbur Pugh, at Capon Bridge.

Surviving are a son and two daughters—Kenzel Oates, and Mrs. Beulah Pugh, of Capon Bridge, and Mrs. Lee Fletcher, of Baltimore; also a brother, Edgar Oates, of Petersburg.

Funeral services were conducted yesterday at the Fairview Lutheran Church conducted by Rev. S. J. Goode and the Rev. S. J. Anderson. Interment was in the adjoining cemetery.

Former Judge Pugh Dead

Columbus Attorney Was Ohio G.A.R. Commander in 1898

COLUMBUS, O., March 23.—(AP)—David F. Pugh, 82, former judge of the Franklin County Common Pleas Court, died at his home here today following an illness of several weeks.

He was a member of the law firm of Pugh & Pugh at the time of his death. He served on the Franklin County bench from 1886 to 1897. He was a veteran of the Civil War. In 1898 he was elected state commander of the G.A.R.

Forty Years Ago— Wednesday, June 12, 1907

Claude Shull, aged 26 years, died Sunday morning about 7 o'clock at the home of his father, Dr. J. W. Shull, at this place. The deceased had been in bad health for more than a year with that dreaded disease, consumption. He was buried Monday at 4 o'clock at Mt. Zion cemetery.

Man Drowns After Rescuing Daughter

On Sunday, July 12, 1948 Dewey Portmess, of Paw Paw lost his life in Cacapo River, near Fork of Capon, after shoving his eleven-year-old daughter to safety on a protruding rock in the middle of the stream.

Mr. Portmess, with his wife and daughter, Jeannie, had gone to the river and Mr. Portmess was teaching his daughter to swim. He left her in shallow water while he went to a picinc spot to dress. As he and the mother sat on the bank the

273

daughter was swept into deep water and the father, fully clothed, leaped in to rescue her. When he got the girl to safety he was too exhausted to pull himself up. Using an artificial respirator, firemen worked for several hours to revive Mr. Portmess, but to no avail.

Besides the widow and one daughter, Mr. Portmess is survived by three other children, Bruce, Ann Lee anl Lorna Mae Portmess.

Mrs. Minne V. Wolfe Dies at Augusta

Mrs. Minne Virginia Wolfe, widow of Ferman Wolfe, died Wednesday of last week at her home at Augusta, after an illness of several weeks. She was 76 years of age. Mrs. Wolfe was a native of Hampshire county.

Surviving are seven children: Mrs. Curtis Ruckman, Augusta; Mrs. Hazel Nealis, at home; Paul Wolfe, at home; Harry Wolfe, Hetzel Wolfe and Reginald Wolfe, all of Cumberland, and Ira Wolfe, Columbus, Ohio.

Funeral services were conducted Saturday afternoon at her late home by the Rev. W. P. Goode, pastor of the Capon Bridge Methodist Church, and burial was in Green Lane cemetery.

George William Riley

George William Riley, a native of Hampshire county, and a son of the late Thomas William and Susan Alabaugh Riley, died at his home in Winchester early yesterday morning. Mr. Riley was 84 years, 7 months and 17 days old. His death was due to infirmities of age.

October 14, 1891, he married Virginia Elizabeth Hawkins, who died in 1925. To this union were born six daughters and three sons. In 1927 he married his second wife, Rosalie Talley Hopkins.

When a young man he was a member of the teaching staff of the public school system and taught in various schools in and near Hampshire county. Following this he became an assessor of this county, a position he held for a number of years. He then entered the mercantile business at Cold Stream and continued in this business at Delray, then Romney and Augusta. While at Augusta he operated large farming interests as well as being postmaster and merchant. He moved to Winchester in 1919 and in 1920 bought out the retail mercantile business of F. W. Quantz.

Surviving are the widow, three sons, Hoye L. Riley, Leonard W. Riley and Wilbur O. Riley, all of Winchester; six daughters, Mrs. Irene Bailey, Romney; Mrs. F. L. Largent, Mrs. C. R. Anderson, Mrs. Claudine Largent, Mrs. Thurman Pierce, and Mrs. Robert Glass, all of Winchester; one brother, C. E. Riley, Martinsburg; three sisters, Mrs. Virgil E. Beery, Augusta; Mrs. Taylor Shanholtz, Cold Stream, and Mrs. George Hott, Long Beach, California; twenty grandchildren and five great grandchildren.

Services will be held tomorrow at 2:30 in the afternoon at the Cork Street Christian Church, Winchester, conducted by the Rev. Charles R. Sine and Rev. S. J. Goode. Interment will be in Mt. Hebron cemetery, Winchester. Pallbearers will be Claude Grove, Curtis Loy, Ray Blosser, Ray Duncan, Robert Hockman and Ray Whitacre.

The body will lie in state the the Jones Funeral Home until Wednesday evening at 6 o'clock when it will be moved to his late home on South Braddock Street, Winchester, where it will remain until the time of the funeral.

Edgar Rowe Zimmerman

Edgar Rowe Zimmerman, died at his home in Baltimore on March 2. He was the son of Rev. George H. Zimmerman, who was presiding elder of the Moorefield district of the Southern Methodist Church some years ago, and Henrietta Rowe Zimmerman, and brother of Prosecuting Attorney J. S. Zimmerman, of this place. He was 72 years old at the time of his death. For many years he had been active in the business life of Baltimore and especially in the general insurance business, being a member of the firm of Tongue, Brooks and Zimmerman, insurance brokers, and Baltimore agents of the Maryland Casualty Company of that city.

Mr. Zimmerman was educated at Randolph-Macon Academy, Front Royal, Va., and at Randolph-Macon College, Ashland, Va., and a member of Phi Delta Theta fraternity at his college. He belonged to the Roland Park Presbyterian Church in which he was a deacon, and was also a member of the Baltimore Country Club for many years.

Funeral services will be conducted at the Mitchell Funeral Home in Baltimore this afternoon, and interment will be in Indian Mound cemetery here in the Caudy family lot at 2 o'clock in the afternoon tomorrow beside his wife, Mrs. Elizabeth Caudy Zimmerman, who pre-deceased him about a month ago.

Certain of his business associates and friends of Baltimore will accompany the remains here and act as active and honorary pallbearers.

Deceased is survived by two children, Mrs. Eleanor Caudy Keeny, of Baltimore, and Edgar Rowe Zimmerman, Jr., of Charlotte, N. C., and his brothers, J. S. Zimmerman, of Romney, and George H. Zimmerman of Whitesburg, Ky.

Services will be conducted at the grave by Rev. Allen Jones, of the Romney Presbyterian Church.

Frank M. Alderton

Word was received of the death on Wednesday, February 18 of Frank M. Alderton at Marion, Indiana. Mr. Alderton who was 75 years of age, was born near Mt. Union, Hampshire county, but when a young man moved to Indiana.

Besides his widow he is survived by one son, Rev. Ivan C. Alderton, of Daleville, Ind., and two daughters, Mrs. Clarence Patch, of Bryand, Ind., and Mrs. George Merrill, of Yeodon, Pa., and seven grandchildren; also two nieces, Mrs. G. C. MacDonald, Cumberland, and Mrs. J. N. Clark, Sebring, Florida.

Mr. and Mrs. MacDonald and son, Rev. Claude R. MacDonald, Lexington, Ky., attended the funeral which was held Saturday, February 21, at Marion, Indiana.

Mrs. Robert Milleson

Mrs. Robert L. Milleson, who was before marriage Miss Lillian A Singhass, of Springfield, died Thursday at her home in

Hagerstown. She had been in failing health for about two years. Before moving to Hagerstown six years ago she lived in Winchester where she was organist at the Braddock Street Methodist Church and was employed in the Shenandoah National Bank.

The survivors are the husband and one sister, Mrs. Percy Middleton, of Arlington, Va. The late Walter F. Singhass, of Romney, was a brother.

The funeral services were held Sunday in Hagerstown and burial was in Mt. Hebron cemetery in Winchester.

Mrs. Elizabeth Zimmerman

Mrs. Elizabeth Caudy Zimmerman, wife of Edgar R. Zimmerman, died at the home in Baltimore, Friday, January 28, 1948.

Mrs. Zimmerman was the daughter of the late Christopher H. Caudy, who was a native of Hampshire county.

The survivors are the husband, one son, E. R. Zimmerman, Jr., of Charlotte, N. C.; a daughter, Mrs. Edmund L. Keeney, Baltimore, and two sisters, Miss Mary Caudy and Mrs. Harry Lepps, of Sarasota, Florida.

Funeral services were held in Baltimore Sunday and the body was brought to Romney Monday and interment was made in Indian Mound cemetery where graveside services were conducted by the Rev. E. S. Wilson, pastor of the Romney Methodist Church.

Those from a distance attending the services here besides the family were Mr. and Mrs. Vance Zimmerman, of Berkeley Springs, and Miss Susan Hawkins, of Baltimore.

Rev. A. R. Spaid Passes Away

Rev. A. R. Spaid, a life-long resident of the Hooks Mill section, died at his home Sunday, November 9, 1947. He was 72 years of age.

He was a son of the late Nicholas and Angeline Spaid, and had been a teacher in Hampshire county schools for a number of years.

The survivors are his widow, four children, Paul and Lyle, at home; Mrs. Ruth Barrett, Fairmont, and Melvin, near home; five brothers, Branson B. and Ora C., of Markle, Ind.; Rosel N., Chenoa, Ill.; Corsa C., Stanford, Il., and Rev. Daniel B. Spaid, of Eglon; and three sisters, Misses Elva C., and Bertha L., and Mrs. Caudy Davis, all of Yellow Springs.

Funeral services were held at Timber Ridge Church today and burial was in the cemetery adjoining, October 12, 1947.

Mrs. Susan J. Selvy

Mrs. Susan J. Selvey, aged 81, died Wednesday, December 10, 1947, at the home of her son, William, in Hickman, Kentucky, after a long illness.

Mrs. Selvey was born near Levels, a daughter of the late Zachariah and Rebecca Johnson, and spent the greater part of her life in Hampshire county. Since last July she had made her home with her son in Hickman. Mrs. Selvey was a life-long member of the Methodist Church and was very active in all organizations of the church as long as her health permitted.

Surviving are two sons, William, of Hickman, Ky., and George, Huntington; and one daughter, Mrs. Tom O'Brien, Akron, Ohio; also one brother, I. T. Johnson, Levels, and one sister, Mrs. Verna Long, Jefferson, Md.

The body was brought to the home of Mrs. A. Z. Ewers here and later taken to Wesley Chapel where funeral services were conducted by the Rev. G. D. Kidner, Friday afternoon with with interment in the cemetery adjoining the church.

Those attending the services from a distance were William Selvey and son, of Hickman, Ky.; Mr. and Mrs. George Selvey and daughters, Janet and Esther, of Huntington; Mr. and Mrs. Tom O'Brien, Akron, Ohio; Mrs. Virginia Lake, Grafton; Mrs. Stanley Fulton, Hancock, Md., and Mrs. Verna Long, Jefferson, Md.

Claudia H. Milleson, daughter of George and Kate Coffman Milleson, born May 16, 1861, died July 5, 1862. Kate Milleson, the mother was born August 8, 1836.

Nancy Milleson, daughter of Wm. and Sarah Milleson, and sister of this author's mother, died April 28, 1853, aged 24 years and 1 day, a recent bride of Elius Ullery.

Margaret Pepper Wolfe, died November 17, 1941, aged 75, buried at Green Lane cemetery, on North River. Her son, Love F. Wolfe, died July 24, 1948 and was buried at Richlands, Va., near Bluefield, W. Va.

John Pugh, died May 31, 1948, and was buried at Malick cemetery, June 2nd, a. m.

R. B. Pugh Passed Away in Oklahoma — 1948

Relatives in Winchester have received the news that R. B. Pugh, of Morris, Oklahoma, passed away Monday at 1 p. m. The funeral will be at 2 p. m. today. Mr. Pugh was the son and only child of the late Mr. and Mrs. A. L. Pugh, of Capon Bridge, and a nephew of Mrs. George Taylor, of 408 Fairmont Avenue, Winchester.

As a young man he assisted his father in the sheriff's office. Later he attended Randolph-Macon College. After his marmiage to Miss Bertha Simmons, daughter of the late Rev. Mr. Simmons, who was stationed at Capon Bridge, Mr. Pugh and his wife went to Morris Oklahoma where he engaged in the hardware business.

Mrs. Martha J. Flory Dies in Florida

Mrs. Martha J. Flory died at her home in Sebring, Florida, September 7, 1948. Funeral services were held Thursday morning, and the body was sent here for burial at the Augusta cemetery. The burial services were held Saturday morning, conducted by the Rev. E. S. Wilson.

Mrs. Flory was 93 years and 10 month old, a native of Hampshire county and the widow of Newton B. Flory. She was the daughter of the late Daniel and Margaret Pugh and an aunt of D. E. Pugh, of Romney. She had been an active member of the Brethren for many years.

John E. Scanlon

Word has been received of the death of John E. Scanlon at his home in Cleveland Friday morning. He was 79 years of age.

He was a native of Hampshire county, born and reared at Three Churches, and was the last of the children of the late Thomas Scanlon, who, with his brother, Michael emigrated from Ireland when a young man. Mr. Scanlon left Three Churches when quite young and became engaged in electrical work, connected with a telegraph system, which carried him to the west coast. His niece, Mrs. Wilson Power, of Martinsburg, went to Cleveland at the time of his death and accompanied the remains "back home".

He is survived by his widow, the former Mrs. Effa Pugh Hildebrant, and three children by a former marriage, Mrs. S. H. Vanden and Richard M. Scanlon, Amarillo, Texas, and Robert D. Scanlon, Downey, California.

Services were held Monday morning at Three churches with interment in the Methodist cemetery there.

Mrs. Jethro S. Watson Dies at Home of Her Son

Mrs. Jethro S. Watson, a native of this county, died Thursday, April 2, 1942, at the home of her son, Paul Watson, in Keyser, and was buried by the side of her husband at Three Churches Saturday afternoon at two-thirty o'clock.

Before marriage Mrs. Watson was Miss Augusta Offutt, eldest daughter of the late Thornton W. Offutt, of near Slanesville, and a sister of the late J. M. Offutt. Her husband, Jethro S. Watson, passed away a decade or more ago.

Mrs. Watson is survived by three fine sons, all successful business men, Paul V. Watson, Keyser; Jethro S. Watson, Wheeling, and Edgar B. Watson, Greenburg, Pa. Also one brother, Henry L. Offutt, Baltimore.

Henry Shanholtz died April 16, 1943, Gettysburg; buried at Malick Cemetery near Hoy, West Virginia, 1:30 p. m., April 19, 1943, aged about 64 years.

George A. Hott, born at Cold Stream, Virginia, August 13, 1852, died at his home, 2129 Lime Avenue, Long Beach, California, December 12, 1941. Old Democrat; member, Disciple Church; teacher, twenty-nine years; member, State Legislature, two terms; wife, Cordelia Riley Hott. Children: Estella and Mrs. Chloe Kilmer, both of Long Beach, and Omer and Ernest Hott, Chicago, Illinois.

Passed Away June 17

Mrs. Cordelia Hott, widow of George A. Hott, died at her home, 602 Dawson Avenue, Long Beach, California, on June 17, 1948, having lived in Southern California for Sixteen years. She was born at Cold Stream (then Virginia) on September 7, 1861.

Surviving her are four children, Mrs. Chloe Kilmer and Miss Estelle V. Hott, of Long Beach, and Omar and Ernest Hott, of Chicago, and five grandchildren.

Margaret Anna Pugh, wife of Alexander L. McKnight, born December 28, 1834, died February 16, 1910.

Alexander L. McKnight (birth date not stated) died 1875. Graves are near Indianapolis, Indiana.

Hamilton Gaver Brill Died Friday Morning at Lehew

Hamilton Gaver Brill, 83, died Friday morning at his home near Lehew, in Hampshire county, in the house in which he was born.

He was a son of the late Jonathan and Elizabeth Brill. Mr. Brill married the former Miss Sallie Arnold, 57 years ago, last December 28. He was a successful farmer and a leading citizen in this community.

In addition to his wife, he is survived by three daughters, Mrs. Minne Fox, Mrs. A. W. Spaid, of Lehew, and Mrs. W. A. Larrick, of Gore, Va.

There are 11 grandchildren and four brothers, Dorsey C. Brill, of Miami, Fla.; Smith R. Brill, Hooks Mill; A. L. Brill and D. C. Brill, of Winchester. One sister, Mrs. Allie Keckley, resides in Washington, D. C.

Final services were held at his late home at 2 o'clock Sunday afternoon and at 3 o'clock in Timber Ridge Church. The Rev. Robert A. Whitten officiated, assisted by the Rev. C. H. Anderson.

King Edward

King Edward was not only King of England, Kaiser Wilhelm of Germany was his nephew, the Empress of Russia was his niece, King Leopold of Belgium was his cousin, one removed. His wife Alexandria was the daughter of the King of Denmark, the King of Greece was his brother-in-law.

The Fifteen Decisive Battles of the World.

Professor Creasy calls these battles "decisive," not alone by reason for their immediate results, but because in each a reversed victory would have changed materially the history of the world.

B. C. 490

The victory at Marathon,
Greece over haughty Persia won.

B. C. 431

At Syracuse the Spartan's name
Attained in Hellas naval fame.

B. C. 331

From Arbela Darius fled,
While Alexander onward sped.

B. C. 207

On the Metaurus Rome foretold
The speedy doom of Carthage old.

A. D. 9

With Varus into wilds decoyed,
Rome's trusted legions were destroyed.

A. D. 431

By Visigoth and Roman spurned,
The "Scourge of God" from Chalons turned.

A. D. 732
At Tours fierce blows from Charles "Martel"
The "Infidels'" retreat compel.

A. D. 1066
At Hastings fought the Saxon lords,
When Norman Williams claimed their swords.

A. D. 1429
Joan of Arc, of France the pride,
At Orleans turned the battle-tide.

A. D. 1588
Spain's huge Armada, greatly feared,
In English waters disappeared.

A. D. 1704
At Blenheim Marlborough held sway,
While Prince Eugene helped win the day.

A. D. 1709
Pultowa saw a triumph famed,
Which Russia over Sweden claimed.

A. D. 1777
At Saratoga in our States,
Burgoyne gave up his sword to Gates.

A. D. 1792
The young democracy of France
At Valmy checked their foes advance.

A. D. 1815
But great Napoleon we view,
Vanquished at last at Watrloo.

—Julia M. Colton, in Christian Advocate

www.ingramcontent.com/pod-product-compliance
Lightning Source LLC
Chambersburg PA
CBHW060141280326
41932CB00012B/1591